Collecting
Rocks, Gems
and Minerals

IDENTIFICATION • VALUES • LAPIDARY USES

Published by

krause publications
A division of F+W Media, Inc.

700 East State Street • Iola, WI 54990-0001
715-445-2214 • 888-457-2873
www.krausebooks.com

To order books or other products call toll-free 1-800-258-0929
or visit us online at www.krausebooks.com or www.Shop.Collect.com

Rock and mineral values are included for the convenience of the reader and are a guide only. The author and publisher are not responsible for typographical errors or losses incurred as a result of consulting this book.

Cover photography by Kris Kandler

Library of Congress Control Number: 2009937509

ISBN-13: 978-1-4402-0415-9
ISBN-10: 1-4402-0415-2

Designed by Heidi Bittner-Zastrow
Edited by Dan Brownell

Printed in China

Contents

Foreword...4

Acknowledgments 5

About This Book...6

Introduction to Collecting Rocks and Minerals..8

What are Rocks and Minerals? 11

How to Locate and Collect Rocks and Minerals 15

Use and Care of Rocks, Minerals, and Gemstones.......................................21

Buying and Selling Rocks, Minerals, and Gemstones 25

Collectible Materials for Lapidary Use and Display.....................................29

Crystalline Quartz...31

Cryptocrystalline Quartz 40

Chalcedony..42

Agate 51

Jasper 90

Pseudomorphs...102

Fossils..103

Petrified Wood 109

Cabochon Materials 113

Faceting Materials 132

Display Materials...146

Carving and Ornamental Materials 150

Architectural Materials 160

Organic Materials..163

Out of This World 168

Just For Fun 171

Mineral Display Specimens 173

Mineral Identification 174

Minerals 177

Glossary..259

Resources 263

Bibliography 265

Photo Credits...266

Index 270

Foreword

The fantastic world of minerals, precious stones and fossils has intrigued people for thousands of years. Even in these extremely technically oriented times, it is still fascinating to watch people be amazed while holding a shiny crystal or an expertly polished agate in their hands. It is even more gratifying to actually be able to find one of these million-year-old treasures in the great outdoors yourself.

In spite of the fact that many established sites have been either totally exhausted or that a find is only possible with a lot of perseverance, hard work and determination, there are still plenty of possibilities to successfully find these natural treasures. The search for a lustrous crystal or a colorful agate is truly a worthwhile and satisfying recreational activity. It is an activity like no other that is good for the body, mind, and soul. This endeavor requires intensive work that broadens the collector's know-how with the use of tools, equipment and skills needed. A wonderful advantage that is attained by this activity is the contact with other like-minded people and the supportive camaraderie that develops. In addition, this is a wonderful pastime for young people to experience exciting, meaningful, and valuable adventures!

In order for a rockhound to be able to excite and motivate people of all ages it is necessary to have a lot of experience, specialized knowledge, and one's own excitement for minerals and stones. Patti Polk, the author of this book, combines these requirements in an exemplary fashion. I remember one of our collecting trips together in the Arizona desert where, with a glimmer in her eyes, she very knowledgably and purposefully was able to find agates even when they were completely hidden. Her jewelry is admirable because it demonstrates the connection between the initial find of the natural treasure, which she has usually found herself, and the completed beauty of the artistic piece.

May this fantastic book give many people support and encouragement to achieve a successful, happy and longlasting alliance with these wonderful stones and minerals.

Johann Zenz
- Author of *Agates I* and *Agates II*
- Editor of ACHAT mineral collectors magazine
Bode Publishing Company, Haltern, Germany

Acknowledgments

My deepest appreciation to all the following people for all their help, without whom this book would not have been possible.

My greatest thanks to my best rockhound buddy Barbara Grill for sharing so many fun, exciting, and crazy adventures with me that have truly been some of the very best times of my life.

To all the wonderful people who contributed their expertise, photos, and collections so generously for me to photograph:

Jason Badgley, who trusted me and went well above the call of duty by taking the time to send me hundreds of beautiful agates and jaspers to photograph; Nancy Bihler, for sharing her fine collection and being such a good friend; Harry Brown, Clara Cohan, Jeff Goebel, Barbara Grill, Linda Kappel, Bob Jones, Val Latham, Pat McMahan, Jim Mills, Dick Moore, Gene Mueller, Helen Serras-Herman, Jim Van Wert, Jeff Weissman, and Glenn Worthington who have all shared their personal collections, experience, and photographs with me.

Extra thanks to Dick Moore, Pat McMahan, and Jim Van Wert for helping me with proofreading for accuracy.

A very special thanks to Sharon Gardner, just for being who she is.

Thank you to John and Barbara Campbell for all your help and support over the years.

Thank you to Johann Zenz for the kind and thoughtful foreword, and last but not least, to Dan Brownell, my ever-patient editor who has so gently guided me through this whole daunting process without a complaint or hint of impatience. Thank you.

About This Book

First and foremost I'd like to introduce myself as your average, garden-variety rockhound. Simply put, I just love the rocks. I have to say that my greatest passion in life today is in collecting rocks, primarily agates, and that once seemingly innocent childhood pastime has gradually accelerated over my lifetime into the full blown, uncontrollable addiction that I now fervently pursue through bad weather, dangerous roads, rough terrain, and sometimes, long lonely journeys to find that ever-elusive next agate, jasper, or mineral specimen that will be the most wonderful and beautiful one for my collection yet!

The author hard at work digging up agates.

Over the years, I have been involved with many rock clubs and associations, and have had the good fortune to get to know many top-notch rock, gem, and mineral collectors, geologists, and lapidaries who have educated me, knowingly or unknowingly, in the finer points of collecting, identifying, and working with rocks and minerals. It is with their help and guidance that I have been able to put a book of this scope together.

My purpose in writing this book was to create a book that combined the many different aspects of the rock and mineral collecting fields into one cohesive work. There have been many books written about collecting rocks, identifying minerals, the lapidary arts and so forth, but they are generally written as completely separate subjects and often as technical texts that are a little daunting to people who are just getting started in mineral collecting. I have found that many people who are interested in the earth sciences often have overlapping interests, and like to collect not only rocks in the field for lapidary use, but also may collect or buy

Petrified wood with a botryoidal coating hand collected in northern Arizona.

mineral specimens for display or study purposes. People also need to know the value of different types of rocks and minerals so if they wish to buy or sell a piece they will have a good idea of what things cost so they can get a fair deal and don't wind up overpaying for their materials.

I have done my best to put this information together in a way that is uncomplicated and easy to understand for the beginning collector, and hopefully, useful for the more advanced collector too. I've also tried to inject some of my own enthusiasm for this hobby into this writing, and share a little of the more fun and playful aspects to collecting too.

The main goal of this book is for it to be used as a hands-on reference guide to refer to when you are out at a gem and mineral show and want to identify and price a specimen, or at home considering an Internet purchase and would like to compare prices with the online values. At the same time, I would also hope to give the beginning collector some ideas about how to start a collection, whether they choose to try their hand personally collecting rocks and minerals in the field, or by purchasing them. I would also like to encourage them to explore the unlimited possibilities of what can be done with any of the fantastic rocks and minerals that we are so lucky to have available to us within the field of the lapidary arts.

A rough agate as found in the field weighing about three pounds.

A silver ring set with a freeform agate cabochon hand collected, cut, and polished by the author.

Introduction to Collecting
Rocks and Minerals

Why do people collect rocks and minerals? There are as many reasons to collect them as there are types of collectors: for their beauty or rarity, for their monetary value, for lapidary or jewelry-making uses, metaphysical purposes, for scientific study, and for fun. Children especially love to pick up pretty and unusual rocks; it seems to come naturally to them.

People have been collecting and using rocks since the beginning of time for adornment and more practical purposes, such as toolmaking or as currency used in trade be-

A child's copper toy horse from the 1950s.

tween tribes or cultures. Materials like obsidian or chert have been used for millennia for making knives, axeheads, and arrowheads; and copper, bronze, or iron was used for many of man's earliest hammers and tools. Some of the very first known uses of stones date to prehistoric times when simple necklaces and bracelets were strung together with pieces of bone, teeth, shell and stones for personal adornment.

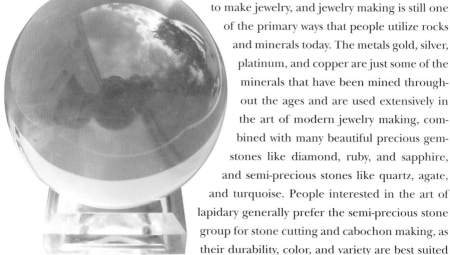

The earliest signs of metallurgy appeared around 7,000 years ago when humans began using forged copper to make jewelry, and jewelry making is still one of the primary ways that people utilize rocks and minerals today. The metals gold, silver, platinum, and copper are just some of the minerals that have been mined throughout the ages and are used extensively in the art of modern jewelry making, combined with many beautiful precious gemstones like diamond, ruby, and sapphire, and semi-precious stones like quartz, agate, and turquoise. People interested in the art of lapidary generally prefer the semi-precious stone group for stone cutting and cabochon making, as their durability, color, and variety are best suited for those purposes.

A quartz crystal ball.

One of the most common uses of gemstones is for faceted gems for fine jewelry. Most people have at one time or another worn a favorite ring or necklace set with a sparkling gemstone large or small that is special and meaningful to them in some way. Almost everyone is familiar with their personal birthstone and the qualities associated with it, and jewelry set with birthstones is often given as a gift for important birthdays and memorable occasions.

Sometimes stones are used in more unusual ways, such as for metaphysical purposes like crystal gazing, healing ceremonies, or wearing as personal amulets. Many people believe in the healing energy of stones, and use them for everything from stimulating their creativity to calming and relaxing their senses.

A decorative selenite wand for metaphysical use.

Another use of minerals is the hobby of collecting specimens for display. People collect them in many ways: by their size, such as micromounts or cabinet specimens; by their locality, mineral group or chemical class; by rarity; or by special properties such as fluorescence, to name just a few.

Gemstone tourmaline in quartz.

Mankind's diverse uses of rocks and minerals has grown over time from crudely chipping stones around a makeshift campfire into a prestigious, multi-million dollar industry, ranging from hometown rockhound or lapidary hobbyists who enjoy hand collecting their material in the field and polishing cabochons for fun or profit, to internationally renowned gemstone experts, jewelers, and mineral collectors who travel around the world to collect and purchase their valuable and prized specimens. Gem and mineral shows are held throughout the year locally, nationally, and internationally and are enthusiastically attended by thousands of people worldwide. In addition, numerous museums,

Gold leaf in a bottle.

clubs, organizations, publications, and websites are dedicated to the various aspects of rock and mineral collecting.

Due to the extensive scope of the rock, gemstone, and mineral collecting field, the focus of this book is primarily on the rocks and minerals that the majority of people would be interested in collecting for jewelry or lapidary use or for mineral specimens to display. As this book is intended to be used as a field guide, ease of use is a priority, with special emphasis on the beginning collector. And, above all else, always remember that rock and mineral collecting is a fun and fascinating hobby full of adventure, enjoyment, and education about the beautiful and enchanting treasures that Earth so generously provides for us.

Early Native American stone axehead.

Antique miner's lamp from the early 1800s.

Stone petroglyphs in Arizona.

What Are Rocks and Minerals?

What are rocks and minerals, and what is the difference between the two? A mineral, by definition, is any naturally occurring inorganic substance generally characterized by a definitive crystal structure that is classified according to the way the atoms of the mineral are arranged. A mineral's chemical composition is determined by the combination, or singularity, of the 103 known chemical elements. All minerals are arranged into groups according to their chemical composition and their crystal structure. Basic elements that occur naturally are also considered minerals.

All minerals belong to a chemical group, which describes their affiliation with certain elements or compounds. The eight main chemical groups are known as: native elements, sulfides, oxides, halides, nitrates, sulfates, phosphates, and silicates. Some of these chemical groups have sub-categories, which may be categorized in some mineral references as separate groups.

Minerals also have distinctive properties, such as color, hardness, crystal habit, specific gravity, luster, fracture, and tenacity. Some minerals exhibit certain properties that others do not, such as fluorescence and radioactivity.

A beautiful quartz crystal druzy-coated mineral specimen.

A typical agate-bearing volcanic field.

A naturally tumbled river agate.

A sedimentary fossiliferous limestone formation.

There are currently about 3,000 different types of known minerals, and new ones are constantly being discovered. Basically, minerals are the individual crystalline substances that are the essential building blocks of all the rocks on Earth.

What is a rock? The best way to define a rock is to say that it is a mixture of two or more naturally occurring mineral elements, and its composition is determined by the combination of minerals and organic materials present when it was formed. Rocks fall into three distinct categories depending on how they were formed: igneous, sedimentary, and metamorphic. Igneous rocks are formed through volcanic activity, both extrusive and intrusive; sedimentary, through weathering and depositing in streambeds and oceans; and metamorphic, which are igneous rocks that have been transformed into a new mineral composition by extreme heat and pressure over time.

Rocks may range in size from tiny pebbles to entire mountainsides and can be composed of tiny microscopic grains of minerals all the way up to large coarse agglomerates of different minerals that are clearly visible to the naked eye.

In less technical terms, rocks are simply aggregates of minerals. Minerals are the individual elements that bind together to form rocks, much like salt, pepper, meat, and vegetables mix together to create a bowl of stew. In other words, rocks are always made of minerals, but minerals are never made of rocks.

Vein agate in matrix.

The Petrified Forest National Park showing petrified wood weathering out of sedimentary deposits.

The red rocks of Sedona, Arizona.
Another sedimentary formation showing extensive weathering and erosion.

Rough agate nodule.

If your interest is in collecting rocks and minerals in the field, it is important to have at least a basic understanding of how they are formed and deposited. You will need to have an idea of where and how to look for the types of rocks or minerals that you're interested in finding.

For more information about the study of rocks (geology) and minerals (mineralogy), there are many excellent classes offered through colleges and clubs throughout the country. Magazines and numerous reference books are available on the subject through your local library or bookstores – see Resources.

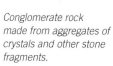

Single amethystine quartz crystal.

Conglomerate rock made from aggregates of crystals and other stone fragments.

How to Locate and Collect Rocks and Minerals

There are basically two main ways to obtain rocks and minerals: either by going into the field and hand collecting them or by purchasing them from a source such as an Internet dealer, a rock shop, a yard or estate sale, or a gem and mineral show. Each option employs different strategies depending on what you're looking for and how you go about getting it.

In this section we will focus on locating and collecting rocks in the field. The first thing you will need is a way to figure out where the rocks and minerals are. Probably the very best way to find out where to go to collecting is to join a local gem and mineral collecting club in your area. There are lapidary clubs and mineral societies in most major cities and within driving distance from most towns throughout the United States, and outside the U.S. as well. Gem and mineral clubs usually have monthly field trips that you can go on with a group and you can not only find out where the minerals are located, but also learn about identifying and collecting them from the other more experienced club members too.

My buddy Barbara collecting in the field.

A flat tire can happen any time you are out in remote areas. Be prepared!

If you prefer not to join a club and want to try your luck on your own, another way to locate where rocks and minerals are is by buying a rock collecting magazine like *Rock and Gem* and using one of their monthly mapped field trip articles, or by buying a rock and mineral field guide book and using the collecting location maps they provide. If you choose to go out collecting on your own, there are a few things you need to know:

- Never go alone! Always let someone know where you will be.
- Never enter open mineshafts or adits!
- What is the difficulty of the terrain? What will the weather be like? Are you prepared? Do you have enough food and water in case of an emergency? Is your vehicle in good operating condition? Do you have a spare tire?
- Know the status of the land you're collecting on. Is it public or private land? If it is private, you must get permission to enter.
- Don't litter or leave open digging holes, and close all gates behind you.
- Know your limitations and don't ever take any unnecessary risks! No rock is worth it!

Collecting in the field is a fun and rewarding experience if you are careful and properly equipped, but a casual outing can turn deadly serious very quickly if you are careless or unprepared. Many collecting locations are in remote areas, accessible only by four wheel drive, with no water or help near by, and can be very hot, cold, windy, wet, steep, crumbly, sharp, or inhabited by poisonous or dangerous animals. The outdoors is a wild place and must always be respected as such.

Backpack for carrying supplies.

Once you have decided what you want to look for and where you want to go, you will need certain tools and supplies for your trip. Because the tools will vary depending on what type of material you are looking for, I will separate them into tools for lapidary or cutting material, and tools for collecting mineral specimens. There are also basic supplies that you will need on any collecting trip you undertake.

Gem Trails guidebook listing collecting locations.

Leather gloves.

Handheld GPS unit.

A topographic map.

Basic supplies:

- Food and water, extra water if you can manage it.
- First aid kit, and sunscreen if you will be out in the sun. Also, insect repellent.
- Appropriate clothing. I like to wear jeans to protect my legs from cactus and sharp rocks, but some people like shorts if it's hot. Sturdy hiking boots and a hat if it's sunny, or a jacket if it's cold.
- Topo maps, compass, and a GPS if you have one.
- Personal hygiene items like toilet paper or wetnaps.
- A cell phone if you are in an area where you can get reception, and walkie-talkies if you will be separated from your friends while collecting.
- A backpack to carry everything in.
- Plenty of gas in your vehicle.

Walkie-talkie.

Compass.

First Aid kit.

Water container.

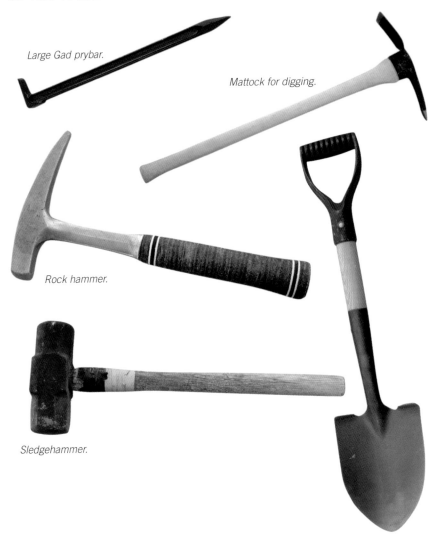

Large Gad prybar.

Mattock for digging.

Rock hammer.

Sledgehammer.

Small shovel.

Supplies for collecting lapidary/cutting material:

- A rock hammer (also known as a geologist's pick), gloves, backpack, and canvas bag to carry your rocks in.
- If you want to dig, you'll need a small shovel (a folding military style is best), and a pick or mattock.
- If you need to break large rocks apart, you'll need gads, chisels, wedges, pry bars (or some combination thereof), and a heavy hammer, such as a striking hammer or a sledge hammer.
- Eye protection if you will be hammering rocks.

Supplies for collecting mineral specimens:

- Rock hammer, gloves, small prybar, and small hand tools such as a three-prong hand rake, a hand weeder or bent screwdriver for cleaning specimens out of cavities.
- Small chisels and gads for prying specimens off the host rock.
- Jeweler's loupe and a streak plate for identifying your specimens. A knife, steel file, and copper penny to test for hardness.
- A portable screen if you need to sift through dirt for small crystals.
- Tissue, egg cartons, or small containers to protect and carry your specimens in.
- UV light for collecting fluorescent minerals at night.
- Note pad and pencil for field notes.

Supplies for collecting gold:

- A gold pan, sluice, or metal detector.
- Small bottles to hold flakes or nuggets.

Multipurpose utility knife.

Jeweler's loupe for magnifying specimens.

Streak plate.

Gold pan.

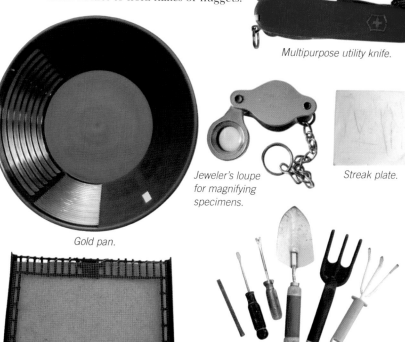

Home made screen for sifting through dirt.

Small hand tools for mineral collecting.

Metal detector.

Once you have done your research and are ready to start collecting, you can begin by going either directly to a known location and start digging or picking up rocks, or go farther afield and do a little prospecting on your own for new deposits. Very often known locations have been picked over, and better material can be found by just going a little bit farther than the last person there. If you do decide to do some prospecting on your own, it is advisable to carry a walkie-talkie, topo map, compass, or a GPS if you have one. This way, you can always navigate back to your camp or vehicle, and also map any new locations you find. If you are a novice collector, you will need to learn how to recognize the material in its natural state, and you can either do that by trial and error in the field, going to a mineral museum and studying their specimens, visiting a local rock shop or show and see what local material is available, reading gem and mineral books, or by joining a gem and mineral club and learning from the other collectors there. Also, if you want to really get to know about how, where, and why rocks

Petrified wood in place on the ground.

and minerals form, you can take classes in geology at a local school or college, and there are also many excellent textbooks on the subject at your public library.

When you are in the field collecting rough lapidary material such as agates or jaspers, it is often hard to tell what the interior will look like, as the exteriors are usually a nondescript color due to weathering, or covered with coatings of desert varnish, soil, or ash. It is common practice for many rockhounds to chip off a small corner of the rock at a 45-degree angle to expose the inner core to get a true picture of what treasure lies inside. However, you never want to indiscriminately smash a rock to break it open, as that would fracture the stone and ruin it. You may also want to carry a small spray bottle of water to rinse off the rock to better see its color or pattern.

Another fascinating branch of collecting rocks or minerals is the collecting of fluorescent minerals. Fluorescent minerals exhibit vivid, glowing colors that are only visible in the dark and are generally collected at night using portable ultraviolet lights. Be sure to check out the terrain in the daylight beforehand though, so as not to fall into any unexpected traps in the dark!

Ultraviolet light for fluorescent mineral hunting.

Use and Care of Rocks, Minerals and Gemstones

Once you have obtained your rocks or minerals, what do you do with them? There are many kinds of ways to use rocks and minerals. They can be used for jewelry making, tumbling, displaying, sculpting or carving, as decorative building materials, and for scientific study. How you plan to use your material will determine what type of equipment you'll need and how you will prepare your specimens.

Lapidary Uses

If you are going to be working with rough, uncut lapidary materials, you will need a rock saw to cut them into useable sized pieces. Rock saws come in a variety of sizes, from small 4" trim saws all the way up to very large 36" ones, or even larger for specialty uses. Most rockhounds use saws in the 6" to 24" range, depending on the size of material they're cutting. If you are cutting rocks simply for display, you may just cut them in half, polish the faces, and place them on a stand. If you are going to use them for creating cabochons for jewelry, you will need to first cut the rough into slices, or slabs, usually about 1/4" thick, then trim the slabs to the size of the cabochon you want. You can either cut them as freeforms, or use a calibrated template to cut precise sizes and shapes like rounds, ovals, rectangles, or squares. If you want to create cabochons, you will need a polishing machine with a graduated set of grinding wheels of increasingly finer grits, generally made of diamond, to polish them; and dop wax, and a dop pot for heating the wax to attach dop sticks to your stones as a handle for polishing them. There are a number of fine polishing machines available on the market by different manufacturers, and they come with a variety of features and attachments.

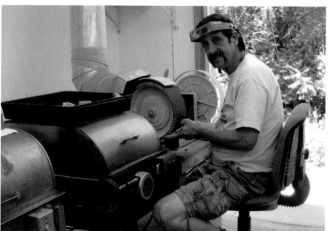

My friend Bob working on a bull wheel high-speed dry sander polisher.

Rough cut slabs.

A vibrating flat lap.

Tumbled stones.

Typical shop supplies from a lapidary rock shop.

If you want to polish flat faces on larger slabs or halves of rocks, like geodes, then you would need a machine called a vibrating lap to polish them. A vibrating lap has a large flat surface infused with grit that the rock sits on and vibrates until it is ground and polished flat. Vibrating laps also come in a range of sizes, from 8" to 27" or larger in diameter. To polish spheres, or round balls of stone in various sizes, there are excellent sphere-making machines available on the market.

If you want to tumble polish your rocks, you will need some patience, a rock tumbler, and an assortment of grit sizes, which range from very coarse 60 grit, up to a fine polishing compound such as cerium or tin oxide. Depending on how rough your rocks are, and whether you use a rotary or vibratory tumbler, it will take anywhere from a week or two to a couple of months to complete a tumbling cycle. Tumbled stones can be used in jewelry like wire-wrapping, or as decorative items displayed in a glass bowl on a tabletop, and make great gifts for children.

For carvers and sculptors, there is a wide range of carving tools. For small jewelry carvings, a hand held Flexshaft or Dremel tool is important, as are a variety of files, sandpapers, and polishing wheels. For larger sculptures, pneumatic tools may be necessary, as well as chisels, rasps, hammers, and polishing equipment.

If your interest is in cutting precious gemstones for jewelry, then you will need a faceting machine. Faceting machines are just what the name implies—a machine that uses various grades of diamond grit impregnated on flat disks to cut and polish facets, or faces, on a gemstone for setting in jewelry. Again, there are many fine manufacturers of faceting machines, and you can usually get any of the related faceting supplies you need from any lapidary supplier.

Many people also like to chip or flake their stones with hand held tools into objects such as arrowheads in a process known as flintknapping. Flint, chert, obsidian, and jasper are just some of the commonly used stones in flintknapping. From the very beginning, native people around the world have fashioned their tools, weapons, and ceremonial objects with the same basic process of knapping that is still in use today. Flintknappers use specialty tools for working and flaking the stone, and these supplies can be found through flintknapping suppliers online, along with rough stones, kits, and instructions for using them.

A diamond grit cabochon polishing machine.

Mineral Specimen Care and Preparation

If you are a mineral collector, due of the multitude of mineral species and varieties, it is usually best to narrow your focus to collecting a particular group or type of mineral. Some of the most common groupings are: by size, such as micromounts; by locality; by rarity; by mineral groups or crystal systems; metallics or fluorescents; and many other ways.

Rock cutting slab saws.

If you have collected your specimens in the field, there are a number of ways to clean and prepare them depending on the chemical composition and fragility of the specimen. If you feel that you can safely trim off any excess matrix without breaking the specimen, you can use a small trim saw, tile

Dop pot, dop wax and sticks.

Tile nippers.

Cabachon marking template.

Vibrating and rotary tumblers with grit.

Household mineral cleaning supplies. Vinegar, dish soap, toothbrush and dental pick.

nippers, chipping hammer, pliers, or chisels. Great care must be taken in the choice of cleaning methods, as many minerals can easily be destroyed by a too harsh cleaning process or inappropriate chemical cleaner. Fine hairlike or tufted mineral specimens can't be cleaned at all, and must be displayed as is. Many minerals can be cleaned by gently brushing with a toothbrush using mild detergent and rinsing in water provided that they are not water-soluble minerals, and high pressure water jets work wonders on more resilient material to remove difficult incrustations. Minerals may be cleaned with vinegar, alcohol, acetone, oxalic acid, muriatic acid, and ultrasonic cleaning. DO NOT use any acids without proper instruction, protective clothing, and understanding of their uses! DO NOT ever add water to acid! ONLY add acids to water – this is the only safe way to dilute them. Acids can be very dangerous and harmful if not used properly, besides destroying your specimens if you use an incompatible solution. There are many excellent reference books on the details of cleaning and preparing minerals, and I strongly suggest you use them.

Once your specimens are clean and prepared, you will want to label and catalog them regarding location, size, variety, date collected, and including any pertinent remarks. One popular way of cataloging is to keep a file of index cards with the information arranged by species with an identifying catalog number for each mineral and the corresponding number written in India ink on a tiny patch of white paint in an inconspicuous place on the specimen.

If your collection is for display, you will need a suitable cabinet for displaying them. An enclosed cabinet is best to keep out excessive light and dust, and to protect them from damage, and glass walls and shelves are desirable so as to be able to view them easily. If the collection isn't for display, minerals can be kept in cabinet drawers in storage trays with individual compartments for each specimen.

Buying and Selling
Rocks, Minerals and Gemstones

Above all else, if you choose to purchase your specimens, always be sure that you are dealing with a reputable person or company, and do as much research as possible beforehand so that you will know what you are getting and buy the best possible material for your money. With that being said, there are some really great options for buying rocks and minerals in today's market. One of the most popular places to buy rocks and minerals these days is on the internet. There are many great mineral and lapidary dealers on the internet, and all you need to do is to type in whatever type of material you're looking for in an online search engine like Google or Yahoo, and go check out their websites. Compare prices among dealers and look at their photographs carefully – established dealers will usually have clear, detailed photos where you can clearly see the actual piece that you would be interested in buying. Online auctions like eBay are another good place to look, and remember, if it seems too good to be true, it probably is!

Another good place to buy rocks and minerals is from a local rock shop. Unfortunately, there aren't quite as many of them as there used to be in the glory days of rockhounding, but they can still be found in many cities and towns. You can usually find them in the Yellow Pages, both print and online, listed under rock or lapidary shops. You can also occasionally find rocks and minerals at neighborhood yard or estate sales, and specialty gift shops.

The storefront of a gem and mineral shop.

A typical booth at the world famous annual Quartzsite Gem and Mineral Show.

One of the best places to find good rocks and mineral specimens is at gem and mineral club shows. These are shows that are held annually by local rock collecting clubs as fundraisers for the club, and usually have a good selection of materials at good prices. There are also larger rock, gem, and mineral trade shows that are held in various parts of the U.S. and abroad, such as the tremendous Tucson Gem and Mineral Show that is held annually in Tucson, Arizona. Large shows like these can encompass hundreds of vendors, with every type of rock, gemstone, or mineral that you can possibly imagine, and people come from every corner of the world to attend them.

Many rock shops offer beads and other jewelry making items.

When buying lapidary materials, such as agate or jasper, you can buy either uncut rough pieces, slabbed (sliced) pieces, or finished cabochons for jewelry making. Prices will vary depending on the size, weight, and quality of the material you're buying. For lapidary materials, good color and pattern is a priority, as is hardness for durability and the ability to take a mirror polish. If you are buying gemstones, you can buy them either rough and uncut, or as completely finished faceted gems. With gemstones, color, clarity, hardness, rarity, and size are all important components of determining their value and cost. Gemstones are usually weighed in carats, semi-precious stones in grams or carats, and lapidary materials in pounds, ounces, or grams.

Cabochons. *Flats of minerals at a rock shop.*

When buying mineral specimens, pieces are usually either sold per single speci-men, or by the flat. A flat is generally a rectangular cardboard box that is filled with a quantity of specimens in compartments or individually wrapped for protection.

If you are interested in selling lapidary or gemstone materials, there are a number of very good venues available to you. You can set up your own personal website store, or sell online at a preexisting store or auction market such as eBay, Overstock, or oth-ers. There are numerous rock and mineral shows throughout the United States, in-cluding both local rock clubs or larger events like the Tucson Gem and Mineral Show or the Quartzsite shows that are held annually or semi-annually. You can also sell your rocks, minerals, or gemstones to brick and mortar rock shops, specialty stores, jewel-ers, lapidary artists, or individual collectors.

In any case, whether you are buying or selling, you always need to be as knowledge-able as you possibly can be about your materials so that you can not only be sure to give your buyers a fair deal if you're selling, but also to not get taken in yourself by an unscrupulous seller if you are buying. Also, you must keep in mind that market prices

Rough rock generally purchased by the pound.

Small scale for weighing stones by the ounce, gram, or carat.

fluctuate both seasonally and yearly on rocks and minerals depending on supply and demand. A particular type of rock that may have cost $2.00 a pound a year ago may now cost $5.00 a pound or more if it has been mined out and is no longer commercially available. Conversely, when a newly discovered deposit enters the market and there is plenty of quality material to be had, that is the optimal time to buy and then sell it later when the supply has markedly dwindled.

A small box of faceted stones.

Ocean Jasper beads.

Collectible Materials for Lapidary Use and Display

Within the lapidary collecting field there are a great many fine materials available for a wide variety of aesthetic applications such as jewelry making, including cabochon cutting and polishing; faceting gemstones; intarsia or inlay; carving decorative items, or simply using as display pieces admired for their beauty or rarity.

The majority of lapidary materials fall within the silicates group, and as such, feature good hardness and durability. For our purposes, this group is generally divided into two categories, crystalline quartz and cryptocrystalline quartz. Quartz is one of the most common minerals on Earth and is the second most abundant mineral in the Earth's continental crust after feldspar. Quartz is composed of silicon dioxide ($SiO2$) with a hardness of 7 on the Mohs scale. When crystalline quartz is pure it is colorless and transparent (commonly known as rock crystal), but when it is infiltrated by other mineral impurities it can exhibit a range of colors and inclusions. Some examples of crystalline quartz include amethyst, citrine, rose quartz, rutilated quartz, and smoky quartz.

Cryptocrystalline quartz is a variety of quartz that is basically the same chemical composition as crystalline quartz, but differs somewhat in its physical properties. The most popular form of cryptocrystalline quartz for lapidary use is called chalcedony (pronounced kal-sid-nee). Chalcedony is tougher than crystalline quartz due to its minute interlocking crystal structure and perpendicular fiber layering. Pure chalcedony is nearly colorless and translucent, but can be colored, banded, and patterned when included with other minerals. When chalcedony has distinctive bands or patterns on a clear or translucent background it is known as agate. When chalcedony is so infiltrated with mineral impurities that it becomes opaque, or nearly so, it is then called jasper. Chert and flint also fall under the category of jasper. Sometimes all three types may be contained in one rock, such as a jasp-agate with some clear translucent areas of chalcedony, areas with agate banding, and opaque jasper or chert sections. Chalcedony, agate, and jasper are among the most favored materials for lapidary use due to their exquisite colors and patterns, excellent hardness, durability, and ability to take a high polish.

Quartz, Chalcedony, Agate and Jasper Values

Generally speaking, prices for rough lapidary materials are valued per pound, per slab, per carat, or by the piece, and categorized by quality. Quality of material for lapidary and display use is determined by a number of factors:

- Hardness and ability to take a good polish without pitting or undercutting.
- Strong color, clarity, or pattern typical of that type of quartz, agate or jasper material. For fine display agates, a complete pattern on the face of the piece is paramount.
- Unusual or rare inclusions.
- Free from flaws such as fractures, breaks, or chips.

When estimating the value of a piece of material for lapidary use, you must first consider what is most important to you. Are you looking to buy a good slab that you can cut yourself into a cabochon for jewelry making, or ready-made cabochons? Are you looking for a world-class polished slab of Laguna agate for your collection to display? Are you looking for large, uncut chunks of rough to make bookends or spheres? What is your budget? If you are buying material for jewelry applications to sell, you will want to buy the best quality pieces that you can afford, but still make a profit once you've cut your stones. Obviously, material of lesser quality will cost less and it will be up to you to find the balance between cost and quality, unless you have unlimited resources to spend.

Typically, slabs that have already been precut from rough rock will cost a little more per pound than the going rate for uncut material due to the time involved in doing the cutting, so be sure to factor that into your expenses too.

If you are buying cabochons, carvings, beads, or other kinds of finished products, the prices will increase depending on the quality and amount of finishing work involved.

Since there can be a wide range of quality within types of material, I am listing the most common retail price range that the average consumer would encounter at an online store, or through a dealer at a gem and mineral show for mid-grade material. Prices can vary considerably depending on fluctuations in the market, and can go sky high for exceptional collector pieces, so always be sure to bring plenty of common sense with you when you are looking to purchase collectible lapidary and display materials!

Quartz, Chalcedony, Agate & Jasper Color Chart

Color chart for quartz, chalcedony, agate, and jasper. Colors are shown at the top of the headers for quick identification.

colorless white gray black brown red orange yellow green blue purple pink metallic

Crystalline Quartz

Crystalline quartz is composed of silicon oxide and is basically clear and colorless, except when tinted by other mineral impurities. Quartz often occurs in clusters with beautiful, well-formed crystals, or in massive form. Quartz crystals are usually hexagonal and prismatic, coming to a point at one end. All members of the quartz family lend themselves to many forms of lapidary uses, such as cabochon cutting, faceting, bead making, and decorative carving. In this section are listed the most commonly found and used types of quartz. As quartz is so commonly found worldwide, only the most popular collectible types of quartz or locations will be listed.

Quartz types are arranged by predominate base color, with secondary colors and inclusions.

Color: Colorless
Group: Silicates
Hardness: 7

Rock Crystal

Clear rock crystal is the purest form of crystalline quartz, with the ideal crystal shape being a six-sided prism terminating with end points having six flat surfaces or facets, known as doubly terminated. In nature, quartz crystals are often twinned, distorted, or so intergrown with adjacent crystals of quartz or other minerals as to only show part of this shape, and are typically formed in hydrothermal veins as a cluster of elongate crystals attached to a wall within a void in the host matrix. Some of the most popular forms of collectible crystals are scepter, doubly terminated, phantom, and Japanese twin. When clear quartz crystal is infiltrated by varying degrees of minerals such as iron oxides, rutile, mica, actinolite, ilmenite, tourmaline or others, the quartz can take on a variety of colors or show inclusions, which then become recognized as their own subspecies, such as rutilated quartz or amethyst quartz.

Clear quartz crystal cluster, Arkansas, USA, 6" x 5".

Single crystal points are commonly used in jewelry wire-wrapped as-is, cut, and polished as cabochons, or faceted as gemstones. Large crystal plates are frequently used by interior designers as decorative display pieces for people's homes or businesses, and many people collect the smaller clusters for their sparkling beauty and, often, for their metaphysical properties.

Some of the very best quartz crystals in the world are located right in the United States in the state of Arkansas within the Ouachita Mountains region where you can go to any of the "dig-your-own" fee-based crystal mines.

Clear quartz crystal with Pyrite flake from Washington Camp, Arizona, 1-1/4" x 1/2".

Strawberry quartz cabochon, 3/4" x 3/4".

Scepter crystal, 2-1/4" x 1".

Occurrences: Arkansas, California, USA; Worldwide.

Value: $7.00 per pound.

Herkimer Diamonds

Color:	Colorless
Group:	Silicates
Hardness:	7.5

"Herkimer diamonds" is the name given to the doubly terminated, water-clear quartz crystals found in Herkimer County, New York, and surrounding areas. Herkimer diamonds have the typical hexagonal habit of quartz, but instead of having a termination on one end they are doubly terminated. Doubly terminated crystals like these are generally quite rare, and this is part of what makes Herkimer diamonds so popular with mineral collectors and jewelry designers worldwide.

Twinned crystals from Herkimer, New York, 3/4" x 1/2".

Although Herkimer County, New York, is the location for which these crystals are named, there are a number of other locations where this type of crystals may be found, including Arizona, USA; Afghanistan, Norway, China, and Ukraine. The crystals from these locations appear almost identical to the Herkimers, but cannot rightfully be called "Herkimer diamonds," as that name refers specifically to that location.

Water-clear Herkimer diamonds are very collectible, but tend to be small ranging in size from 1/8" to usually no more than 1" in length, although crystals up to 6" have been found. For this reason, they are generally used as small display specimens, or wire-wrapped in jewelry unaltered to preserve the integrity of the double termination; or cut and faceted as gemstones for high-end jewelry.

Clear quartz crystal in matrix from Payson, Arizona, 2-1/4" x 1".

Herkimer diamonds can be mined for a fee at a number of privately owned mines in the Herkimer, New York, area.

Occurrences: Herkimer, NY, USA.

Value: $12.00 for a Grade A, 1/2" single crystal.

Rutilated Quartz

Color:	Colorless
Group:	Silicates
Hardness:	6-7

Rutilated quartz contains red and/or yellow rutile inclusions that grow in acicular, prismatic, slender strands that float like fine hairs or golden needles within the clear quartz background.

Rutile and quartz have different levels of hardness on the Mohs scale, quartz being 7 and rutile being 6-6.5. For this reason, it can be difficult to polish the stone properly, as the softer areas of rutile may undercut and leave pitting if the rutiles are within the surface of the stone. But, if the rutiles are entirely encased in quartz, the stone can then be cut for beautiful cabochons or faceted gemstones.

Clear rutilated quartz with red and orange/gold needles, 2" x 1-1/2".

Occurrences: Australia, Brazil, Madagascar, Russia, USA.

Value: $10.00 to $20.00 per pound.

| Color: Colorless |
| Group: Silicates |
| Hardness: 7 |

Tourmalinated Quartz

Clear quartz included with floating, criss-crossing black tourmaline (schorl) needles is known as tourmalinated quartz. It is most commonly used as faceted stones and cabochons for setting in jewelry, and often cut as beads. Tourmalinated quartz also displays beautifully as a mineral specimen, and is frequently used for metaphysical purposes.

Small slab of tourmalinated quartz, 2" x 1".

Tourmalinated quartz fish sculpture, 3-1/2" x 1-3/4".

Occurrences: Brazil, Madagascar, USA.

    Value: $1.00 per carat.

| Color: White |
| Group: Silicates |
| Hardness: 7 |

Milky Quartz

Milky quartz is probably one of the most common varieties of quartz on the planet. Milky quartz is cloudy to opaque with a greasy luster and colored white by numerous, minute internal gas bubbles and impurities. Milky quartz is generally massive in form, occurring in veins. Some milky quartz may include mineral ores such as gold, silver, pyrite, or copper which when cut and polished make exquisite cabochons for jewelry setting.

Milky quartz with copper inclusions, Arizona, 2" x 2".

Milky quartz with schorl tourmaline, 4" x 2-3/4".

Occurrences: Worldwide.

    Value: $1.00 to $2.00 per pound.

Quartz with Gold

| Color: White |
| Group: Silicates |
| Hardness: 7 |

Milky quartz with veins of gold included is one of the rarest forms of natural gold. Milky quartz with gold is highly prized and usually cut as cabochons for fine, high-end jewelry. Quartz with gold is quarried underground by hard rock mining in only a few locations in the world. The majority of the world's production comes from a handful of privately owned mines in Northern California, and you can purchase material from mine operated stores and mineral dealers.

Oval gold in quartz ring, 1" x 1/2", $1,450.00.

Occurrences: Alaska, California, USA; Australia.

Value: Slabs are sold by the troy ounce, ranging from $600.00 to $1,400.00.

Smoky Quartz

| Color: Brown/Black |
| Group: Silicates |
| Hardness: 7 |

Smoky quartz is colored a brownish-black by mineral impurities and exposure to natural radioactivity. Colors can range from light smoky gray to deep chocolate brown, with tints of yellow and copper color. Many of the commercially faceted stones available are not genuine smoky quartz; the material is natural quartz, but it is often irradiated to obtain the smoky color. Smoky quartz is often faceted, cut as cabochons, and made into beads.

Faceted smoky quartz crystal beads, 16" strand.

75 carats smoky quartz wire-wrapped pendant.

Petrified wood with smoky quartz crystals, 5" x 2-3/4".

Occurrences: Argentina, Australia, Brazil; Maine, Colorado, Utah, USA.

Value: $8.00 to $10.00 per pound.

Color: Brown/Gold
Group: Silicates
Hardness: 7

Tiger Eye Quartz

Tiger eye is a chatoyant form of quartz and is a classic example of pseudomorphic replacement by silica of fibrous crocidolite (asbestos). Chatoyant tiger eye exhibits a changeable silky luster as light is reflected within the thin parallel fibrous bands in the structure of the material. Colors are generally yellow to red-brown, and occasionally grayish-blue. Red stones are created through heat treating.

Tiger eye is very popular as a semi-precious gemstone and is usually cut as cabochons for jewelry in order to best display its chatoyancy. Tiger eye is fairly common and inexpensive, and is used for beads, carvings, and other decorative pieces.

Rough chunk of golden tiger eye, 3" x 1".

Occurrences: Australia, Africa, India.

Value: $7.00 to $9.00 per pound.

Color: Yellow
Group: Silicates
Hardness: 7

Citrine Quartz

Citrine is a variety of quartz whose color ranges from a pale yellow to rich golden yellow to dark orange or brown, and gets its color from inclusions of colloidal iron hydrates. Citrine is rarely found naturally. Most commercial citrine is artificially heated amethyst or smoky quartz. Darker colors are more highly prized, including medium golden orange and dark sherry-colored Madeira citrine. It commonly occurs as clusters or druzy coatings, and is most often faceted for jewelry. Citrine crystal clusters make lovely display pieces, and are sometimes used for metaphysical purposes.

Single citrine crystal from Brazil, 1-1/2" x 3/4".

Occurrences: Africa, Brazil, Madagascar, Uruguay.

Value: Mine run: $6.00 per pound.

Aventurine Quartz

Color:	Green
Group:	Silicates
Hardness:	6.5

Aventurine is a tough, granular, green semi-translucent to mostly opaque stone with inclusions of small flakes of mica or hematite that reflect light and give it a shimmering or glistening effect termed aventurescence, and a variety of colors. The most common color of aventurine is green, but it may also be orange, brown, yellow, blue, or gray. Chrome-bearing fuchsite is the classic inclusion, and gives a silvery green or blue sheen. Oranges and browns are attributed to hematite or goethite.

Aventurine is usually cut for cabochons and beads for jewelry. Aventurine has been used for many centuries for jewelry, sculpture, and other ornamental objects. Aventurine is a useful and inexpensive stone and is very popular with jewelry makers.

Polished aventurine quartz, 1-1/4" x 1-3/4".

Occurrences: Africa, Chile, India, Russia; Montana, USA.

Value: $3.00 to $4.00 per pound.

Green Quartz

Color:	Green
Group:	Silicates
Hardness:	7

Green quartz is clear to opaque and colored by a variety of minerals including iron, nickel, copper, chlorite and actinolite. True green quartz is fairly rare and is used in jewelry making or as a display specimen.

Green quartz specimen from Greece, 4" x 1-1/2".

Occurrences: Africa, Greece, India, Mexico; Arizona, Idaho, Michigan, USA.

Value: Brazil, $4.00 per pound.

| Color: Blue |
| Group: Silicates |
| Hardness: 7 |

Blue Quartz

Blue quartz is translucent to opaque, generally massive in form, and also forms as surface crystals. Blue quartz may range from a light blue-gray to a fairly dark periwinkle blue in clear crystals, and may show asterism due to the inclusion of finely dispersed rutile needles. The blue color is due to microscopic inclusions of fibrous magnesiorie-beckite, aerinite, or crocidolite. Blue quartz can be polished as a cabochon, or faceted as a gemstone if the crystal is sufficiently clear.

Blue quartz crystal, Arizona, 3/4" x 1/2".

Massive blue quartz from Quartzsite, Arizona, 5" x 4".

Occurrences: Brazil, India, Madagascar; Alabama, Arizona, Georgia, Vermont, USA.

Value: Brazil, $5.00 per pound.

| Color: Purple |
| Group: Silicates |
| Hardness: 7 |

Amethyst Quartz

Amethyst is quartz colored purple by trace amounts of ferric iron and is one of the most popular gemstones in history. Its color varies from pale lavender to deep purple with red highlights. Amethyst is generally abundant and quite inexpensive, although fine, large Siberian amethyst crystals are rather scarce and may command prices of several tens of dollars per carat. When exposed to strong sunlight for extended periods, amethyst may fade in color. Recently, gem markets have been flooded with inexpensive synthetic amethyst, so be sure that you are dealing with a reputable seller.

Chevron amethyst cut chunk, Mexico, 3-1/2" x 3".

Amethyst is most popularly used in jewelry, and can be either polished as a cabochon, or faceted as a gemstone. Amethyst crystal clusters or points are also used for small carvings, or for decorative and metaphysical purposes. Large amethyst geodes standing many feet tall are highly prized by interior designers and are often displayed as art objects.

Ametrine quartz is a combination of amethyst and citrine within a single crystal. Such bi-colored stones are fairly unusual and can be very striking in appearance. Bi-color crystals combining amethyst and citrine are mainly used as faceted stones for jewelry.

Cactus ametrine cluster, Africa, 4-1/2" x 3".

Amethyst stalagtite slice, Uruguay, 1-1/2" x 1-1/4".

Occurrences: Africa, Brazil, Uruguay.

Value: African mine run: $6.00 to $7.00 per pound.

Rose Quartz

| Color: Pink |
| Group: Silicates |
| Hardness: 7 |

Rose quartz metaphysical pendulum, 1-1/2" x 1".

Rose quartz is a translucent to opaque, massive form of quartz that is colored in shades of pink by traces of manganese, iron, or titanium. Most rose quartz is translucent rather than transparent, and some rose quartz is almost entirely opaque. Colors range from pale pink, to rose pink, lavender pink, and rose red. Some rose quartz may display asterism when heavily included with rutile needles. Specimen rose quartz crystals are very rare in nature but can occasionally be found in Brazil, Maine, and California. Because of its massive size, rose quartz can yield large blocks of material that are suitable for architectural uses, sculpture, and decorative products. Rose quartz is a popular material with lapidaries and jewelry makers, and can be cut for cabochons, beads, spheres, bookends, and carvings. Rose quartz is readily available, and quite inexpensive for most lapidary needs.

Massive rose quartz, 3" x 2-1/2".

Occurrences: Africa, Australia, Brazil, India, Mexico; California, Colorado, South Dakota, Virginia, USA.

Value: $3.00 to $5.00 per pound.

Cryptocrystalline Quartz

This section includes the chalcedonies, agates, and jaspers. Chalcedony is listed by color, and the agates and jaspers are listed by pattern, as they are generally recognized and identified in this way.

Chalcedony, Agate, and Jasper Forms

Shown here are the most common forms, shapes, or structures of chalcedony, agate, and jasper.

Form	Description
Geode	Solid round rock with an open center cavity, often crystal-lined.
Massive	An amorphous structure, thick and dense; often in large solid chunks or seams.
Nodule	Rock with an agatized center, almond, oval or football shaped; Amygdaloidal.
Polyhedral	A sharply geometric or angularly shaped nodule.
Pseudomorph	Silica or another mineral replacing and taking the form of a previous mineral.
Thunderegg	Rock with a solid agatized internal center cavity surrounded by matrix, usually round.
Vein	Rock formed within a crack or fissure, flat or rectangular shaped.

Chalcedony, Agate, and Jasper Characteristics

Some common characteristics of chalcedony, agate, and jasper.

Characteristic	Description
Botryoidal	Rock with a bubbly or grape-like surface coating. Mammillary.
Chatoyance	Shifting Cat's Eye effect created by parallel fibers.
Druze or Druzy	A coating of fine crystals on the surface of a rock.
Enhydro	Solid rock with an internal water-filled cavity, often with a visible air bubble.
Fire	Displays shimmering iridescence within surface layers.
Fluorescent	Exhibits bright colors under ultraviolet light in darkness.
Iris	Rock when cut thin and backlit displays iridescence within its bands.
Opalescence	Displays fiery flashes of color within surface layers.

Parallax	Shadowy effect exposed within tight agate banding when rotated.
Schiller	Broad flashing iridescence due to internal reflection.

Chalcedony, Agate, and Jasper Patterns

Commonly found patterns occurring in chalcedony, agate, and jasper.

Pattern	**Description**
Aggregate Stalks	Fingerlike structures in a row emanating from one direction on one plane.
Banded	Smooth, concentric, unbroken rings.
Brecciated or Ruin	Broken fragments recemented into a random pattern.
Clear	Transparent or translucent.
Cloud	Cloud-like wispy patterns.
Dendritic	Two-dimensional tree or branchlike inclusions.
Dot	Small solid round dots, like a polka dot.
Eye or Orbicular	Small concentric rings or circles, like an eye. Spherulites.
Floater	Small floating banded section in the center of a nodule surrounded by euhedral quartz.
Flower or Bouquet	Singular flowers or groups of puffy clusters resembling flower bouquets.
Fortification	Concentric rings with complex angular or curving patterns.
Lace	Delicate, lacy patterns throughout.
Lattice	Angular, bladed sections in a zigzag or lattice-like pattern.
Moss	Strings, seaweed, or mossy looking inclusions.
Mottled	Irregularly marked with splotches of color.
Plume	Single, three-dimensional feather-like inclusions.
Sagenite	Sprays of needles, hairlike, or fan-like inclusions.
Scenic or Picture	Patterns or lines that resemble landscape formations.
Snowflake	Small floating groups of dots or flakes like snow.
Spiderweb	Criss-cross or woven patterns like a spiderweb.
Tube	Elongated tube-like structures, usually with internal concentric rings.
Waterline	Straight parallel lines of banding.

Chalcedony

Chalcedony is a cryptocrystalline variety of quartz. It is composed of silicon dioxide and has a hardness of 7 on the Mohs scale. It is tough, amorphous, without cleavage, and has a conchoidal fracture. Chalcedony is formed in a number of different environments usually near the surface of the Earth where temperatures are relatively low. Chalcedony develops as veins or nodules from precipitating aqueous solutions within cooled volcanic flows, and is commonly found in the zone of alteration of lode and massive hydrothermal deposits, and as bodies of chert or flint in sedimentary rock deposits. Chalcedony has a dull to waxy luster and often forms as botryoidal or mammilary crusts on the surface of the host rock. In its purest form it is transparent and colorless. It can be colored by mineral impurities that give it a wide range of colors and patterns that are highly desirable for lapidary use.

Chalcedony is also the most common mineral found in pseudomorphic replacements such as petrified wood and fossils.

Chalcedony

Color:	Colorless
Pattern:	None/All
Group:	Silicates
Hardness:	7

Chalcedony can be virtually any color of the rainbow depending on the mineral inclusions that are present within it. It is commonly a clear, pale gray color when not imbued with quantites of other minerals, and is the basic ingredient of all agates, jaspers, and cherts.

When chalcedony is concentrically banded, it is called by the subvariety name agate. When there are flat layers or bands, it is often called by the subvariety name onyx or waterline agate. Many non-banded forms of chalcedony, such as plume, dendritic, sagenitic, or moss agate, are often erroneously called "agates," but only concentrically banded chalcedony is officially what is considered as true "agate." Mottled and included chalcedonies in reality should be called chalcedony with inclusions, but most people typically know these chalcedonies as agates, so I have categorized the included chalcedonies as agates or jaspers for sake of convenience.

Throughout history, chalcedony has been the stone most used by the gem carver, and many colored varieties are cut and polished today as semi-precious gemstones for jewelry making. Very often the surface of chalcedony is covered by fine druzy quartz crystals, and these stones can be cut into beautiful and desirable cabochons.

Chalcedony pseudomorphs after other minerals often give rise to very interesting specimens and are highly collectible as fascinating display pieces.

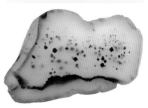

Slab of clear chalcedony with dark, snowflake-like dendritic inclusions, Montana, 2-1/2" x 1-1/2".

Stalactitic chalcedony replacement from central Arizona, 2" x 2".

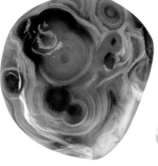

Polished enhydro chalcedony nodule. You can see the trapped air bubble in the large eye area just to the right of center in the photo, Mexico, 1-1/2" x 1-1/4".

Tumble polished snakeskin nodule, Oregon, 1-3/4" x 1-3/4".

Small slab of chalcedony with white sagenite needles, Oregon, 2-1/2" x 1-3/4".

Occurrences: Worldwide.

Value: $1.00 to $5.00 per pound.

| Color: White/Pink |
| Pattern: None |
| Group: Silicates |
| Hardness: 7 |

Chalcedony Rose

A form of gobular chalcedony that has a generally flat shape with rounded hills and valleys that may resemble the shape of a rose. Colors are usually white to pink, and occasionally lavender. Chalcedony roses are often surface coated by sparkling crystals and make pretty display specimens. Sizes can range from 1" up to the size of dinner plates. When collecting chalcedony roses, look for a waxy surface, pink or white color, and unusual undulating shapes.

White and pink chalcedony rose, Arizona, 2" x 1-3/4".

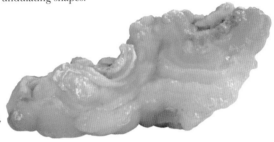

Large pink chalcedony rose, New Mexico, 6" x 3".

Occurrences: Worldwide.

Value: .50 to $3.00 per pound.

| Color: Black |
| Pattern: None/Banded/Cloud |
| Group: Silicates |
| Hardness: 7 |

Black Chalcedony

This form of chalcedony is colored black by mineral inclusions, often with white banding or wispy, cloud-like patterns. A type of black chalcedony geode known as Oco from Brazil is popular for slicing into polished slabs for jewelry making. True black chalcedony is fairly rare, and much clear chalcedony is dyed to create a synthetic black chalcedony.

Brazilian black chalcedony geode with crystal center and cloud patterns, 1-1/2" x 1/2".

Occurrences: Brazil, Mexico, Uruguay; Florida, South Dakota, USA.

Value: $3.00 to $8.00 per pound.

Fire Agate

Color: Brown/White	
Pattern: None/Banded	
Group: Silicates	
Hardness: 7	

Fire agate is a variety of chalcedony containing a transparent quartz layer over a thin layer of goethite or limonite, that produces an iridescent or "fiery" effect when cut and polished properly. The most common colors are brown, gold, red, green and orange, with purple and blue being the rarest.

Fire agates, at their best, have all the brilliant flash of opals and are often confused with opal, although they differ in color and composition from opal in a number of ways, most obviously in that their background color is usually a brown color not found in precious opal. Fire agate is most commonly used in fine jewelry, cut as cabochons.

Large rough chunk of fire agate, Arizona, 3" x 2".

Polished fire agate cabochon. Arizona, 1-3/4" x 1-1/4".

Occurrences: Arizona, California, USA. Mexico.

Value: $10.00 to $18.00 per pound.

Carnelian

Color: Orange/Red	
Pattern: None/Banded	
Group: Silicates	
Hardness: 7	

Carnelian is a translucent variety of chalcedony that owes its orange, red, and reddish-brown color to colloidally dispersed hematite, and it may contain the full spectrum of inclusions. It is a close relative of sard, which is harder, more opaque, duller, and darker, with shades ranging from a deep reddish-brown to almost black. Both carnelian and sard have been used as a favorite lapidary material for centuries. Carnelian lends itself well to cutting for cabochons and beads, and for carving many types of decorative objects. Carnelian is often heat treated or dyed with iron salts to enhance color. Carnelian is a fairly common and inexpensive stone.

Carved and polished carnelian rooster, 1-1/2" x 1-1/4".

Rough carnelian, New Mexico, 6" x 5".

Occurrences: Australia, Brazil; India, Mexico; Oregon, New Jersey, New Mexico, Tennessee, USA.

Value: $3.00 to $8.00 per pound.

Color:	Green
Pattern:	None
Group:	Silicates
Hardness:	7

Chrysoprase

Chrysoprase is a translucent form of chalcedony that is colored green by trace amounts of nickel. The color varies from a bright apple green to dark green. Because of its semi-opaque green color, it is often mistaken for Imperial Jadeite. Chrysoprase is one of the most valuable of all the chalcedony gemstones, and is most often used as cabochons for jewelry making. A very similar mineral to chrysoprase is chrome chalcedony, in which the color is provided by chromium rather than nickel.

Polished piece of chrysoprase, Australia, 3-3/8" x 1-3/8".

Carved chrysoprase lizard on matrix, 3" x 2" x 1".

Occurrences: Australia; Brazil; Poland; California, Colorado, USA.

Value: $1.50 to $6.00 per gram.

Chrysocolla

Color:	Blue/Green
Pattern:	None
Group:	Silicates
Hardness:	7

   Chrysocolla is an attractive blue-green mineral that forms in the oxidation zones of copper rich ore bodies.

   Pure chrysocolla is quite soft and fragile (2 - 4 on the Mohs scale) so, therefore, on its own, it is not appropriate for use in lapidary applications. However, chrysocolla often is "agatized" by silica and it is the silica that provides the stone with its strength and durability. Gem silica is the highest grade of silicified chrysocolla, and is very desirable as a lapidary material. Cabochons of unpolished druzy or botryoidal chrysocolla are also often used as-is in designer jewelry.

Rare, double terminated chrysocolla crystal, Arizona, 3/4" x 3/8".

Rough gem chrysocolla, 3" x 4"

Polished chrysocolla/malachite massage wand, Arizona, 3-5/8" x 5/8".

Occurrences: Africa; Australia; Mexico; Russia; Arizona, USA.

Value: Gem silica: $100.00 to $400.00 per pound.

| Color: Blue |
| Pattern: None/Banded |
| Group: Silicates |
| Hardness: 7 |

Blue Chalcedony

Blue chalcedony is a clear to translucent chalcedony colored blue by traces of iron, titanium, manganese, or copper. Most blue chalcedony is actually more gray than blue, but material from a number of locations displays true shades of blue, ranging from a lovely violet-blue to sky blue to robin's-egg blue. True blue chalcedony is uncommon and highly desirable as a lapidary material. Some blue chalcedonies have light banding, dendrites, or other inclusions within them, and can sometimes exhibit chatoyancy. Blue chalcedony is mainly used as cut stones in jewelry making. Clear chalcedony is often dyed or heat treated to imitate blue chalcedony.

Light blue chalcedony polished half nodule, 1-3/4" x 1-1/2".

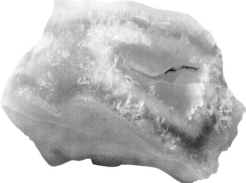

Blue banded chalcedony nodule, Arizona, 1-3/4" x 1-1/4".

Rough piece of blue Mt. Airy chalcedony, Nevada, 5" x 3-1/2".

Rough chunk of rare California Mojave blue agate, 2-3/4" x 1-3/4".

Occurrences: Africa; California, Nebraska, Oregon, South Dakota, Washington, USA.

Value: $15.00 to $30.00 per pound.

Purple Chalcedony

| Color: Purple/Lavender |
| Pattern: None/All |
| Group: Silicates |
| Hardness: 7 |

A clear to translucent chalcedony colored by trace impurities, such as manganese or iron oxides. Purple chalcedony is an uncommon stone and fairly expensive. Some purple chalcedonies have light banding, dendrites, or other inclusions within them, such as the dendritic Amethyst Sage from Nevada. Purple chalcedony is most often used in jewelry as cabochons and beads. Clear chalcedony is often dyed or heat treated to imitate purple chalcedony.

Purple chalcedony beads and cabochon, 1/2" x 3/8".

Purple chalcedony slab, California, 2-1/2" x 2-1/2".

Purple chalcedony with dendrites, commercially known as Amethyst Sage, Denio, Nevada, 3" x 1-1/2".

Occurrences: Africa, Indonesia, Turkey; Arizona, California, Nevada, USA.

Value: Nevada material: $20.00 per pound.

Color: Pink	
Pattern: None/Banded	
Group: Silicates	
Hardness: 7	

Pink Chalcedony

Pink chalcedony is a clear to translucent chalcedony colored pink by traces of iron oxides, manganese, or other minerals. Pink chalcedony often occurs in a gobular, botryoidal form known as chalcedony rose; as nodules, or as a replacement after wood as seen in the famous Texas Springs, Nevada, limb casts. Some pink chalcedonies have light banding, dendrites, or other inclusions within them. Pink chalcedony makes lovely cabochons, beads, and carvings. Pink chalcedony roses make interesting display pieces.

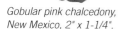

Gobular pink chalcedony, New Mexico, 2" x 1-1/4".

Pink chalcedony limb cast, Texas Springs, Nevada, 3-1/4" x 1-1/2".

Rare pink banded nodule with snowflakes, Arizona, 2-1/2" x 2-1/2".

Occurrences: Africa, India; Arizona, California, Nevada, Oregon, South Dakota, USA.

Value: 2" pink chalcedony rose, $3.00; Texas Spring, Nevada, pink limb cast: $18.00 per pound.

Agate

Historically by definition, true agate is a transparent form of chalcedony with only concentric banding, but today the term agate is commonly used to include chalcedonies with many different kinds of mineral inclusions, patterns, and colors. Agates of many different types may be found throughout the world, and exceptionally fine and desirable agates may be collected in a number of locations.

Agate is present primarily in volcanic flows, but can occur in other environments, and forms as veins, masses, nodules, or interstitial fillings.

As I am predominately an agate collector, I am extremely fortunate to live in the state of Arizona where I am in close proximity to many excellent agate collecting locations that occur not only within Arizona itself, but also in the neighboring states of California, New Mexico, Utah, and Texas. Due to its specific types of volcanic geology, the Southwest United States is a prime location for finding good agate, jasper, and many other fine collectible materials. You may notice that many of the specimens in this section come from this region since it includes a portion from my own personal collection that I've hand collected myself, and other pieces contributed by rockhound friends of mine who are also located in this area.

Due to the numerous varieties of agates that are identified either by their location and/or their pattern type, I am grouping them by common patterns and including types specifically recognized by their locations, in the way that they would be most commonly known and identified.

Agate types are arranged in order by the most common pattern or inclusions associated with that type of agate. Some agates may contain more than one pattern, and are listed by their primary pattern or attribute. Agate sizes are the height and width across the face of the specimen.

Group: Silicates

Hardness: 7

Banded Agate

Banded agates are recognized by their parallel, concentric banding, and nodular shape. Most banded agates are not overly colorful, usually occurring in subtle shades of white, gray, or tan. There are exceptions, though, at certain locations where vividly colored agates can be found with hues of vibrant reds, pinks, purples, yellow, and more.

When banded and fortification agates have very tight banding, an interesting phenomena occurs called "parallax." This is a visual effect that resembles a shadowy movement within the stone's bands when it is slowly rotated in the light.

Banded agates make beautiful cabochons and are a very popular lapidary material.

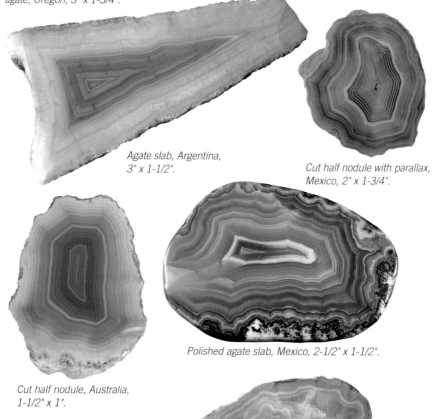

Rough chunk of Holley blue agate, Oregon, 3" x 1-3/4".

Agate slab, Argentina, 3" x 1-1/2".

Cut half nodule with parallax, Mexico, 2" x 1-3/4".

Polished agate slab, Mexico, 2-1/2" x 1-1/2".

Cut half nodule, Australia, 1-1/2" x 1".

Banded agate, Mississippi, 3" x 1-1/2".

Cut Botswana nodule, Africa, 2" x 1-1/2".

Polished agate slab, Brazil, 4" x 2-1/2".

Rough Brazilian agate, 4" x 5".

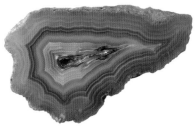

Polished coyamito nodule, Mexico, 2" x 1-1/4".

Agate nodule with center floater, Mexico, 2" x 1-1/2".

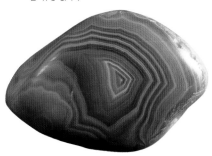

Lake Superior agate, Michigan, 2" x 1-1/2".

Nodule with two separate pattern centers, Arizona, 2-1/4" x 1-1/2".

Purple banded nodule, Arizona, 4" x 3 1/2".

Occurrences: Africa, Australia, Brazil, Germany, Mexico, Scotland; Arizona, California, Michigan, Minnesota, New Mexico, USA.

Value: Brazillian agate: $3.00 per pound.

Group: Silicates

Hardness: 7

Brecciated Agate

Brecciated agate is an agate in which previously broken angular pieces of agate or jasper are recemented with chalcedony to form a new type of agate. The recemented pieces are randomly arranged and the internal agate pattern often has a jagged, mosaic look with clear lines of demarcation between the more solid fragments. Brecciated agate is usually cut for cabochons and is also known by the name ruin agate.

Burro Creek pastelite slab, Arizona, 5" x 4-1/2".

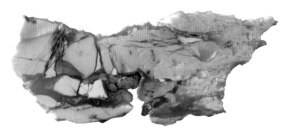

Burro Creek slab, Arizona, 3" x 1-1/4".

Brecciated rough with fortification, California, 2-1/2" x 1-1/2".

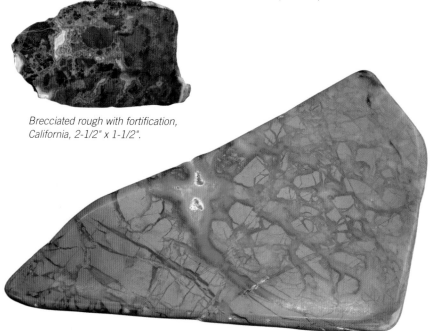

Stone Canyon polished slab, California, 3-1/2" x 1-3/4".

Occurrences: Brazil, Germany, Mexico; Arizona, California, Wyoming, USA.

Value: $2.00 to $4.00 per pound.

Dendritic Agate

Group: Silicates
Hardness: 7

Dendritic agate is a type of agate that displays sharply defined, two-dimensional, tree-like branching patterns within the stone. The very best dendritic agate has the dendrites floating in clear chalcedony, like the picturesque and well known Montana agates or the beautifully patterned dendritic agates from India. Dendrites also occur as surface coatings on the exterior of agates and other materials like limestone or slate.

Dendrites are usually inclusions of manganese minerals that have infiltrated and filled cracks between flat layers or bands within the chalcedony, creating the lovely patterns that lapidaries find so desirable for cabochon cutting.

Unpolished slab, New Mexico, 2-3/4" x 2-1/2".

Contour polished slab, California, 6" x 4".

Polyhedroid with dendrites, Brazil.

Unpolished dendritic slab, Arizona, 2-1/2" x 2".

Rough exterior of Montana agate, 3" x 2-1/4".

Tumble polished agate slab, Montana, 2" x 1-1/4".

Polished Owl Hole agate, California, 2-1/2" x 2".

Polished agate slab, Montana, 2-1/2" x 1-3/4".

Polished agate slab, Arizona, 1-1/2" x 1-1/4".

Tumble polished slab, Arizona, 1-3/4" x 3/4".

Occurrences: Brazil, India, Kazakhstan, Mexico; Arizona, California, Montana, Nevada, Oregon, USA.

Value: $5.00+ per pound.

Dot and Eye Agate

Group: Silicates
Hardness: 7

Dot agates consist of random floating solid round dots of varying size and color on a plain background, and Eye agates contain spherulites or orbs of one or more concentric round rings that resemble eyeballs. An Eye agate with one large eye is often called a "bullseye" agate. In some display agates, the eyes are actually internal pseudomorphic replacement tube structures that have been cut perpendicular to the tube to create the eye pattern. Dot and eye agates make beautiful display specimens and are frequently cut as cabochons for jewelry.

Rough eye agate, California, 5" x 3".

Polished eye agate, Arizona, 1-1/2" x 1".

Polished crazy lace agate, Mexico, 3/4" x 3/4".

Polished eye agate, California, 3" x 2".

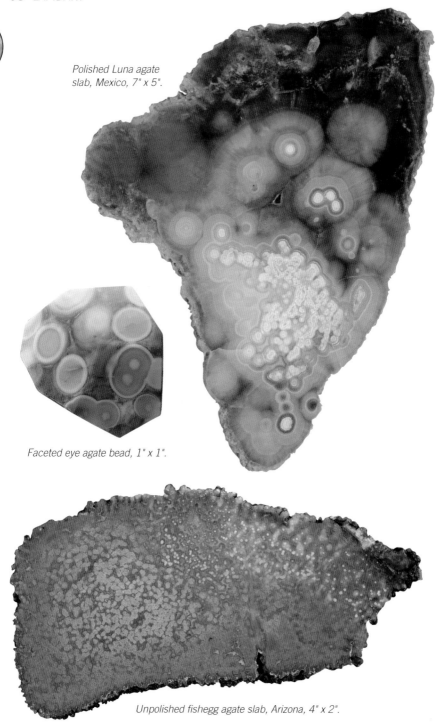

Polished Luna agate
slab, Mexico, 7" x 5".

Faceted eye agate bead, 1" x 1".

Unpolished fishegg agate slab, Arizona, 4" x 2".

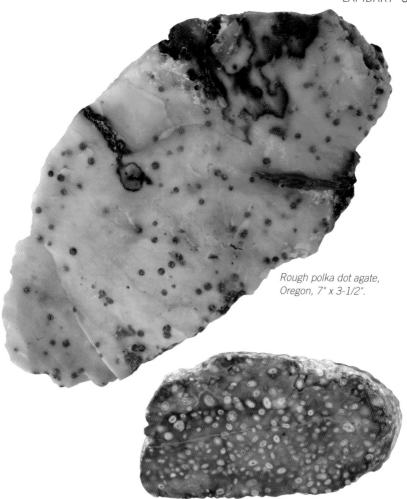

Rough polka dot agate,
Oregon, 7" x 3-1/2".

Oolitic agate, Arizona, 2" x 1".

Rough fishegg agate, Arizona,
3" x 1-1/2".

Occurrences: Brazil, China, Hungary, Mexico; Arizona, California, Michigan, Oregon, USA.

Value: Polka dot agate; $10.00 per pound.

| Group: Silicates |
| Hardness: 7 |

Flame Agate

Flame agate is generally a vein agate with patterns shaped like flames of fire. The flame patterns generally run along the outside edges of the agate with the flames pointing inward, with the center of the agate usually fairly clear and transparent. Flame agate comes in a variety of colors, and occurs in many locations where varietal agate is found. Flame agate is customarily cut for cabochons or polished as display pieces.

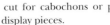

Polished agate chunk, Nova Scotia, Canada, 6-1/4" x 1-3/4".

Unpolished slab, Mexico, 4-1/2" x 4".

Occurrences: Australia, Brazil, Germany, Mexico; Arizona, California, New Mexico, USA.

Value: $3.00 to $8.00 per pound.

Flower or Bouquet Agate

Group: Silicates
Hardness: 7

Flower agate is a nodular or vein agate with inclusions that look like flowers, bouquets, or round puffy plumes on a clear chalcedony background. Flower agate patterns make beautiful cabochons for jewelry making, and flower agates from Texas and Oregon are highly prized by collectors and lapidaries.

Bouquet agate slab, Marfa, Texas, 6-1/4" x 4-1/4".

Rough cut agate chunk, Arizona, 3" x 1-3/4".

Wingate agate slab, California, 4" x 2".

Rough cut agate chunk, Arizona, 3" x 1-3/4".

Magnesite flower agate slab, Anderson Lake, California, 6" x 4".

Occurrences: Mexico; Arizona, California, Oregon, Texas, USA.

Value: $10.00+ per pound.

Group: Silicates
Hardness: 7

Fortification Agate

Fortification agate differs from banded agate in that the bands are much more complex and irregular with scallops, angles, and sharp curving patterns, and often containing other inclusions. Fortification agate is also generally gray or white, but can have spectacular displays of color such as found in the best Mexican agates or boldly striking patterns such as the Fairburns of the South Dakota Badlands.

Fortification agates are mainly cut as cabochons for jewelry, and the finest fortification agates when face polished make outstanding display specimens.

Polished slab with quartz center, Mexico, 3" x 2-1/4".

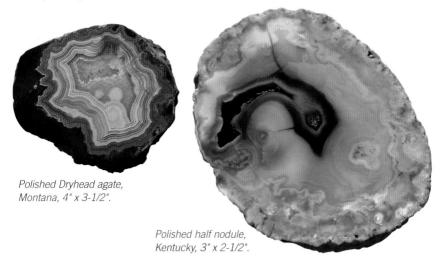

Polished Dryhead agate, Montana, 4" x 3-1/2".

Polished half nodule, Kentucky, 3" x 2-1/2".

Polished Agua Nueva agate, Mexico.

Polished Fairburn agate,
Nebraska, 3-1/4" x 1-3/4".

Unpolished cut nodule,
Germany, 3-1/2" x 1-3/4".

Polished fortification agate with stalk aggregates,
California, 2-1/4" x 1".

Polished Laguna agate,
Mexico.

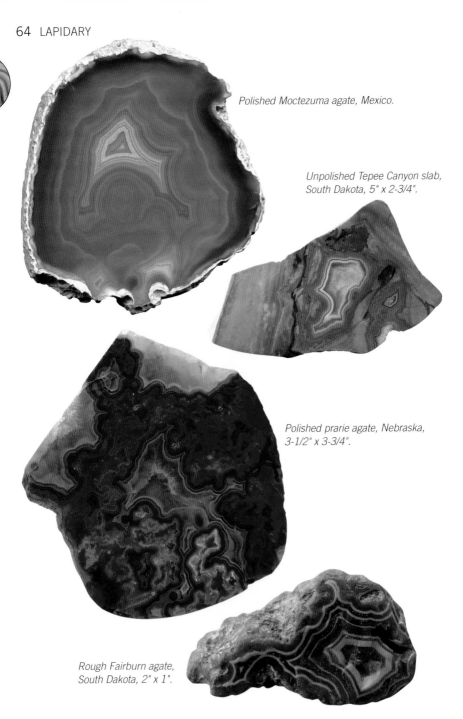

Polished Moctezuma agate, Mexico.

Unpolished Tepee Canyon slab,
South Dakota, 5" x 2-3/4".

Polished prarie agate, Nebraska,
3-1/2" x 3-3/4".

Rough Fairburn agate,
South Dakota, 2" x 1".

Occurrences: Argentina, Australia, Germany, Mexico; Arizona, California,
Kentucky, New Mexico, South Dakota, Wyoming, USA.

Value: Laguna agate: $16.00 to $25.00 per pound.

Lace and Lattice Agate

Group: Silicates
Hardness: 7

Lace agate is an agate that has an overall lacy pattern that may include eyes, swirls, banding, scallops, and zigzags. When lace agate is almost entirely composed of a zigzag pattern, it is known as lattice agate. Lace agate is generally a vein agate, and comes in a variety of colors from a number of locations worldwide, some of the most famous being the colorful Mexican crazy lace and softly beautiful African blue lace. Lace agates tend to be hard and take an excellent polish for lapidary work.

Rough lace agate, Georgia, 3" x 2".

African blue lace slab, 4-1/2" x 1-1/2".

Red crazy lace agate polished slab, Mexico, 2-3/4" x 1-1/2".

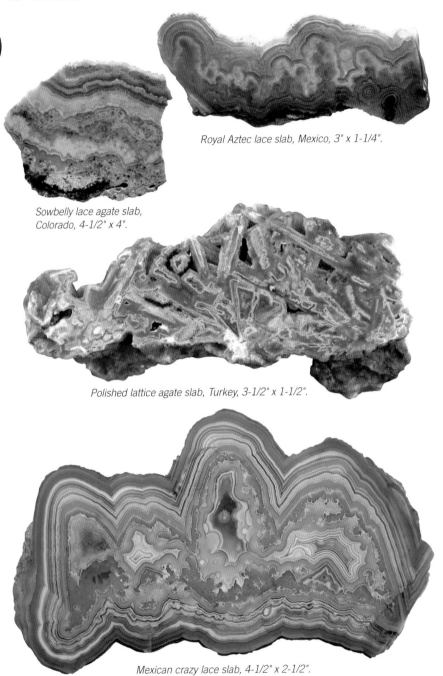

Royal Aztec lace slab, Mexico, 3" x 1-1/4".

Sowbelly lace agate slab, Colorado, 4-1/2" x 4".

Polished lattice agate slab, Turkey, 3-1/2" x 1-1/2".

Mexican crazy lace slab, 4-1/2" x 2-1/2".

Occurrences: Africa, Mexico; Arizona, California, Colorado, Missouri, USA.

Value: African Blue lace: $15.00 per pound.

Moss Agate

Group: Silicates
Hardness: 7

Moss agate is a vein or nodular agate that contains colorful and delicate inclusions that resemble seaweed, moss, strings, or filaments on a clear chalcedony background. Moss agate can occur in a variety of colors including green, red, yellow, orange, black, and white. The moss inclusions are created by different mineral impurities such as manganese, chlorite, or iron oxides. Moss agate has been worked for centuries and is still a favorite of lapidaries today for cabochon cutting and polished display specimens.

Polished half nodule, Klama, Washington, 2-1/2" x 2".

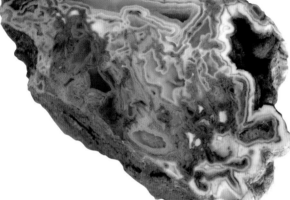

Horse Canyon agate chunk, California, 3-1/4" x 1-3/4".

Green moss agate slab, India, 2-1/2" x 2".

Polished slab,
Scotland,
2-1/2" x 1-1/4".

Colorful unpolished moss agate,
Oregon, 3-1/2" x 2".

Moss agate half nodule,
California, 4" x 2-3/4".

Polished Rio Grande agate,
Texas, 3-1/2" x 2-1/2".

Unpolished agate slab,
California, 2-1/2" x 1-3/4".

Polished agate slab, Arizona,
2-1/2" x 1-1/4".

Cut unpolished agate chunk,
Oregon, 4" x 2-1/2".

Unpolished Brenda agate,
Arizona, 2" x 1-3/4".

Tumble polished lavender moss agate,
Arizona, 2" x 1-3/4".

Occurrences: Africa, India, Mexico; Arizona, California, Nevada, Montana, Oregon, Texas, USA.

Value: Indian green moss agate: $4.00 per pound.

Plume Agate

Group: Silicates
Hardness: 7

Plume agate is a vein or nodular agate that displays graceful, three-dimensional, feather or plume-like inclusions on a clear chalcedony background. The plume patterns may consist of only one single plume, or a small grouping of plumes. Either way, the plumes are distinctive, individual plumes similar to an ostrich feather, and top quality plume agate material is highly prized by lapidaries and collectors of fine agate specimens. Plumes can occur in a variety of colors and may have a submetallic luster due to minerals such as pyrolusite, goethite, or manganese.

Canadian River agate slab, Texas, 4-1/2" x 3-1/2".

Graveyard Point rough chunk, Idaho, 4-1/2" x 2-1/2".

Polished Del Norte agate, Colorado, 5-3/4" x 3".

Polished Horse Canyon agate, California, 4" x 2".

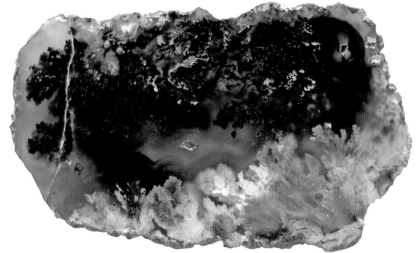

Polished Marfa plume agate, Texas, 3-1/4" x 2".

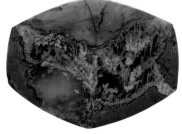

Priday plume cabochon, Oregon, 1-3/4" x 1-1/4".

Unpolished plume slab, New Mexico, 3-3/4" x 2-1/2".

Unpolished cut plume agate, California, 4" x 3".

Unpolished Butte Creek agate, Oregon, 3" x 3".

Polished Owl Hole agate, California, 3" x 1-3/4".

Polished Woodward Ranch cabochon, Texas, 2" x 1-1/2".

Unpolished Woodward Ranch biscuit, Texas, 3" x 1-1/2".

Polished Stinking Water slab, Oregon, 8-1/4" x 2".

Occurrences: Argentina, Brazil, India, Morocco, Mexico; Arizona, California, Nevada, Oregon, Texas, USA.

Value: Woodward Ranch plume agate: $12.00 per pound.

| Group: Silicates |
| Hardness: 7 |

Sagenite Agate

Sagenite agate is a vein or nodular agate with needle-like inclusions, occurring loosely dispersed, or collectively in sprays or fan shapes. The best sagenite agate has a clear chalcedony background where the needles are uninterrupted and appear to be floating freely. Sagenite needles are composed of a variety of minerals, including rutile, manganese, chlorite, actinolite, or goethite, and are often pseudomorphic replacements of other minerals such as barite or aragonite. Sagenite agate in another example of a highly collectible and much sought-after agate for both jewelry applications and display.

Polished half nodule, California, 2-1/2" x 2".

Polished slab, Oregon, 5-3/4" x4".

Million Dollar Hill polished half nodule, Idaho, 3-1/2" x 3-1/2".

Rough nodule showing external spray, Arizona, 3" x 2".

Unpolished half nodule, Arizona, 2" x 1-1/2".

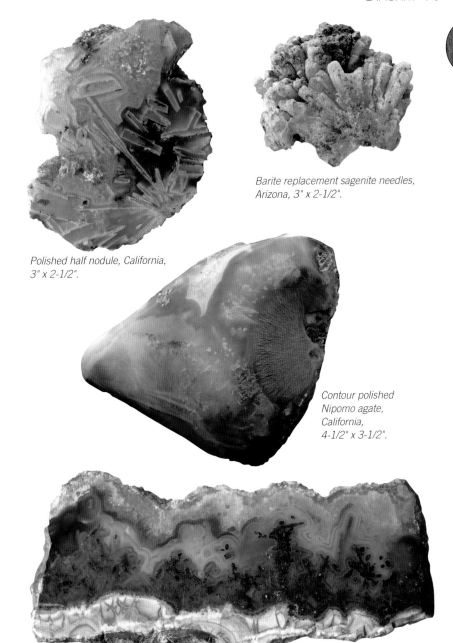

Barite replacement sagenite needles,
Arizona, 3" x 2-1/2".

Polished half nodule, California,
3" x 2-1/2".

Contour polished
Nipomo agate,
California,
4-1/2" x 3-1/2".

Agate slab with stibnite needles, Oregon, 4-1/4" x 1-3/4".

Occurrences: Brazil, Germany, Mexico; Arizona, California, Nevada,
Oregon, New Mexico, USA.

Value: $6.00+ per pound.

Group: Silicates

Hardness: 7

Snowflake Agate

Snowflake agate is a vein or nodular agate that has little floating white flecks or flakes in clear chalcedony that look like snowflakes. Some of the flakes can have a lenticular shape and look like tiny spaceships. Snowflakes have a tendency to occur in banded agates, but can appear with almost any of the other agate types. In some of the dendritic agates there are snowflakes that are colored black and brown by different mineral inclusions.

Snowflake agates are used primarily for cabochon cutting and occasionally for polished display pieces.

Banded snowflake half nodule, California, 2-1/2" x 2".

Banded snowflake half nodule, Arizona, 2-1/2" x 1-1/2".

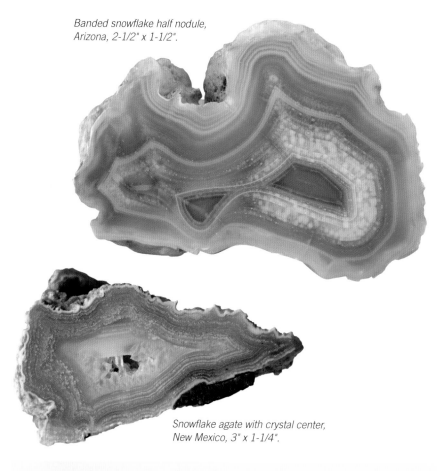

Snowflake agate with crystal center, New Mexico, 3" x 1-1/4".

Occurrences: Brazil, Mexico; Arizona, California, New Mexico, Montana, USA.

Value: $6.00 per pound.

Tube Agate

Group: Silicates
Hardness: 7

Tube agate is a nodular or vein agate with internal pseudomorphic replacements of crystals or needles that create stalagtitic or tube-like formations within the stone. When tube agate is cut parallel to the pattern, it reveals a long finger-like tube, and when cut perpendicular, or across the tube, creates an eye or orbicular pattern. Tube agates make fascinating display specimens, and when properly cut, exquisite cabochons.

Slab cut across the tube for bull's eye, New Mexico, 4-1/2" x 3-1/2".

Polished Agua Nueva agate, Mexico, 4-3/4" x 2-3/4".

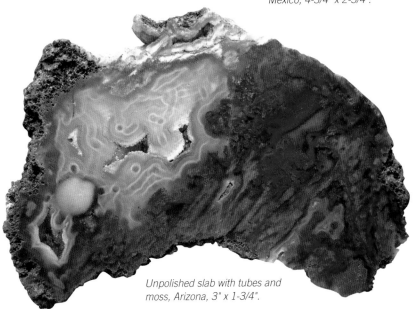

Unpolished slab with tubes and moss, Arizona, 3" x 1-3/4".

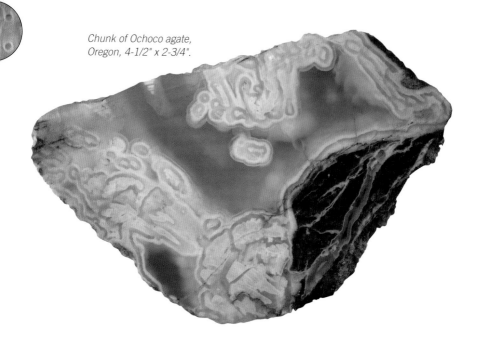

Chunk of Ochoco agate, Oregon, 4-1/2" x 2-3/4".

Paul Bunyon agate slab, California, 4" x 2-1/2".

Unpolished cut rough agate, Nevada, 3-1/2" x 2".

Tube formation with druzy coating, New Mexico, 4" x 2-1/2".

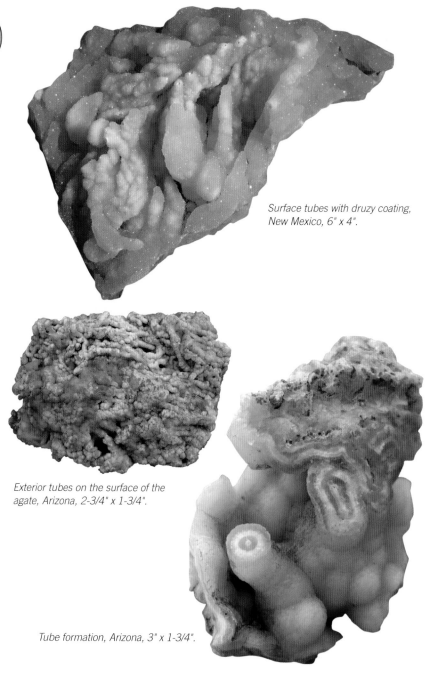

Surface tubes with druzy coating, New Mexico, 6" x 4".

Exterior tubes on the surface of the agate, Arizona, 2-3/4" x 1-3/4".

Tube formation, Arizona, 3" x 1-3/4".

Occurrences: Argentina, Brazil, Mexico, Morocco; Arizona, California, Nevada, Oregon, Texas, USA.

Value: Brazillian agate: $6.00 to $12.00 per pound.

Waterline Agate

Group: Silicates
Hardness: 7

Waterline agate is a nodular or vein agate that exhibits straight rows of colored lines, usually white, on a clear chalcedony background. Waterline agate can occur with other agate patterns, such as banded, dendritic, or moss types. Waterline agate is also known as onyx agate or Uruguay banding.

Waterline agate is generally cut as cabochons or beads for jewelry making.

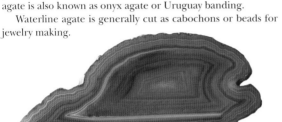

Polished Australian half nodule, 1-1/2" x 1".

Polished agate slab, Brazil, 4-1/2" x 2".

Unpolished half nodule with moss, California, 1-1/2" x 1-1/2".

Unpolished half nodule, California, 2" x 1-1/2".

Polished Red Top agate, Washington, 4-1/2" x 2".

Occurrences: Argentina, Australia, Germany, Scotland; Arizona, California, Idaho, New Mexico, USA.

Value: $4.00 to $6.00 per pound.

| Group: Silicates |
| Hardness: 7 |

Iris Agate

Iris agate isn't a particular type of agate, but rather a visual phenomenon that occurs rarely in certain agates. The iris effect is usually found in colorless banded nodular agates, often with a quartz filled center. The iris effect is caused by extremely fine banding that diffracts light as it passes through the stone and produces a spectrum of rainbow colors. The iris effect is not visible to the naked eye under ordinary conditions, and the agate must be cut into very thin slices (1/16" - 3/32") and viewed in front of a light source at the correct angle to see the fire within.

Backlit slice the showing iris effect, California, 2" x 1-1/2".

Iris agate is primarily of interest to collectors as display specimens.

Another backlit slice showing iris, California, 1" x 1-1/2".

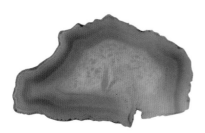

Iris agate in plain daylight, California, 2-1/2" x 1-3/4".

The same agate comes alive when viewed in the proper light.

Occurrences: Argentina, Mexico; Arizona, California, Oregon, Montana, Tennessee, USA.

Value: $25.00+ per specimen slice.

Pseudomorphic Agate

Group: Silicates
Hardness: 7

Pseudomorphic agate is agate that has sections that are replacements of previous minerals or crystal forms with silica, the prime ingredient of chalcedony. Tube agate, as previously described, is a pseudomorph, as are petrified wood and many of the fossils that are popularly collected today. Included here are examples of pseudomorphic replacement of mineral or crystal forms. Petrified wood and fossils are covered in another chapter.

Polished pseudomorphic coyamito agate, Mexico, 3" x 4-1/4".

Coyamito agate with aragonite replacement, Mexico.

Agate with replacement after barite, Arizona, 3" x 2".

Pseudomorphic display specimen, Arizona, 8" x 4".

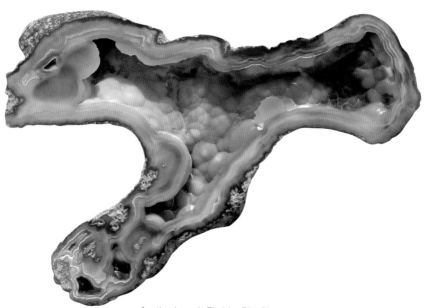

Agatized coral, Florida, 5" x 3".

Occurrences: Argentina, Germany, Mexico, Turkey; Arizona, California, Florida, Georgia, New Mexico, USA.

Value: $5.00+ per pound.

Geodes

Group: Silicates
Hardness: 7

Geodes are formed by chalcedony that is deposited in rhyolite vugs, or cavities, leaving a hollow center. Geodes are frequently lined with beautiful crystal formations, including amethyst, and are primarily cut in half and polished as display specimens. Some small geode slices are used in jewelry making and geodes are a perennial favorite among children as collectibles.

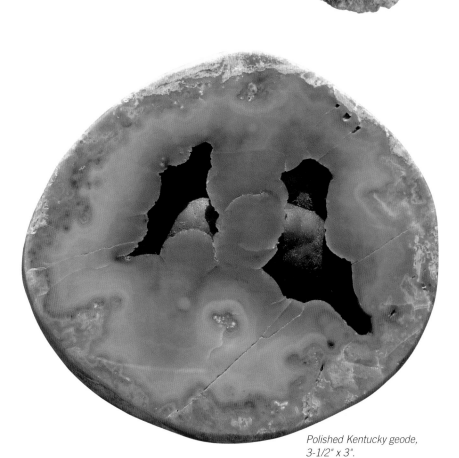

Exterior of Mexican coconut geode, 3".

Polished Kentucky geode, 3-1/2" x 3".

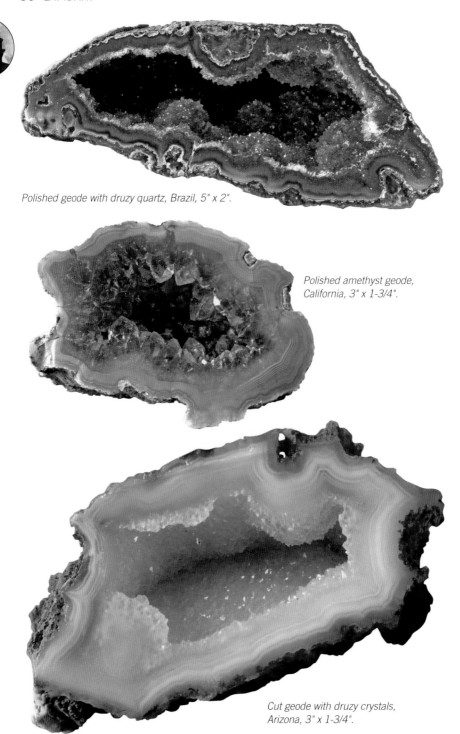

Polished geode with druzy quartz, Brazil, 5" x 2".

Polished amethyst geode, California, 3" x 1-3/4".

Cut geode with druzy crystals, Arizona, 3" x 1-3/4".

Polished geode, Argentina, 3" x 2".

Dugway geode, Utah, 8-1/2" x 5-1/2".

Occurrences: Brazil, Germany, Mexico; Arizona, California, Kentucky, Oregon, Nevada, Texas, Utah, USA.

Value: Dugway geodes: $3.50 per pound.

Group: Silicates
Hardness: 7

Thundereggs

Thundereggs are solid, spherical-shaped nodules that are agate-filled, with an external rind, generally of a rhyolite type. Thundereggs occur in decomposed volcanic ash beds, and are usually hidden beneath the surface, just waiting to be uncovered by an enthusiastic rock digger. The chalcedony interiors of thundereggs often contain beautiful inclusions of plume, sagenite, moss, or fortification banding, and on occasion, opal.

Thundereggs must be cut in half to reveal what lies within. Thundereggs are commonly used for cutting cabochons and for polished display pieces.

Unpolished Del Norte thunderegg, Colorado, 4" x 3-1/2".

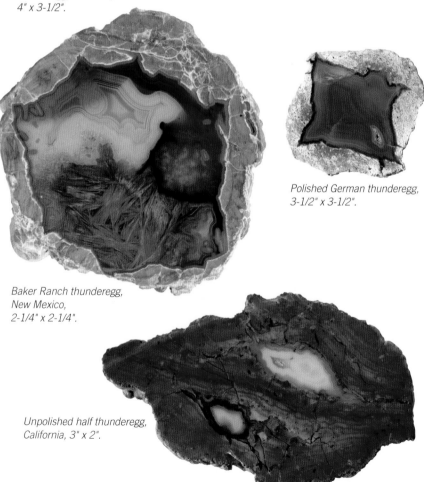

Baker Ranch thunderegg, New Mexico, 2-1/4" x 2-1/4".

Polished German thunderegg, 3-1/2" x 3-1/2".

Unpolished half thunderegg, California, 3" x 2".

Typical thunderegg exterior, 8".

Unpolished Arizona thunderegg, 3-1/2" x 3".

Unpolished half thunderegg, unknown location, 2" x 2".

Occurrences: Australia, Germany, Mexico; Arizona, California, Colorado, Idaho, Nevada, New Mexico, Oregon, USA.

Value: Opal Butte thundereggs: $8.00 per pound.

Jasper

Jasper is also a form of chalcedony that is opaque, tough, fibrous, and massive with a greater density of mineral inclusions—such as iron oxides and earthy clays—than agate. Jasper can occur as nodules or veins in bedded sedimentary or metamorphic deposits, and altered igneous rock deposits. Jasper is often found in conjunction with agate and the two are often intermingled (called jasp-agate), creating colorful and striking specimens that make gem cabochons of great beauty. Jasper has many of the same types of patterns as agate, although they are usually not quite as fine as those seen in agate due to the more granular and less transparent nature of jasper.

As with the agates, there is an almost infinite variety of jaspers that are found throughout the world.

The jaspers are identified by their pattern type, and grouped by their patterns with their recognized locations, in the way that they would be most commonly known and identified.

For quick identification, jasper types are arranged in order of the most common pattern associated with that type.

Banded Jasper

Group: Silicates
Hardness: 6-7

Banded jaspers have parallel banding much the same as banded agates, except that while agates are transparent or translucent, jaspers are opaque and more granular. Most banded jaspers are not very colorful, usually occurring in subtle shades of white, cream, gray, tan, or brown. Jasper is a tough stone and will take a good polish if sufficiently silicified. Also known as ribbonstone.

Banded jasper can be cut and polished for cabochons, beads, and ornamental uses.

Tumble polished jasper, New Mexico, 2-1/2" x 1-1/2".

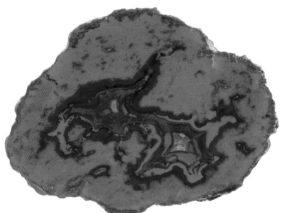

Paint Rock, Tennessee.

Rough jasper chunk, California, 2" x 1-1/2".

Unpolished jasper chunk, Michigan, 4-1/2" x 1-1/4".

Occurrences: Australia, India, New Zealand; Arizona, California, Michigan, Nevada, New Mexico, USA.

Value: $3.00 per pound.

| Group: Silicates |
| Hardness: 6-7 |

Brecciated Jasper

Brecciated jasper is a jasper that has been previously broken into angular pieces and recemented together again with chalcedony to form a new type of jasper. The recemented pieces are randomly arranged and the internal pattern often has a jagged, broken look with clear lines of demarcation between the more solid jasper fragments. Some brecciated jasper is so well silicified as to be considered more of an agate than a jasper. Brecciated jasper makes attractive cabochons and is a popular stone to collect.

Burro Creek pastelite slab, Arizona, 2-3/4" x 2 1".

Unpolished brecciated chunk, California, 10" x 5".

Youngite polished end view showing brecciation, Wyoming, 3-1/2" x 3".

Youngite top view showing druzy surface, Wyoming, 3-1/2" x 3".

Occurrences: Brazil, Germany, Mexico; Arizona, California, Wyoming, USA.

Value: $2.00 to $4.00 per pound.

Chert

Group: Silicates
Hardness: 6-7

Chert is a light yellow, beige, or off-white colored form of jasper with little color or patterning, which makes it generally undesirable for most lapidary use, although occasionally chert does contain fossils, which are interesting to collect. Chert is mentioned here due to its long history of use by native peoples who have used it for tools such as arrowheads or knives, and people still use it today when flintknapping arrowheads.

Chert arrowhead, Kentucky, 2" x 1".

Chert with banding, 3-1/2" x 3".

Chert with fossil sponge, Arizona.

Occurrences: Worldwide; Arizona, Arkansas, Kansas, Nevada, Ohio, USA.

Value: $2.00 to $3.00 per pound.

| Group: Silicates |
| Hardness: 6-7 |

Dendritic Jasper

Dendritic jasper is a jasper that contains inclusions of dendritic patterns within the stone. Dendritic jaspers tend to be earthy colors such as tans, browns, and creams with black to brown dendrites. Some dendritic jaspers tend towards a form of opalite and are somewhat glassier and more brittle than the average jasper.

Dendritic jaspers make beautiful display specimens and are frequently cut as cabochons for jewelry.

Rough slab with unusual dendrites, 5" x 3".

Dendritic jasper slab, 3" x 2-1/2".

Dendritic jasp-agate slab, California, 5" x 3-1/2".

Inlaid dendritic jasper bracelet.

Occurrences: Brazil, China, Mexico; Arizona, California, Michigan, Oregon, USA.

Value: $8.00 per pound.

| Group: Silicates |
| Hardness: 6-7 |

Flint

Flint is another form of jasper and close relative of chert. Flint comes in a greater variety of colors than chert such as black, gray, and brown, and is slightly more finely grained. Flint may also contain fossils. In primitive times flintstones were used in combination with pyrite to make fire, and flint was used for striking a spark in early flintlock rifles. Flint is a popular stone for flintknappers to work into arrowheads.

Flint specimen, Arizona, 4-1/2" x 4".

Occurrences: Africa, England, Germany, New Zealand; Missouri, Nevada, New York, Ohio, Texas, USA.

Value: Keokuk flint: $3.00 to $4.00 per pound.

Fossiliferous Jasper

Group: Silicates
Hardness: 6-7

Fossiliferous jasper may contain fossil remnants of ancient plants, marine life, shells, or skeletons. Colors may include gray, white, black, brown, green, and red. Fossiliferous jaspers are very collectible and may be polished as display pieces or cut for cabochons for jewelry making.

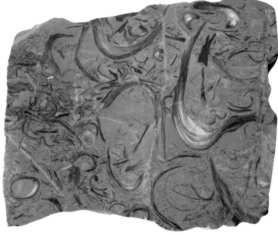

Mary Ellen jasper slab with stromatolites, Minnesota, 6-1/4" x 4-1/4".

Coquina jasper slab with shell fragments, California, 2-3/4" x 2".

Algal jasper chunk, California, 2-1/2" x 1-1/2".

Occurrences: Africa, Canada; California, Minnesota, Oklahoma, Wyoming, USA.

Value: Mary Ellen jasper: $3.00 per pound.

Group: Silicates
Hardness: 6-7

Jasp-Agate

Jasp-agate is a jasper that falls somewhere between agate and jasper due to the high amount of chalcedony present in the stone. Jasp-agates tend to be very colorful, hard, and well patterned and are a highly desirable lapidary stone. Good examples of jasp-agate include material found at Lavic Siding, California, and the well known Stone Canyon brecciated material also located in California.

Jasp-agates are mainly cut as cabochons for jewelry, and many jasp-agates make outstanding display specimens when face polished.

Stone Canyon chunk, California, 4" x 1-1/2".

Polished Lavic jasper, California, 4" x 2-1/2".

Jasp-agate slab, California, 3-1/2" x 2-1/2".

Occurrences: Argentina, Australia, Germany, Mexico; Arizona, California, Kentucky, New Mexico, Wyoming, USA.

Value: Stone Canyon jasper: $10.00 per pound.

Mottled Jasper

Group: Silicates
Hardness: 6-7

Mottled jasper is a jasper that has a blotchy appearance. It can come in a wide array of colors including red, green, brown, yellow, orange, and gray. Mottled jasper is an attractive stone and is used for a variety of lapidary purposes including cutting cabochons and beads for jewelry making, and decorative items.

Mottled pastelite chunk, Arizona, 3" x 3".

Mottled jasper slab, California, 3" x 2".

Occurrences: Africa, Mexico; Arizona, California, Colorado, Missouri, USA.

Value: $2.00 per pound.

Orbicular Jasper

Group: Silicates
Hardness: 6-7

Orbicular jasper is a popular material with jasper collectors. Orbs can range from small dots or spherules to larger undulating patterns of concentric, overlapping rings of great beauty, as seen in the patterns of Mexico's fine Royal Imperial jaspers, or the famous Bruneau jaspers from Idaho in the United States.

Orbicular jaspers are usually cut as cabochons or polished as striking display specimens.

Polished Royal Imperial picture jasper, Mexico.

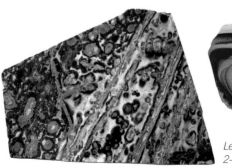

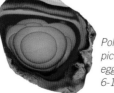

Polished Bruneau picture jasper with egg patterns, Idaho, 6-1/4" x 5-1/4".

Leopardskin jasper slab, Mexico, 2-1/2" x 2".

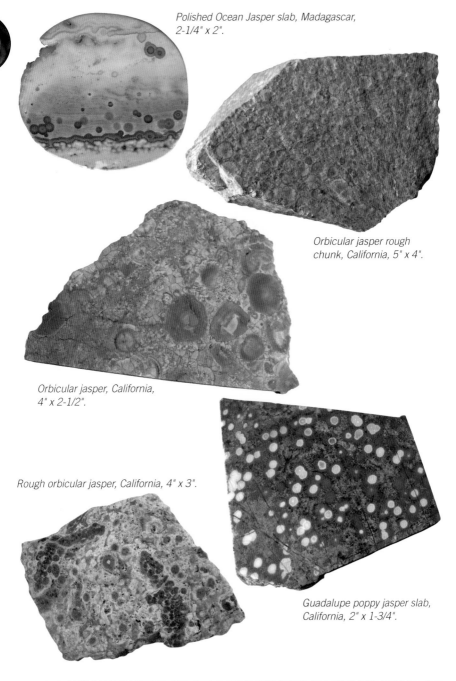

Polished Ocean Jasper slab, Madagascar, 2-1/4" x 2".

Orbicular jasper rough chunk, California, 5" x 4".

Orbicular jasper, California, 4" x 2-1/2".

Rough orbicular jasper, California, 4" x 3".

Guadalupe poppy jasper slab, California, 2" x 1-3/4".

Occurrences: Africa, India, Mexico; Arizona, California, Nevada, Montana, Oregon, Texas, USA.

Value: Ocean jasper, mid-grade: $12.00 per pound.

Picture Jasper

Picture, or scenic jaspers are some of the most popular gem materials on the market today for lapidary artists. Picture jaspers occur in a dazzling array of colors and exquisitely detailed patterns that resemble skies, mountain vistas, desert landscapes, hills and valleys, and forest horizons. Colors include warm tones of tan, gold, yellow, blue, green, and browns all swirled together in strikingly outlined picturesque scenes.

Most picture jaspers will take a high polish and make extraordinary cabochons or display pieces.

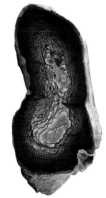

Succor Creek jasper rough, Oregon, 6" x 5-1/2".

Polished Biggs jasper, Oregon.

Polished picture jasper slab, Oregon, 3-1/2" x 2".

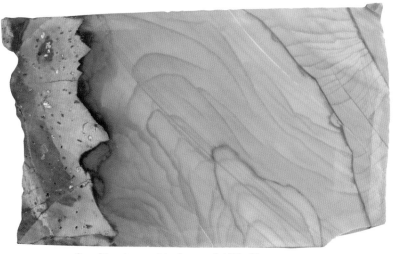

Gray Biggs jasper slab, Oregon, 3-1/2" x 2".

Unpolished Biggs jasper slab, Oregon, 6-1/4" x 2-1/2".

Mookaite jasper slab,
Australia, 5-1/2" x 2-1/2".

Owyhee jasper, Oregon, 3" x 1-1/2".

Rough Willow Creek chunk,
Idaho, 4" x 1-3/4".

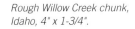

Porcelain jasper slab, Utah, 6-3/4" x 7".

Polished Willow Creek jasper, Idaho.

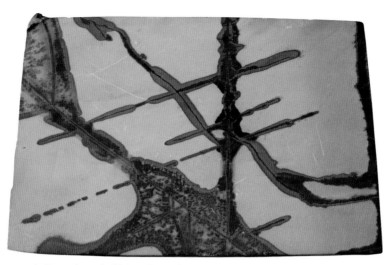

Indian paint rock, Mojave Desert (closed location), California, 4" x 2-1/2".

Occurrences: Africa, China, Egypt; California, Idaho, Nevada, Oregon, Texas, Utah, USA.

Value: Owyhee jasper: $6.00 per pound.

Spiderweb Jasper

Group: Silicates
Hardness: 6-7

Spiderweb jasper is exactly what the name implies—a criss-cross, or woven type of spiderweb pattern overlaying a solid color background. Spiderweb jaspers can occur in colors of green, red, black, cream, and brown. Some spiderweb patterns are small and delicate, and others are larger and more intense as in the flashy patterns seen in Utah's bold Picasso stone.

Most Spiderweb jasper is well silicified and takes an excellent polish. Spiderweb jasper is commonly used in the making of cabochons, beads, and decorative items.

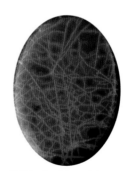

Polished spiderweb jasper cabochon, 1" x 3/4".

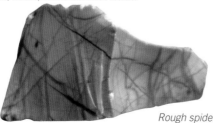

Rough spiderweb jasper piece, 2" x 1".

Occurrences: Mexico; Arizona, California, Nevada, Oregon, New Mexico, USA.

Value: $6.00 per pound.

Pseudomorphs

Pseudomorphs are formed when minerals, usually in the form of chalcedony, replace another mineral or organic substance and the shape is retained of the original object, but its chemical composition has been permanently altered. The item replaced may be animal, such as dinosaur bone or marine corals; plant, such as petrified wood or fossilzed ferns; or other minerals, such as barite or aragonite crystals replaced and filled by chalcedony. Other minerals such as calcite, pyrite, azurite, malachite, and goethite may also form as replacement materials, but it is the harder silicifed chalcedony forms that are of interest to the lapidary artist for cutting and polishing.

Collecting pseudomorphs in the form of fossils and petrified wood is, and has been for a very long time, an important and popular part of the rock and mineral collecting hobby. These materials are not only used by the lapidary for cutting cabochons of great beauty and quality, but are also important to collectors of mineral specimens as fascinating display pieces or for scientific and geologic study,

Animal Fossils

Animal fossils include the fossilized bones and remains of many different land animals including dinosaurs of all types, and other extinct animal species such as woolly mammoths, mastodons, horses, camels, sabertooth tigers, reptiles, birds, and insects. Dinosaur bone is especially prized by lapidaries for its beautiful color and strikingly preserved bone cell structure. People also collect other dinosaur artifacts, such as gastroliths (gizzard stones) and coprolite (dinosaur poop).

Most animal fossils are prepared as collectible display specimens, or studied by paleontologists for their historic significance.

Polished coprolite, Utah, 4-1/2" x 3".

Polished whale bone, California, 2" x 1".

Fossil alligator tooth, 4" x 3-1/2".

Dinosaur bone slab, Utah, 4-1/2" x 3".

Fossil worm casing, North Carolina, 4" x 1".

Occurrences: Africa, Australia, China; California, Colorado, Utah, Wyoming, USA.

Value: Lapidary grade dinosaur bone: $20.00 per pound.

Marine Fossils

Ammolite with iridescence, Canada, 2-1/2" x 2".

Marine fossils occur in marine environments such as ancient oceans, lakes, and streambeds, and include a variety of animal and plant types including corals, crinoids (also known as sea-lilies), fish, sharks, whales, crabs, mollusks, shells, and trilobites. Crinoids, trilobites, fish, shells, and other marine fossils are popular display items when prepared and exhibited on slabs of stone, usually limestone or another sedimentary form of rock, that they are found encased in. Crinoid stem sections are also used occasionally as beads in jewelry making, as they generally have hollow centers. and some living forms of crinoids still exist today. Sharks teeth are commonly used in wire-wrapping, and the beautifully patterned fossil corals of Indonesia make lovely beads and excellent cutting material for lapidaries. Fossilized ammonite shell, displaying iridescence, is a prime lapidary material and commands high prices. The agatized fossil coral geodes of Florida are well known and regarded as handsome display pieces, and are highly collectible.

Fossil clam, Oregon, 1-1/2" x 2".

Chain coral, Michigan, 3" x 2-1/4".

Fossil crinoids, Arkansas, 2-1/2" x 5".

Fossil bivalve shell, Oregon, 1-1/2" x 2-1/4".

"The Owl" agatized fossil coral, Georgia, 8" x 6".

Shark tooth, North Carolina, 2" x 1-1/2".

Fossil horn coral, Utah, 1" x 1".

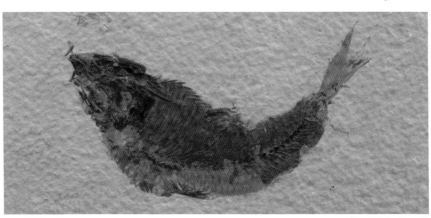

Fossil fish, 3" x 4".

Trilobite, Morocco, 5-1/2" x 5".

Fossil whale vertebrate, 7" x 3-1/2".

Fossil coral head, Indonesia, 3" x 3".

Pyritized sand dollar, Illinois, 3-1/2" x 3-1/2".

Trilobite in limestone, 4" x 3".

Shell conglomerate, 6" x 4".

Turritella shell agate, Wyoming, 4" x 3".

Occurrences: Morocco, worldwide; Canada, Florida, Michigan, Wyoming, USA.

Value: 1" x 3" sliced (two halves) Tampa Bay coral geode: $20.00

Plant Fossils

Fossil leaf, Utah, 6" x 3".

Fossil plants are usually found as individual leaves or fronds, not complete structures, due to their fragility and rate of decomposition. Some modern leaf species that have been found as fossils are maples, oaks, sycamores, willows, poplars, and ginkos, as well as many others. Some of these species had unique shapes and leaf structures not found in their living descendants today, and sometimes fossilized examples exhibit disease scarring or insect predation. Most leaf fossils are about 2″ to 6″ long, and complete fossil leaves, with venation preserved and petiole (stem) intact, are prized by collectors as fine display specimens.

Fossil ferns are probably the most abundant and recognizable of all the fossil plants. Almost all of the so-called fossil ferns are actually extinct seed ferns that reproduced by seeds rather than spores as in modern ferns. During the Pennsylvanian period, billions of fern plants covered the forest floors and swamps over a great part of the Earth, and once fossilized, these plants formed dense, fossil-rich layers of bog dozens of feet thick and miles long that were compressed over millions of years to create many of the vast coal deposits of Pennsylvania and West Virginia in the United States that we see today. A particularly unique fossilized fern specimen that occurs as a white imprint on black shale from the St. Clair, Pennsylvania, coal mining district is highly collectible as a display specimen, and is quite affordable for the beginning collector.

Fossil fern, Illinois, 8-1/2" x 2-1/2".

Occurrences: China, Canada, India; Illinois, Kansas, Louisiana, Pennsylvania, Utah, USA.

Value: 8-1/2" x 3" St. Clair, Pennsylvania, fossil fern plate: $15.00

Petrified Wood

Petrified wood occupies an important and time-honored place in the world of the lapidary arts and rock and mineral collecting fields. Petrified wood is probably one of the most collected and appreciated of all the collectible fossilized pseudomorphic materials for its many aesthetic applications in jewelry making and for display. The incredible variety of different wood types, patterns, and colors are bound to enthrall even the most expert and seasoned specimen collectors. Whole books have been devoted to the study of the various species of petrified wood, and I recommend that you get one of them if you are seriously interested in acquiring petrified wood for your personal collection. Just a few of the collecting possibilities include cycad, elm, holly, maple, oak, palm, pine, redwood, and reed. When collecting petrified wood for specimen display, complete, unbroken rounds of branches or trunks with bark attached are always the most desirable. Spectacular opalized petrified wood occurs in Virgin Valley, Nevada, and can be collected at a number of fee-based mine sites. Another collectible pseudomorph related to petrified wood is known as a limb cast. This cast is formed by an ancient piece of wood that decomposes in the soil, leaving a hollow negative mold of itself that is later filled in with aqueous chalcedony that solidifies and creates a positive replica of the original limb. Beautiful pink chalcedony limb casts are collected by lapidaries and specimen collectors alike.

When cutting and polishing petrified wood for lapidary use, it is important to check for fractures, as it is common in wood, especially if has been weathering on the surface of the ground for a long period of time.

Polished petrified wood makes beautiful display specimens and wonderful cabochons or beads for jewelry making.

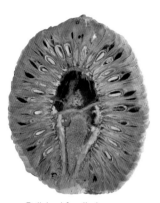

Polished fossil pine cone, Argentina, 3-1/4" x 2-1/2".

Rare chromium green petrified wood, Arizona, 2-1/2".

Petrified palm, 3" x 1".

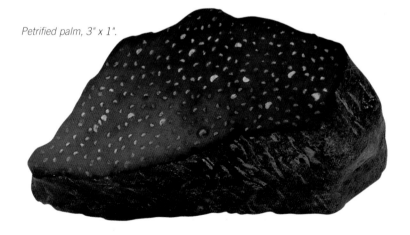

Redwood, Oregon, 9" x 8".

Juniper with teredo shipworm borings, Texas, 7" x 6".

Quartz crystal coated limb section, Arizona, 4-1/2" x 2-1/2".

Cycad, Utah, 12" x 6".

Ancient conifer, rainbow wood, Arizona, 11".

Blue Forest pepper tree, Wyoming, 5".

Conifer cone in barite sand nodule, Germany, 5" x 3".

Full wood round, 4-1/2" x 4".

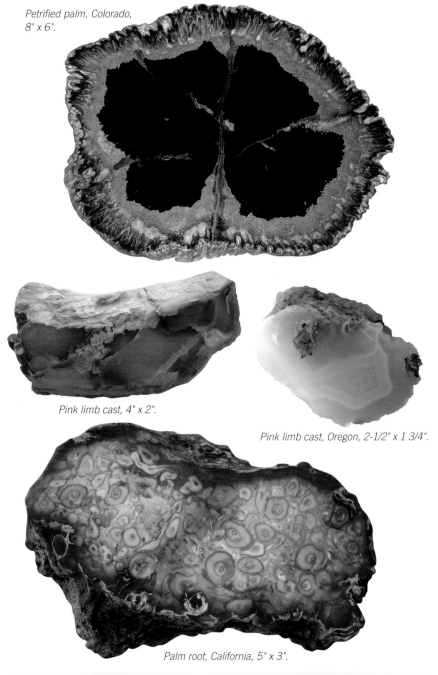

Petrified palm, Colorado, 8" x 6".

Pink limb cast, 4" x 2".

Pink limb cast, Oregon, 2-1/2" x 1 3/4".

Palm root, California, 5" x 3".

Occurrences: Argentina, Australia, Canada, China, Greece; Arizona, Colorado, Montana, Nevada, Oregon, Washington, USA.

Value: Lapidary quality Arizona petrified wood: $5.00 per pound.

Cabochon Materials

A wide variety of lapidary materials can be used to cut, polish, or carve for cabochon making, from inexpensive, semi-precious material such as rose quartz or obsidian to precious black opal or even emeralds or rubies. Cabochons are typically domed, with a flat back, and round or oval shaped, although they can be cut in other shapes like squares, rectangles, diamonds, crosses, or freeforms. The geometric shapes are usually cut from calibrated templates so they fit in standard-size jewelry settings.

Lapidary material for cabochon cutting can be opaque to transparent, and solidly colored or patterned; it's up to you. The main requirement, however, is that the material be of a hardness and strength suitable for your jewelry making purposes. Some cabochon materials are quite soft—such as opal with a hardness of 5.5 and turquoise with a hardness of 5.6 on the Mohs scale—but are still commonly used in jewelry making as long as they are in a setting that protects them from being chipped or damaged, or in jewelry as earrings or pendants where there's less wear and tear. Even then, there is still no guarantee that they won't be broken or cracked if they are accidentally banged against something. It is best to use material of a hardness of 6.5 or higher if possible for the greatest durability in your cabochons, especially for rings and bracelets.

Cabochons can also be carved into delicate designs, such as cameos or small sculptural pieces, and some stones are simply shaped around the sides, leaving their surface unpolished to display a druzy coating of fine sparkling crystals, a bubbly botryoidal surface, or unusual formations. Many cabochons are cut from the precious gemstone group, especially if the material isn't sufficiently clear for faceting quality stones. Overall, cabochon cutting is probably the most popular and favored skills of all the lapidary arts.

Included here alphabetically are many, but certainly not all, of the materials that are well suited for cabochon making, prized for their color, durability, or pattern, and have a long history of lapidary use. Also mentioned are a few of the more uncommon, or more recently recognized stones that are gaining popularity as they become more accessible and affordable for the general public.

Agate, Chalcedony, and Jasper

To my eye, many of the agates, chalcedonies, and jaspers are some of the prettiest cabochons of all due to their extraordinary range of color and pattern, such as the brilliantly colored fortification agates of Mexico, or the strikingly graceful plumes or fan-like sprays of sagenite found in certain agates, such as the famous California, Oregon, or Texas agates found in the U.S.A.; and the beautiful orbicular Ocean Jasper from Madagascar. Many fine agates are found in the western region of the United States due to the volcanic environment there that is favorable to their formation. Agate, chalcedony, and jasper have a hardness of 7 on the Mohs scale and generally take an excellent polish. Chalcedony replacements such as petrified wood, dinosaur bone, and fossilized corals all make exceptionally beautiful cabochons too.

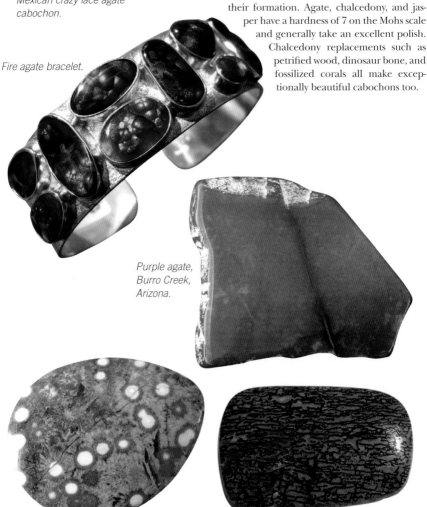

Mexican crazy lace agate cabochon.

Fire agate bracelet.

Purple agate, Burro Creek, Arizona.

Guadalupe poppy jasper, California.

Dinosaur bone cabochon.

Chrysocolla cabochon.

Zebra jasper cabochon.

Petrified wood cabochon, Arizona.

Fossil coral slab, Indonesia.

Sonoran Sunset slab (cuprite in chalcedony).

Owyhee jasper cabochon.

Occurrences: Africa, Australia, Brazil, Madagascar, Mexico; Arizona, California, Michigan, New Mexico, Oregon, Texas, USA.

Value: Ocean jasper: $8.00 per pound.

Feldspar Group

The feldspar group includes the microcline (var. amazonite), orthoclase (var. adularia moonstone), and plagioclase feldspars (var. labradorite, bytownite, and sunstone). They commonly occur as prismatic crystals in aggregate groups. Some of these stones exhibit the characteristics of adularescence, as in moonstone, or labradorescence, as in labradorite. These effects create rich plays of color or light in the stones when they are rotated at different angles in the light, and are very popular cabochons for jewelry making. Most members of the feldspar group are translucent to semi-opaque, and colors can be gray, pink, white, yellow, or in the case of amazonite, a lovely aqua blue color. Hardness averages around 6-6.5 and most feldspars take a very good polish.

Moonstone cabochon.

Amazonite crystals, Colorado, 3-1/2" x 2-1/2".

Labradorite cabochon.

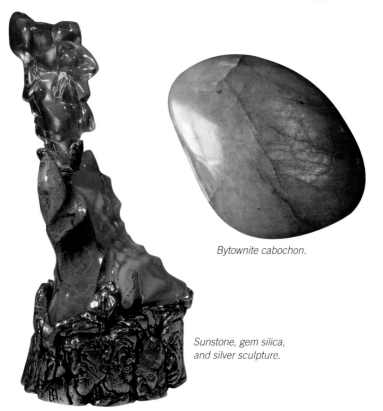

Bytownite cabochon.

Sunstone, gem silica, and silver sculpture.

Occurrences: Australia, Brazil, Burma, Canada, Finland, Madagascar; Colorado, Virginia, USA.

Value: Moonstone: $8.00 per carat.

Gaspeite

Gaspeite is considered a rare mineral, being found in only a few localities as a secondary mineral around nickel sulfide deposits, but gaspeite is fast becoming popular as a cabochon material in design combination with stones such as turquoise, malachite, coral, and spiny oyster in sterling silver Southwest-style jewelry. Gaspeite's color is a pale green to lime or apple green, and has a hardness of 4.5-5.

Gaspeite with turquoise earring.

Occurrences: Australia, Canada.

Value: Australian gaspeite: $60.00 per pound.

Jade/Jadeite/Nephrite

The stone commonly referred to as jade includes two mineral groups: jadeite (sodium aluminum silicate) and nephrite (calcium magnesium iron silicate). Jadeite is harder (7 on the Mohs scale) and the colors are brighter and more varied than nephrite, with a slightly different chemical composition. Richly colored translucent imperial jade has been a prized lapidary material for centuries. Jadeite is a tough material, translucent to opaque, occurring in granular masses, and ranges from white to apple green or emerald green, with tones of lavender, yellow, brown, red, and blue. Jadeite is popular not only as a cabochon material, but also as an exceptional carving material for ornamental objects, sculptures, and beads. Nephrite is more commonly found, slightly softer (6.5) than jadeite, and can exhibit many patterns including dendrites, snowflakes, swirls, and inclusions of quartz crystals, pyrite, or other minerals. Colors range from light greens to brown, red, and black. Nephrite has also been a favorite material for lapidary use since prehistoric times, and is used for the same purposes as jadeite.

Carved jade cabochon.

Jade cabochon, China.

Carved jade pendant.

Jadeite pendant.

Occurrences: Burma, Canada, Guatemala, Russia; Alaska, California, Utah, Washington, Wyoming, USA.

Value: Burmese jadeite: $3.00 per gram.

Lazurite (Lapis Lazuli)

Lazurite is a admired for its deep, royal blue color, and is a silicate of sodium and aluminun, and a member of the sodalite group. In lapidary use, lazurite is known by the name of lapis lazuli, and it occurs as aggregates of crystals and compact masses, and is tough and opaque. Lazurite has a hardness of 5-5.5, and has been used as an ornamental stone for hundreds of years. In early times, it was ground into powder and used as the pigment ultramarine for paintings. Lapis lazuli makes beautiful cabochons, beads, and carvings, especially when included with metallic yellow pyrite and polished to a high sheen.

Rough lazurite, Afghanistan.

Occurrences: Afghanistan, Burma, Canada, Chile, Russia; California, Colorado, USA.

Value: $2.00 per gram.

Malachite/Azurite

Both malachite and azurite are basic hydrous copper carbonates, most often found in conjunction with copper deposits. They often occur together, and azurite, over time, eventually alters into malachite. Both materials are quite soft, 3.5-4 on the Mohs scale, yet with careful polishing, they can be used for lapidary work. Azurite is prized for its deep, intense blue color, and malachite for its rich greens and patterns of swirling bands and bull's eyes. Malachite occurs in fibrous, radiating masses of acicular needles, and botryoidal crusts or masses. Azurite forms as elongated or tabular striated, prismatic crystals, and radiating aggregates or earthy or granular concretionary masses. Both are semi-translucent to opaque, and are sometimes combined with chrysocolla to form beautiful color groupings of aquas, greens, and blues. Although it can be difficult to work, malachite can be polished to a high sheen, and has been used extensively for many types of ornamental objects, especially in Russia. Both azurite and malachite are toxic to work with, so care must be taken when working with these materials, and wearing a protective mask is very important, as is keeping the material wet when polishing. Malachite and azurite are also often collected as display specimens.

Malachite cabochon.

Occurrences: Africa, Mexico, Russia; Arizona, California, Nevada, Pennsylvania, Tennessee, Utah, USA.

Value: African malachite: $20.00 per pound.

Metallic Materials
(Hematite, Psilomelane, Pyrite and Marcasite)

These stones have a high content of metallic minerals and when polished have a bright, metallic shine. They tend to be very dirty to cut and work with, but make beautiful cabochons when polished to a high sheen.

Hematite

Hematite is composed of iron oxide and has a hardness of 5.5. Hematite occurs as lamellar or lenticular polyhedral crystals, and mammilary aggregates or concretionary masses. Hematite is colored black, is opaque and metallic, with a silvery-gray shine when polished. Some hematite is mixed with other materials, such as jasper, which creates nicely banded patterns that make for attractive cabochons. When hematite is ground into a powder, it has a deep red color that has been used as a paint pigment since prehistoric times.

Rough hematite with jasper, Arizona, 4" x 3".

Occurrences: Australia, Brazil, Canada, Germany; Arizona, Michigan, Minnesota, Wisconsin, USA.

Value: $5.00 per pound.

Psilomelane (Romanechite)

Psilomelane is composed of manganese oxide and occurs as botryoidal, and stalactitic or dendritic aggregrates. Psilomelane is opaque and metallic, and has a hardness of 5-5.5 on the Mohs scale. When cut properly, across the botryoidal surface, psilomelane cabochons exhibit a striking sliver and black swirling, orbicular pattern similar to that of malachite. A popular form of highly silicified psilomelane, known as Crown Silver from Mexico, still periodically becomes available on the market, but is a fairly expensive stone.

Psilomelane cabochon.

Occurrences: Brazil, France, Mexico; California, Michigan, USA.

Value: Crown Silver, Mexico: $22.00 per pound.

Pyrite and Marcasite

Pyrite and marcasite are closely related, both being composed of iron sulfide, and pyrite being a dimorph of marcasite. Both are 6-6.5 on the Mohs scale, opaque and metallic, with pyrite occurring as brassy yellow cubic crystals, groups of pentagonal dodecahedra, and nodules or concretions with aggregates of tiny crystals. Marcasite occurs as pale, greenish yellow flattened prismatic crystals, often in the shape of "spearheads" and "cockscombs"; and radiating, concretionary masses, nodules, and stalactitic aggregates. Marcasite is frequently found as an attractive inclusion in agate, forming lovely plumes or flowers. Pyritized fossils are often used as-is in jewelry settings, and pyrite can be cut as domed or faceted cabochons and beads.

Marcasite in agate, California.

Marcasite in agate knife handle.

Occurrences: Bolivia, Canada, Chile, Mexico, Peru; Arizona, Colorado, Idaho, Illinois, USA.

Value: Pyrite: $5.00 per pound.

Obsidian

*Snowflake obsidian slab,
2" x 3-1/2".*

Rough obsidian.

Obsidian is a natural form of volcanic glass, composed of various combinations of basalt, andesite, rhyolite, and trachyte; other minerals; and a high percentage of silica. Obsidian has a hardness of 6-7, is amorphous with conchoidal fracture, glassy, and translucent to semi-opaque. Basic colors range from smoky gray to red or reddish brown, and black. Due to its sharp conchoidal fracture, obsidian has been used extensively since Paleolithic times as a cutting tool or weapon, and is still used today by flintknappers to make arrowheads and knives. Obsidian comes in a number of colors and patterns including banded, snowflake (small white bursts resembling snowflakes), mahogany (includes streaks of mahogany colored bands), rainbow or peacock (contains layers of iridescent colors), and sheen (colors such as gold, silver, or blue sheen seen in certain light). Obsidian occurs in masses, and sometimes in small nodules known as Apache Tears. Obsidian can be cut as cabochons or beads, faceted, and carved into ornamental objects. Obsidian is widely available and is an inexpensive stone.

*Rough mahogany obsidian,
6-1/2" x 10".*

Occurrences: Hungary, Italy, Japan, Mexico; Arizona, California, Idaho, Oregon, Utah, USA.

Value: Snowflake obsidian: $4.00 per pound.

Onyx

Onyx is a form of calcite, or calcium carbonate, that forms in large, fibrous, compact masses and is very popular as an ornamental stone. It is quite soft (3 on the Mohs scale), yet can take a fairly good polish. It is translucent to opaque and comes in a wide range of colors including white, yellow, red, brown, green, and orange, and can be banded or exhibit a number of patterns including swirls, dendrites, and plumes. Onyx carves well, and is frequently used for larger ornamental objects, such as spheres or eggs; architectural purposes, and cabochons or beads.

Carved onyx pendant, Arizona.

Flower onyx slab, Utah, 4" x 3-3/4".

Occurrences: Africa, Canada, Mexico, Pakistan; Arizona, California, New Mexico, Utah, USA.

Value: Rainbow calcite onyx: $4.00 per pound.

Opal

Opal has the same chemical composition as quartz (silicon dioxide), but contains from 1 to 2 percent water, and is not crystallized. Opal has a hardness of 5.5-6.5, is transparent to semi-opaque, with conchoidal fracture, and occurs as veins or nodules inside cavities or cracks of silica-rich rocks. There are two main types of opal: common and precious. Common opal doesn't have the play of internal colors that precious opal does, but is pretty in its own right with a translucence and palette of colors including honey, orange, blue, green, and red. Common opal is widely used for cabochons, beads, and carvings, and can be faceted if sufficiently clear. Precious opal exhibits a variety of flashing colors, called fire or opalescence, on backgrounds of white, black, dark brown, or colorless. The fire appears as flecks or sparkles of vivid colors of the spectrum floating on top of the background, often giving it a blue or purplish tone overall. The opal "fire" is caused by the diffraction of light within the stone by alignments of small silica spheres, and the opalescent colors are determined by the size and distance apart of the spheres. Within the precious opal group, there are a variety of sub groups determined by the various colors and patterns, such as black opal, boulder opal, and white opal; and by locations such as Lightning Ridge or Coober Pedy in Australia. Precious opal is used almost exclusively for cabochon making, and gem-quality precious opal is quite expensive.

Precious opal intarsia ring.

Rough precious opal, Nevada, 2-1/2" x 4-1/2".

Occurrences: Australia, Brazil, Honduras, Mexico; Nevada, Idaho, USA.

Value: Australian black opal: $5.00 per carat.

Pectolite (Larimar)

Pectolite is a member of the zeolite group and is composed of hydrous sodium calcium slilicate and has a hardness of 5 on the Mohs scale. A particular form of light blue pectolite, so far found only in the Dominican Republic, has been named Larimar and is fast becoming a favorite gemstone among lapidary artists. Larimar is a tough stone that can take a high polish, and often will include dendritic patterns, or exhibit chatoyancy. Larimar has a lovely soft blue color, and is increasing in demand as a lapidary material. Larimar is primarily cut as a cabochon.

Larimar pendant.

Occurrences: Dominican Republic.

Value: $.80 per gram.

Quartz

Crystalline quartz (silicon dioxide), which includes the varieties rock crystal, amethyst, citrine, smoky quartz, rose quartz, aventurine, and tiger-eye, is probably used more than any other stone for so many purposes in lapidary work. All members of the quartz family are of an excellent hardness, 7 on the Mohs scale, and take a brilliant polish. Quartz occurs as hexagonal, prismatic crystals or in massive form, is transparent to semi-opaque, and comes in an array of colors including colorless, pink, purple, green, yellow, white, brown, gray, and black. When quartz contains silky, fibrous inclusions of crocidolite, it exhibits chatoyancy and is called tiger-eye, hawk's-eye, or ox-eye, depending on the prevailing colors of gold, brown, or blue. All forms of quartz are used for many lapidary applications, such as for cabochon and bead making, carving decorative objects, and faceting. Quartz crystal clusters are highly collectible as beautiful display specimens.

Tiger eye cabochon.

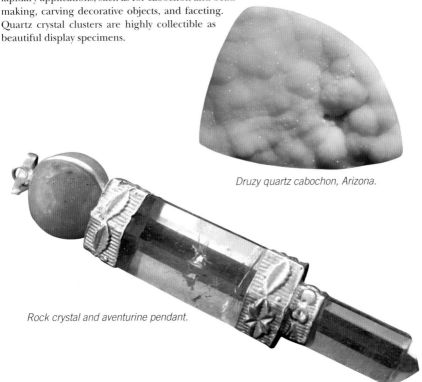

Druzy quartz cabochon, Arizona.

Rock crystal and aventurine pendant.

Occurrences: Africa, Australia, Brazil, Uruguay; Alaska, Arkansas, California, USA.

Value: African golden tiger eye: $9.00 per pound.

Rhodochrosite

Rhodochrosite freeform cabochon.

Rhodochrosite is composed of manganese carbonate and has a hardness of 4 on the Mohs scale. Rhodochrosite occurs as semitransparent rhombohedral crystals, stalagtites, or as concretionary masses, and is translucent to opaque. Despite its softness, rhodochrosite is valued because of its beautiful pink and rose colors and delicate swirling or banded patterns, similar to those found in lace agates or malachite. Massive rhodochrosite is often used for many decorative items, including carvings, bowls, spheres, and bookends. Rhodochrosite also makes for beautiful cabochons and beads, and is a favorite with lapidary artists. Due to its softness, rhodochrosite is best used in pendants or earrings where it has less chance of being damaged.

Rhodochrosite stalagtite.

Occurrences: Africa, Argentina, Brazil, Peru, Russia; Colorado, Montana, USA.

Value: $.50 per gram.

Rhodonite

Rhodonite cabochon.

Rhodonite is a silicate of manganese and occasionally occurs as translucent to semi-opaque crystals, but usually forms as compact crystalline masses, in colors of rose pink with brown and red mottling, and patches of black veining due to oxidation of the manganese. Rhodonite has a hardness of 5.5-6.5, and massive rhodonite is a popular lapidary material useful for making cabochons and beads, carvings, bowls, and other decorative items.

Rhodonite slab.

Occurrences: Australia, England, India, Russia; California, Massachusetts, USA.

Value: $6.00 per pound.

Sodalite

Sodalite is composed of sodium aluminum silicate and occurs in compact masses, and very rarely as dodecahedral crystals. Sodalite has a hardness of 5.5-6, is translucent to opaque, and is colored a bright blue with white or gray streaks. Due to its vibrant blue color, sodalite is a very popular lapidary material with many uses, including cutting cabochons and beads for jewelry, and for carving decorative items. Some sodalite can be transparent enough for faceting.

Rough sodalite, Canada, 3" x 2".

Occurrences: Brazil, Canada, India, Norway; Colorado, Maine, South Dakota, USA.

Value: $6.00 per pound.

Star Ruby and Star Sapphire

Star ruby and star sapphire are both part of the corundum (aluminum oxide) group of gemstones and display the phenomenon of asterism, or a six-rayed star when held in bright light. The star effect is created by very fine needles of rutile arranged in intersecting lines parallel with the symmetry of the crystal. Star rubies and sapphires can be transparent to semi-opaque, and are very hard, 9 on the Mohs scale. Star rubies and sapphires take an excellent polish, and are generally always cut as cabochons to display their stars. Star rubies and sapphires are quite expensive.

The quality of asterism also occurs in other gemstones, including garnet and quartz.

Star sapphire cabochon ring.

Occurrences: Africa, Asia, Canada, Russia; Alaska, Nebraska, USA.

Value: Star Sapphire: $30.00 per carat.

Sugilite

Sugilite pendant.

Sugilite is a relatively new gemstone, first introduced into the lapidary market in the late 1970s. Sugilite is composed of manganese silicate, is massive and tough, translucent to opaque, and has a hardness of 6.5 on the Mohs scale. Sugilite is prized for its striking purple to red-violet color, and it is becoming a highly sought after material for cabochon cutting, intarsia, and high-end designer jewelry. Authentic sugilite can be a little on the pricy side, and sugilite is now being synthesized, so buyer beware when purchasing sugilite.

Occurrences: Africa.

Value: $4.00 per gram.

Turquoise

Turquoise ring.

Rough turquoise, Kingman, Arizona, 4" x 3".

Turquoise has a long and illustrious history as a gemstone, its origins of use dating back to early Egypt and beyond. Turquoise is composed of hydrous copper and aluminum phosphate, is opaque, and has a hardness of 5-6. Turquoise occurs in thin veins and small nodules, and varies in color from dark greenish-blue to sky blue, or robin's-egg blue, and some varieties display a desirable fine black or brown spider web-like matrix pattern. Some turquoise grades into a soft, pale chalky type, which is frequently dyed and hardened with resin, or otherwise stabilized, waxed, and reconstituted. Also, other materials such as howlite or magnesite are dyed to imitate turquoise, so pay close attention when you are buying turquoise and don't be afraid to ask the seller questions. Turquoise is one of the most popular of all the cabochon materials, and is also used for bead making, and small carvings or sculptures.

Occurrences: China, Iran, Tibet; Arizona, Nevada, New Mexico, USA.

Value: Sleeping Beauty, Arizona, stabilized: $1.10 per gram.

Variscite

Variscite is composed of aluminum phosphate and occurs as fine-grained masses, nodules, veins, and crusts. Variscite has a hardness of 4.5, has a conchoidal fracture, is opaque, with good toughness, and comes in various shades of green from pale green to an almost emerald green. Variscite is sometimes confused with turquoise, but turquoise generally has a bluer tint and is slightly denser than variscite. Like turquoise, some variscite has a delicate spider-web pattern that is highly desirable. Variscite is most often used for cabochons, although it can be used for small carvings too.

Variscite cabochon, Utah.

Rough variscite, Utah, 3" x 2-1/2".

Occurrences: Australia, Brazil, Spain, Canada, Russia; Nevada, Utah, USA.

Value: $.50 per gram.

Uncommon Materials
(Datolite, Moldavite, Seraphinite, Thomsonite, and Thulite)

These are stones that have been more rarely used due to limited supply, greater cost, or are of a more recent discovery. Some of these materials are gaining in popularity and becoming more accessible as new deposits are discovered and demand increases.

Datolite

Datolite is a calcium borosilicate with a hardness of 5-5.5 that occurs as fine-grained nodules found in old copper mine dumps in the Keweenaw Peninsula of upper Michigan. Datolite is colored by iron oxide, copper, and silver, giving a range of soft hues of pink, peach, red, green, and violet on a white, opaque, porcelain-like background, sometimes with lacy inclusions of native copper or silver. Good datolite nodules are very rare, and are not normally used for jewelry, but rather cut and polished as display specimens. Smaller pieces are sometimes cut as cabochons, though, and the crystal form of datolite is also collected as a display specimen. Datolite nodules rarely appear on the market.

Polished datolite nodule, Michigan, 1" x 1-1/2".

Occurrences: Michigan, USA.

Value: $20.00 per ounce.

Moldavite

Moldavite is a transparent green type of glass tektite that is believed to be formed from an impact by a meteor or other extraterrestrial object on the Earth's surface that causes the soil to melt, cool, and recrystallize into a tektite. Tektites are high in silica, colored by iron oxides or other minerals, have a hardness of 5.5-6, and are transparent to translucent. True moldavites are found near the Moldau River in Czechoslovakia, hence the name. Tektites occur in a number of other areas worldwide, but the moldavites are prized for their good transparency and bottle green color. Moldavite can be used for cabochons, and if very transparent, for faceting.

Natural moldavite pendant.

Occurrences: Czechoslovakia.

Value: $8.00 per gram.

Seraphinite

Seraphinite is the gem variety of clinochlore in the chlorite group and is composed of magnesium iron aluminum silicate hydroxide, has a hardness of 2-2.5, is opaque, and crystallizes in the form of foliated or granular masses and also as tabular crystals. Seraphinite is usually a deep forest green with feathery silver-colored inclusions of mica, but also found in yellow, red, brown, tan or white. The mica inclusions give seraphinite a chatoyant effect, or shimmery sheen, that is quite beautiful. Although soft, seraphinite can be cut into cabochons, and it is much sought after as collector specimen and by the metaphysical community for its resemblance to angel's wings.

Polished seraphinite slab.

Occurrences: Russia.

Value: $22.00 per pound.

Thomsonite

Thomsonite is composed of hydrous sodium calcium aluminum silicate and is a member of the zeolite group. Thomsonite has a hardness of 5-5.5, is transparent to translucent, and occurs as small, radiating balls of needles or globular aggregates in basalt pockets that have orbicular patterns and resemble eyeballs when cut. Colors are usually pink, red, or green with black accents on a white background. Thomsonite can be cut into interesting and unusual cabochons, and is also collected as a mineral specimen for display.

Thomsonite cabochon.

Occurrences: Canada, Denmark, Switzerland; Michigan, Minnesota, USA.

Value: $1.00 per gram.

Thulite

Thulite is composed of calcium aluminum silicate and is a member of the zoisite group. Thulite has a hardness of 6.5 and occurs in compact, granular, or fibrous masses, and rod-like aggregates. Thulite is pink to rose colored, occasionally with accents of green; translucent to semi-opaque, and often resembles rhodonite. Thulite is often erroneously called pink jade, and is used for cabochons, beads, and carvings.

Rough thulite, Washington, 2-1/2" x 2".

Occurrences: Australia, Italy, Norway; New Mexico, Tennessee, Washington, Wyoming, USA.

Value: Norway: $1.50 per ounce.

Faceting Materials

Faceting material is the general name for the type of stones that are used for cutting faceted gemstones. The sparkling beauty of faceted stones comes from the way the transparent stone reacts to transmitted light by bending and reflecting light rays through the angles of the faceted faces on the surface of the stone to create the brilliant effects that have made gemstones so precious and admired for centuries. The most important qualities that a gemstone exhibits are known as the four C's: color, clarity, cut, and carat weight. These characteristics are essential to evaluating the quality and value of colored gemstones.

1. Color is the most important factor in determining the value of colored gemstones and most dealers assess the color component of a stone at between 50 and 70 percent of its value. In general, a bright, rich, intense, pure, and vivid color is always best. Gemstones should not be too dark or too light. Ideally, they should look good under any light conditions.

2. Clarity in gemstones is always an important consideration, second only to color in importance. Colored stones are almost never as clean as diamonds and they should not be judged by the same criteria. Important stones like emeralds, rubies, alexandrites, and tourmaline are rarely ever clean, and many gemstones are frequently fairly heavily included. Clarity and transparency are always desirable but color is still of primary importance.

3. The cut is what gives a gemstone its beauty and brilliance. A cut that reflects all the light in an even pattern without any darkness or windowing is ideal. In faceting stones, specific indices and critical angles are what produce the maximum brilliance.

4. A carat is a metric unit of weight used in the gemstone industry to describe how much a gemstone weighs. A carat is one fifth of a gram, so one gram is five carats. When referring to decimal fractions of a carat, a point is equal to .01 (1/100th) of a carat.

Valuable gemstones are generally sold by weight and not by size. Less valuable materials can be cut into standard calibrated sizes commonly used by jewelry designers. When choosing rough gemstone material for faceting, look for a high refractive index and hardness of at least 6 or more on the Mohs hardness scale. Softer materials can be used, but must be protected or used as pendants or earrings rather than in rings or bracelets where they may be damaged.

Included here are most, but not all, of the various types of materials that can be faceted into gemstones. Some of these materials of lesser quality may also be cut into cabochons, but faceting of these stones is usually preferable if they are of better quality. Values given are for average grade, eye clean, rough faceting material, except for diamond, which is for a finished gemstone. Stones are arranged by hardness, from hardest to softest.

Diamond

Colors:	Colorless, yellow, brown, gray, pink, black.
Luster:	Adamantine.
Refractive Index:	2.4175–2.4178
Hardness:	10
System:	Isometric

Diamond generally occurs as octahedral, rounded crystals, and is composed of carbon. Diamond is transparent to translucent, and is the most famous and precious of gemstones next to ruby and emerald. Diamond is the hardest of the gemstones and is used extensively in the jewelry making field. Diamond has been imitated by glass, colorless spinel, corundum, and cubic zirconia, but all of these are distinguished from diamond by their lower density and hardness. Today's diamond market is strictly controlled and about the only real opportunity for any person to be able to actually collect a diamond is by visiting the Crater of Diamonds State Park located in Arkansas, USA, and being lucky enough to stumble upon one.

Rough yellow diamond, 2+ carats, Arkansas.

Occurrences: Africa, Brazil, Canada, India; Arkansas, California, USA.

Value: Round cut, .30 carat, VS2, I, $480.00.

Corundum
(Ruby, Sapphire)

Colors: Colorless, red, blue, pink, yellow, green, violet, colorless.

Luster: Vitreous to adamantine.

Refractive Index: 1.77-1.76

Hardness: 9

System: Trigonal

The corundum group occurs in semiopaque masses, and also in distinct prismatic or tapered crystals with close transverse striations. Corundum is composed of aluminum oxide and is transparent to opaque. Members of the corundum group include ruby (red), and sapphire (blue, pink, yellow, green, violet, orange, padparadschah, colorless). Some rubies and sapphires exhibit the phenomena of asterism, or the appearance of a six-rayed star within the stone, an effect caused by very fine included needles of rutile that shimmer across the stone when held in the light. Most star rubies and sapphires are cut as cabochons, as the effect would be lost in a faceted stone.

Faceted ruby.

Blue sapphire ring.

Pink sapphire crystal, Sri Lanka, 1" x 1".

Ruby in zoisite, India, 1-1/4" x 1".

Occurrences: Australia, Burma, Sri Lanka, Thailand; Montana, North Carolina, Pennsylvania, USA.

Value: Sapphire: $5.00 per carat.

Chrysoberyl (Alexandrite)

Colors: Yellow, yellow-green, green, green-brown.
Luster: Vitreous.
Refractive Index: 1.75-1.74
Hardness: 8.5
System: Orthorhombic.

The chrysoberyl group generally occurs as V-shaped twinned or flattened crystals, with singular crystals being rare. Chrysoberyl is primarily composed of beryllium aluminum oxide and is transparent to translucent. Members of the chrysoberyl group include golden chrysoberyl; Alexandrite, a rare green variety that can exhibit color change to red when held in the proper light; and cat's-eye or cymophane, a variety that exhibits chatoyancy, or cat's-eye effect, due to the inclusion of fine parallel needles. Cat's-eye chrysoberyl is generally cut as a cabochon.

Faceted yellow chrysoberyl.

Occurrences: Brazil, Italy, Madagascar, Russia; Colorado, New York, USA.

Value: Yellow: $20.00 per carat.

Topaz

Colors: Colorless, yellow, pink, blue, green, violet.
Luster: Vitreous.
Refractive Index: 1.606-1.638
Hardness: 8
System: Orthorhombic.

Topaz occurs as orthorhombic, prismatic crystals, often with vertical striations on prism faces. Topaz is a silicate of aluminum containing fluorine and hydroxyl, and is transparent to translucent. True golden-yellow topaz is the most highly prized, with pink and blue also being very popular with faceters. Both the pink and blue varieties of topaz are frequently irradiated to produce stronger colors, but this is a generally accepted practice in the gem trade with these particular gemstones, so this should not create any concerns in purchasing unless you personally object to any kind of artificial treatment to gemstones.

Imperial topaz crystal, 1" x 1/2".

Faceted blue topaz ring.

Occurrences: Africa, Brazil, Russia, Sri Lanka; California, Colorado, Utah, USA.

Value: Natural Swiss blue: $2.25 per carat.

| Colors: Grayish-white, yellow-white, pale blue-green. |
| Luster: Vitreous. |
| Refractive Index: 1.56-1.57 |
| Hardness: 7.5-8 |
| System: Hexagonal |

Beryl (Aquamarine, Emerald)

The beryl group occurs as hexagonal crystals composed of beryllium aluminum silicate, and is transparent to translucent. When transparent beryl is colored by certain minerals, it takes on a number of colors that are recognized as some of the most beautiful and popular of all gemstones including emerald (green), aquamarine (blue), heliodor (yellow), bixbite (red), and morganite (pink).

"Portrait of Queen Sikirit of Thailand," 547.7 carats carved aquamarine, Pakistan, 2-1/2" x 1.5".

Aquamarine crystal in quartz, 2" x 1-1/2".

Emerald crystal with pyrite. Brazil, 3-1/2" x 2-1/2".

Heliodor in quartz, 6" x 3".

Occurrences: Africa, Brazil, Columbia, Madagascar; California, Massachusetts, Virginia, USA.

Value: Aquamarine: $1.50 per carat.

Spinel

Spinel occurs generally as small, perfect octahedrons, frequently twinned. Spinel is also common in aggregates and rounded grains, and can be found as small pebbles in alluvium. Spinel is composed of magnesium aluminum oxide and is transparent to opaque, sometimes fluorescent. As secondary gems go, brilliant red spinels comparable in color to rubies are quite valuable, although they are only about one-tenth or so of the price of rubies.

Colors: Red, pink, blue, brown, violet.

Luster: Vitreous.

Refractive Index: 1.712-1.762

Hardness: 7.5-8

System: Isometric

Spinel crystal, Burma, 1/4".

Occurrences: Afghanistan, Brazil, Burma, Sri Lanka; California, New Jersey, New York, USA.

Value: $5.00 per carat.

Zircon

Colors: Colorless, red, blue, yellow, orange, green, brown, violet, black.

Luster: Adamantine to vitreous.

Refractive Index: 2.01-1.96

Hardness: 7.5

System: Tetragonal

Zircon occurs as small isolated or twin crystals in the form of stubby prisms with bipyramidal terminations, and as irregular lumps or grains in alluvial deposits. Zircon is a silicate of zirconium, also containing thorium and uranium, and is transparent to opaque. Zircon has the property of birefringence, or double refraction, which distinguishes it from other gemstones which it is often mistaken for. Transparent, colored zircon has been a popular gemstone throughout the ages, and continues to be so today.

Zircon crystal, Canada, 1" x 1".

Occurrences: Burma, Canada, Russia, Sri Lanka; Colorado, Oklahoma, New Jersey, USA.

Value: $6.00 per carat.

Cordierite (Iolite)

Colors: Colorless, gray, pale to dark blue or violet.

Luster: Vitreous

Refractive Index: 1.54-1.53

Hardness: 7 – 7.5

System: Orthorhombic

Cordierite occurs as short, multifaceted prismatic crystals, and granular masses. Cordierite is composed of magnesium aluminum silicate and is transparent to translucent. Cordierite is known as the gemstone iolite and exhibits the property of dichroism, the ability to apparently change color when viewed from different angles. Because of this powerful characteristic, the Vikings used it for navigational purposes, as it was able to indicate the direction of the sun on overcast days, hence the name "Viking's compass." Cordierite is also known as water sapphire.

Cordierite crystal mass, Connecticut, 2" x 1-1/2".

Occurrences: Brazil, Finland, Norway, Madagascar; Connecticut, USA.

Value: $2.00 per carat.

Garnet

Colors: Red, orange, green, brown, yellow, black.
Luster: Vitreous.
Refractive Index: 1.80
Hardness: 6.5-7.5
System: Isometric

The Garnet group is a collection of very closely related mineral groups, occurring as dodecahedral or trapezohedral crystals, and granular masses:

Pyrope: Magnesium aluminum silicate. **Colors:** Blood-red, purplish-red (var. rhodolite).

Almandine: Iron aluminum silicate. **Colors:** Red with violet or brown tints.

Spessartine: Manganese aluminum silicate. **Colors:** Orange-pink, orange-red, brownish-yellow.

Grossular: Calcium aluminum silicate. **Colors:** Colorless, green (var. tsavorite), brown-orange (var. hessonite).

Andradite: Calcium iron silicate. **Colors:** Brown, red, yellow, green (var. demantoid), black.

Uvarovite: Calcium chromium silicate. **Colors:** Green.

Demantoid andradite garnet, California, 2-1/4" x 1-1/2".

Garnets are popular and commonly used gemstones both faceted and as cabochons. Garnet cluster specimens are also collected as beautiful display pieces.

Faceted pyrope garnet ring.

Spessartine garnet, China, 2-1/2" x 1-1/2".

Uvarovite garnet, Russia, 5" x 2-1/4".

Pyrope garnet crystal, 3" x 1-3/4".

Grossular garnet, Canada, 2-1/2" x 1-3/4".

Occurrences: Africa, Czechoslovakia, India, Mexico, Russia; Arizona, California, New Mexico, Virginia, USA.

Value: Rhodolite garnet: $3.00-$10.00 per carat..

Colors: Colorless, pale yellow, peach, orange-brown. Luster: Vitreous. Refractive Index: 1.622-1.670 Hardness: 7 System: Orthorhombic	# Danburite

Danburite occurs as prismatic, striated crystals closely resembling topaz. Danburite is composed of calcium borosilicate and is transparent to translucent. Danburite is named for its first reported occurrence in Danbury, Connecticut, but the original locality has been long since been buried by the growth of the city. Danburite cuts lovely, clear faceted stones.

Danburite crystal, Mexico,
1-1/2" x 1/2".

Occurrences: Burma, Japan, Mexico, Sri Lanka; Connecticut, New York, USA.

Value: $3.50 per carat.

Quartz (Amethyst, Citrine)

Colors: Colorless, yellow (citrine), violet (amethyst), violet-yellow (ametrine), brownish-black (smoky).
Luster: Vitreous.
Refractive Index: 1.55-1.54
Hardness: 7
System: Hexagonal

The quartz group occurs as prismatic crystals, often with pyramidal or bipyramidal terminations. Quartz is composed of silicon dioxide and is transparent to subtranslucent. When clear crystalline quartz is imbued with other minerals it takes on the various colors and characteristics that form the subvarieties so widely valued and used by lapidary artists. For faceting purposes, rock crystal, amethyst, citrine, ametrine, and smoky quartz are the most commonly used, and occasionally, if sufficiently clear, rose quartz and the variously colored cryptocrystalline chalcedonies can be faceted too.

Rock crystal quartz collected,
faceted, and set by the author,
Arizona.

Occurrences: Brazil, Canada, Russia, Uruguay; Arkansas, Colorado, North Carolina, USA.

Value: Amethyst: $1.75 per carat.

Tourmaline

Colors: Red, pink, green, brown, black.
Luster: Vitreous to adamantine.
Refractive Index: 1.64-1.62
Hardness: 7
System: Orthorhombic

The tourmaline group is a complex borosilicate of aluminum and alkali, with iron, magnesium, and other cations in varying combinations. Tourmaline occurs as prismatic crystals, often very elongated with vertical striations and sometimes hemimorphic; and in aggregates of parallel, columnar, or radiating individuals. Tourmaline is transparent to semi-opaque and some varieties are pleochroic or chatoyant. At present, there are six members of the tourmaline group:

Elbaite: Sodium lithium aluminum rich. **Colors:** Pink to red (var. rubellite), green-pink bicolor (var. watermelon), blue (var. indicolite), green.
Schorl: Sodium iron rich. **Colors:** Black (usually opaque).
Buergerite: Sodium iron rich. **Colors:** Brown, black.
Dravite: Sodium magnesium rich. **Colors:** Brown.
Uvite: Calcium iron silicate. **Colors:** Green, colorless, white, light brown or black.
Liddicoatite: Calcium lithium aluminum rich. **Colors:** Green, pink.

Schorl in quartz, Arizona, 4" x 2-3/4".

In tourmaline, usually only the elbaite varieties are faceted as gemstones, the others are commonly collected as mineral display pieces.

Faceted rubellite tourmaline, 3 carats.

Tourmaline cluster, Brazil, 3" x 2-1/2".

Indicolite in matrix, Africa, 2" x 1-3/4".

Occurrences: Brazil, Italy, Mexico, Russia; California, Connecticut, Maine, USA.

Value: Rubellite tourmaline: $10.00 per carat.

Olivine (Peridot)

Colors:	Yellow green (var. chrysotile), green, yellow brown.
Luster:	Vitreous
Refractive Index:	1.69-1.65
Hardness:	6.5-7
System:	Orthorhombic

A silicate series consisting of two end members, forsterite and fayalite, which occur separately in variable proportions of magnesium and iron. In combination, they are commonly called olivine. Olivine is transparent to translucent, and the transparent green gem quality olivine is known as peridot. Olivine occurs very rarely as anhedral or prismatic crystals, and is most commonly found as rounded grains and granular masses. Olivine is also an important rock-forming mineral and occurs as an essential constituent of gabbro, peridotite, and basalt.

Faceted peridot gemstone, Arizona.

Occurrences: Burma, Brazil, Egypt, Norway; Arizona, California, USA.

Value: Pyrite: $2.00 per carat.

Spodumene (Kunzite, Hiddenite)

Colors:	White, gray, pale yellow, green, pink, violet.
Luster:	Vitreous to pearly.
Refractive Index:	1.632-1.646
Hardness:	6.5-7
System:	Monoclinic

Spodumene frequently occurs as very long, unevenly terminated, flat-sided crystals, often with longitudinal striations. Spodumene is a member of the pyroxene group, and is a silicate of lithium and aluminum. Spodumene is transparent to opaque, and is a trichroic mineral, changing color depending on the angle from which it is viewed. The transparent gemstone varieties of spodumene include kunzite, a pink to violet color; and hiddenite, pale to dark green in color. Spodumene is found only in granite pegmatites, often occurring with tourmaline, albite, and lepidolite.

Kunzite crystal, California, 3" x 1-1/4".

Occurrences: Brazil, Canada, Madagascar; California, Maine, North Carolina, South Dakota, USA.

Value: Kunzite: $1.00 per carat.

Benitoite

Color: Blue.
Luster: Vitreous to subadamantine.
Refractive Index: 1.8
Hardness: 6.5
System: Hexagonal

Benitoite is a rare and unique gemstone that occurs in a single known location in San Benito County, California. Benitoite occurs as stubby, prismatic, dipyramidal crystals, and is composed of barium titanium silicate. Benitoite is translucent to transparent, and due to scarce amounts of available material, cut gemstones or crystals are difficult and expensive to obtain.

Benitoite specimen with faceted stone, California.

Occurrences: California, USA.

Value: Small 1/2-1 carat pieces: $8.00 per carat.

Vesuvianite (Idocrase)

Colors: Brown, olive green, yellow, red, blue (var. cyprine)
Luster: Vitreous.
Refractive Index: 1.702-1.742
Hardness: 6.5
System: Tetragonal

Vesuvianite occurs as short prismatic crystals with a square cross-section; sometimes columnar with finely striated faces, and compact granular masses. Vesuvianite is commonly known as idocrase and is composed of hydrous calcium magnesium aluminum silicate. Vesuvianite is transparent to opaque and a compact, massive form of vesuvianite is known as californite, which is often sold as "California Jade" and cut into cabochons. Vesuvianite is used both as a gemstone and as display specimens for mineral collectors.

Vesuvianite crystal, Italy, 1" x 1/2".

Occurrences: Canada, Mexico, Russia; California, Montana, New Jersey, USA.

Value: $1.50 per carat.

Zoisite (Tanzanite)

Colors: White, green, pink, blue-violet.

Luster: Vitreous

Refractive Index: 1.70-1.69

Hardness: 6.5

System: Orthorhombic

Zoisite occurs as elongated, prismatic crystals, finely striated on the prism faces, often poorly terminated; and, as rod-like aggregates and granular masses. Zoisite is part of the epidote group and is a silicate of calcium and aluminum. Zoisite is transparent to opaque. The transparent blue-violet variety of zoisite is known as tanzanite and is a highly valuable and desirable faceting gemstone. The granular, massive forms of zoisite, which include thulite (a pink variety colored by manganese); and green zoisite with ruby inclusions, are sometimes cut as cabochons, and in the case of green zoisite, also used as an ornamental carving stone.

Faceted tanzanite, 1.42 carats.

Tanzanite crystal, Pakistan, 1/4".

Occurrences: Africa, Austria, Norway, Russia; California, South Carolina, Tennessee, Wyoming, USA.

Value: Tanzanite: $72.00 per carat.

Fire Opal

Colors: Off-white, yellow, orange, red-orange.

Luster: Vitreous.

Refractive Index: 1.37–1.43

Hardness: 5.5-6.5

System: Non-crystalline.

Fire opal is a form of common opal that doesn't exhibit the typical fire of precious opal. Fire opal occurs as amorphous, compact masses, and is composed of hydrous silica, often colored by iron and aluminum. Fire opal is transparent to translucent, and is often cut either as a faceted stone or as a cabochon. Occasionally there will be some flecks of fire visible in the stone, or a slight iridescence. Most fire opal comes from Mexico.

Faceted white fire opal, 6.53 carats.

Tumbled orange fire opal, Mexico, 1-1/4" x 1/2".

Occurrences: Australia, Guatemala, Honduras, Mexico; Arizona, USA.

Value: Kunzite: $6.00 per carat.

Apatite

Colors: Colorless, yellow, green, blue, brown, violet.
Luster: Vitreous to subresinous
Refractive Index: 1.632-1.646
Hardness: 5
System: Hexagonal

The apatite group occurs as prismatic or tabular crystals, granular masses, and botryoidal crusts. Members of the apatite group include hydroxylapatite, chloroapatite, or fluorapatite. Apatite is primarily composed of calcium phosphate and is transparent to opaque. Some included apatite is also used for cat's-eye cabochons.

Apatite crystals, Mexico, 4-1/4" x 3".

Blue apatite, Brazil, 1-1/2" x 1-1/4".

Occurrences: Austria, Canada, Italy, Mexico; Idaho, Maine, South Dakota, USA.

Value: Yellow apatite: $3.00 per carat.

Dioptase

Color: Bright emerald green.
Luster: Vitreous.
Refractive Index: 1.65–1.71
Hardness: 5
System: Hexagonal

Dioptase occurs as stubby, prismatic crystals with rhombohedral terminations. Dioptase is composed of hydrous copper silicate and is transparent to translucent. Dioptase is not only faceted as gemstones for jewelry but is also collected as a beautiful mineral display specimens. When dioptase was first discovered, it was believed to be emerald due to its vivid emerald-green color.

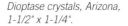

Dioptase crystals, Arizona, 1-1/2" x 1-1/4".

Occurrences: Africa, Chile, Russia; Arizona, USA.

Value: $100.00 per carat.

Display, Carving, and Ornamental Materials

A wide variety of lapidary materials can be used for display, carving, and ornamental purposes.

For display, many people collect rocks or minerals that stand alone on their own merit, or in other words, they are displayed as-is without any kind of processes applied to them in any way, other than cleaning them. This includes rocks or minerals that are displayed for their natural beauty, such as colorful mineral specimens or unusually patterned or shaped rocks. Display materials can range from anything like a small quartz crystal cluster resting prettily on a windowsill to precisely placed boulders arranged in an outdoor space for specific purposes, such as in a Zen garden, or a landscaped yard or public park. Carving and ornamental materials run the gamut too—everything from small carved cabochons or beads used in jewelry making, to decorative stone bowls, boxes, pipes, and numerous small objects, to small tabletop carvings or monumental sculptures. Ornamental stone is also used extensively for architectural and building purposes, such as for kitchen counters, floors, and tiles, and as the raw material for stone buildings, exterior walkways, and structural columns.

Display Materials

Included here are just a few examples of the types of rocks or minerals that people may collect for display, and there are certainly many more collecting options than this. Truly, the sky is the limit when it comes to the variety of possibilities for rock and mineral collections. Mineral specimen collecting is an enormously important and popular aspect of the rock and mineral collecting field in its own right, and is included in its own separate section in this book.

Fetishes

Fetishes are small stone animal carvings or totems, most famously made by the Zuni Indians of New Mexico. Fetishes have symbolic and spiritual meanings, and are used for healing, protection, spiritual guidance, good luck and longevity. Fetishes are believed to embody the strengths and characteristics of the animals they represent, and are able to endow those qualities to those that possess them. Zuni fetishes are not only spiritually significant, but wonderful works of art to be honored, respected, and cherished.

Carved serpentine fetish.

Carved jasper fetish.

Carved marble fetish.

Occurrences: New Mexico, USA.

Value: Depending on the carver, material, and detail, from $40.00 to hundreds of dollars.

Fluorescent Materials

Frankin, New Jersey, specimen in daylight, 4" x 3".

Collecting fluorescent minerals constitutes a large sector of the mineral collector's group. When viewed under natural light, most fluorescent minerals appear drab, ordinary, and uninteresting, but when fluorescent minerals are viewed under ultraviolet light, they come alive with extreme neon colors such as red, bright blue, lime green and orange, and make fascinating and beautiful display specimens. The neon colors are determined by the mineral content of the rock. For instance, calcite fluoresces red, fluorite fluoresces blue, and willamite fluoresces green. Certain localities are famous for their fluorescent minerals, such as Franklin, New Jersey, and are well known among collectors. If you want to collect fluorescent minerals in the field yourself, you will need a hand-held fluorescent UV light, and be prepared to wander around in the dark at night looking for them.

Same specimen under black light.

Occurrences: Worldwide; Arizona, California, New Jersey, USA.

Value: Multi-color, Franklin, New Jersey: $20.00 per 3" x 3" x 2" specimen.

Natural Display Rocks

These are rocks that are collected simply because they are beautiful, or exhibit a unique pattern, shape, or design. Included here are examples of a Chinese chrysthanthemum stone (a limestone porphyry) showing the exquisitely bold flower pattern that it is known for, and a septarian nodule from Utah (actually a concretion), collectible for its distinctive cracked pattern and hollow center lined with sparkling calcite crystals. Septarian nodules are often quite large and are cut and polished as bookends, spheres, eggs, ands small sculptures.

Polished septarian nodule, Utah, 4" x 3".

Chrysanthemum stone, China.

Occurrences: Worldwide.

Value: Chrysthanthemum stone: $30.00 per 3" x 3" x 3" specimen.

Carving and Ornamental Materials
Agate, Chalcedony, and Jasper

Although much harder than most materials used for decorative items, agates, chalcedonies, and jaspers are commonly used for carved cabochons and beads, small sculptural objects, and some larger pieces including bookends, spheres, and slabs for inlay projects. The choice of colors and patterns available, durability, and ability to take a high polish make them very desirable for all types of ornamental and functional adornments.

Crazy lace agate heart cabochon.

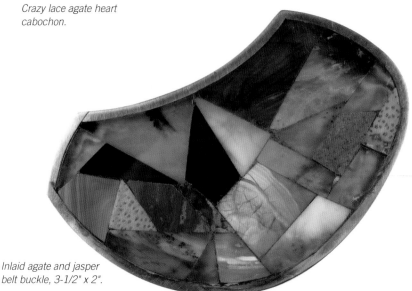

Inlaid agate and jasper belt buckle, 3-1/2" x 2".

Petrified wood handled knife.

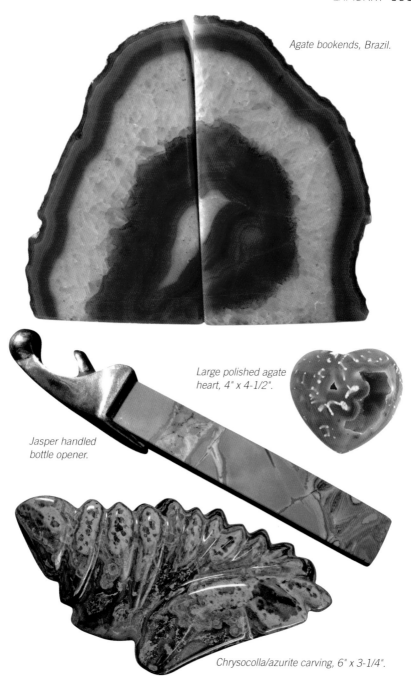

Agate bookends, Brazil.

Large polished agate heart, 4" x 4-1/2".

Jasper handled bottle opener.

Chrysocolla/azurite carving, 6" x 3-1/4".

Occurrences: Worldwide.

Value: Owyhee picture jasper: $6.00 per pound.

Alabaster

Alabaster is composed of hydrous calcium sulfate and is quite soft with a hardness of 2 on the Mohs scale. Alabaster is a dense, granular form of gypsum, and is a favorite carving material among artists due to its translucency, delicate colors, ease of use, and availability. Alabaster typically occurs in soft colors of white, pink, peach, and gray, and some alabaster has attractive light banding or veining. Alabaster is a commonly used sculptural material.

Rough alabaster, 4-1/2" x 2-1/2".

Carved alabaster, by the author, 3" x 1-3/4".

Occurrences: Australia, England, Italy, New Zealand; Colorado, Michigan, South Dakota, Utah, USA.

Value: $3.00-$5.00 per pound.

Calcite Onyx

Calcite onyx is composed of calcium carbonate with a hardness of 3 on the Mohs scale, is translucent to semi-opaque, compact and massive, and comes in a wide range of colors including gold, tan, pink, white, yellow, brown, gray, and green. Calcite onyx generally has intricate patterns of banding, swirls, lace, and dendrites, and due to its massive size, can be used for larger applications such as tabletops, lamps, bookends, or clocks, as well as for smaller objects like cabochons and beads. Calcite onyx is very popular with carvers.

Mayer onyx, Arizona, 7" x 4-1/2".

Honey onyx sculpture, "Contemplation," 15" x 8".

Occurrences: Africa, Argentina, Mexico, Pakistan; Arizona, California, Kentucky, North Carolina, Utah, USA.

Value: Honey calcite onyx, Mexico: $1.75 per pound.

Catlinite (Pipestone)

Catlinite, more commonly known as pipestone, is a form of argillite (metamorphosed mudstone), and is composed of a compact, fine-grained clay that is quite soft with a hardness of 2.5-3 on the Mohs scale. Due to its softness, it is a material that is very easily worked, and catlinite has been prized throughout history by Native Americans for its use in making sacred pipes and ceremonial objects, and is still quarried by hand in certain locations today. Catlinite is usually brownish-red to red in color, but can also occur in black.

Rough pipestone.

Carved pipestone fetish.

Occurrences: Canada; Arizona, Minnesota, South Dakota, Utah, USA.

Value: Minnesota red pipestone: $8.00 per pound.

Dumortierite

Dumortierite is an aluminum borosilicate mineral that can occur as prismatic crystals, but is more commonly massive, columnar, and fibrous, with a hardness of 7-8.5. When dumortierite forms as included crystals in massive quartz, it is known as dumortierite quartz. Dumortierite quartz is opaque and tough, occurring in an attractive deep violet to blue color, and also pink and brown. Massive dumortierite is popular as an ornamental stone and can be carved into cabochons, beads, sculptures, eggs, and spheres.

Rough dumortierite, California, 6" x 2-3/4".

Occurrences: Brazil, Madagascar, Russia; Arizona, California, Colorado, Nevada, USA.

Value: $9.00 per pound.

Fluorite

Fluorite is composed calcium fluoride, is transparent to translucent, and has a hardness of 4 on the Mohs scale. Fluorite occurs as cubes, octahedrons, and dodecahedrons; and compact concretionary masses with banding and variable color zoning. Fluorite can be colorless, yellow, green, blue, pink, and purple, or combinations thereof. Fluorite is especially popular for small carvings and is also used for making cabochons and beads.

Carved fluorite Buddha.

Carved fluorite fish.

Occurrences: Canada, China, Mexico, Russia; Arizona, Illinois, Kentucky, USA.

Value: Purple/green fluorite, Mexico: $10.00 per pound.

Howlite

Howlite is composed of hydrous calcium borate, is opaque, with a hardness of 3.5., and occurs in compact, fine-grained nodules. Howlite is generally white to cream with fine grayish black veining. White howlite is often used for cabochons, beads, and small carvings, and is frequently dyed to imitate many other materials such as turquoise, lapis lazuli, coral, and others.

Polished howlite pendant.

Occurrences: California, USA.

Value: $2.00 per pound.

Jade

The stone commonly referred to as jade includes two different mineral groups: nephrite and jadeite. Jadeite is harder and the colors are brighter and more varied than nephrite, with a slightly different chemical composition. Jadeite and nephrite are both tough, translucent to opaque, and occur in granular masses. Jadeite ranges from white to apple green or emerald green, with tones of lavender, yellow, brown, red, and blue. Nephrite is more commonly used, slightly softer than jadeite, and not quite as deep in color. Colors range from light greens to brown, red, and black. Nephrite and jadeite have been a favorite material for lapidary use since prehistoric times, and jade is popular as an exceptional carving material for ornamental objects, sculptures, cabochons, and beads.

Rough California jade, 2-1/2" x 1-1/2".

Purple jade frog.

Occurrences: Burma, Canada, Guatemala, Russia; Alaska, California, Utah, Washington, Wyoming, USA.

Value: Burmese jadeite: $3.00 per gram.

Labradorite

Labradorite is a member of the oligoclase feldspar group and is composed of sodium calcium aluminum silicate, is massive, translucent to semi-opaque, and has a hardness of 6-6.5 on the Mohs scale. The attraction of labradorite comes from its phenomenal quality of peacock-like iridescence, caused by internal twinning striations and a lamellar structure within the stone. The groundmass color of labradorite is colorless, gray, yellowish, green, or occasionally reddish. Labradorite is a strikingly beautiful material and is mainly used for cabochons, beads, and small, highly polished sculptural objects such as paperweights. Some labradorite is facetable if sufficiently transparent.

Polished labradorite paperweight.

Occurrences: Canada, Finland, Madagascar; Nevada, New Mexico, North Carolina, Texas, USA.

Value: Madagascar labradorite: $8.00 per pound.

Malachite

Malachite is a basic hydrous copper carbonate most often found in conjunction with copper deposits. Malachite is semi-opaque to opaque, and quite soft at 3.5-4 on the Mohs scale. Malachite occurs in fibrous, radiating masses of acicular needles, and botryoidal crusts or masses. Malachite is prized for its rich green colors, swirling bands, and bull's-eye patterns. Although it can be difficult to work with due to undercutting, malachite can be polished to a high sheen, and is used extensively for many types of ornamental objects, including cabochons and beads, inlay work, and carvings. Malachite is toxic to work with, so care must be taken when working with it, and wearing a protective mask is very important, as is keeping the material wet when polishing. Malachite is often collected as a display specimen, either natural or polished.

Polished malachite slab, Africa, 3" x 2-1/4".

Occurrences: Africa, Mexico, Russia; Arizona, California, Nevada, Pennsylvania, Tennessee, Utah, USA.

Value: African malachite: $20.00 per pound.

Obsidian

Obsidian is a natural form of volcanic glass, with a hardness of 6-7, conchoidal fracture, and is translucent to semi-opaque. Obsidian comes in a number of colors and patterns including banded, snowflake (exhibiting small white bursts resembling snowflakes on a black background), mahogany (having streaks of mahogany red colored bands), rainbow or peacock (containing layers of iridescent colors), and sheen (exhibiting shiny colors such as gold, silver, or blue in certain light). Obsidian occurs in masses and sometimes in small nodules known as Apache Tears. Obsidian can be cut and polished as cabochons or beads, and carved into a variety of decorative objects.

Rainbow obsidian paperweight.

Occurrences: Hungary, Italy, Japan, Mexico; Arizona, California, Idaho, Oregon, Utah, USA.

Value: Snowflake obsidian: $4.00 per pound.

Quartz

Crystalline quartz (silicon dioxide) includes the varieties rock crystal, amethyst, citrine, smoky quartz, rose quartz, aventurine, and tiger-eye. All forms of quartz are 7 on the Mohs scale, and take a brilliant polish. Quartz is transparent to opaque and comes in an array of colors including colorless, pink, purple, green, yellow, white, brown, and gray. When quartz contains silky, fibrous inclusions of crocidolite, it exhibits the quality of chatoyancy and is called tiger-eye, hawk's-eye, or ox-eye, depending on the prevailing colors of gold, brown, or blue. All forms of quartz are used for cabochon and bead making, carving decorative objects, and faceting. Quartz crystal clusters are highly collectible as beautiful display specimens.

Carved quartz bird sculpture, 4" x 2".

Occurrences: Africa, Australia, Brazil, Uruguay; Alaska, Arkansas, California, USA.

Value: African golden tiger eye: $9.00 per pound.

Rhodochrosite

Rhodochrosite is composed of manganese carbonate and has a hardness of 4 on the Mohs scale. Rhodochrosite occurs as semitransparent rhombohedral crystals, stalagtites, or as concretionary masses, and is translucent to opaque. Despite its softness, rhodochrosite is valued because of its beautiful pink and rose colors and delicate swirling or banded patterns. Massive rhodochrosite is often used for many larger decorative items, including carvings, bowls, spheres, and bookends.

Carved rhodochrosite Buddha, 3-1/2" x 3-1/2".

Occurrences: Africa, Argentina, Brazil, Peru, Russia; Colorado, Montana, USA.

Value: $.50 per gram.

Serpentine

Serpentine is a general name for a group of closely related metamorphic rocks with a hardness of 5, translucent to opaque, waxy, tough and massive, and frequently occurring in veins. Serpentines are often mistaken for jade, as they are similar in color and texture. Serpentine colors run from translucent green, to yellow green, pale green, gray green, and mixed with brownish black inclusions. Some serpentines contains asbestos fibers and exhibit chatoyancy. Serpentine, also known as green marble, is a popular lapidary material useful for making carvings, bowls, spheres, decorative items, and can also be used as a building material. An altered, white, porous form of serpentine with magnesite is known as sepiolite, commonly called meerschaum, that has been used to carve finely detailed smoking pipes for centuries.

Rough serpentine, Arizona, 4" x 3".

Carved serpentine, 2-1/2" x 1-3/8".

Occurrences: Afghanistan, Africa, China, New Zealand, Turkey; California, Michigan, Rhode Island, Vermont, USA.

Value: Verde antique, California: $6.00 per pound.

Soapstone

Soapstone (steatite) is a metamorphic stone composed of hydrous magnesium silicate closely related to talc and serpentine. Soapstone is massive, fine-grained, compact, and very soft, only 1 on the Mohs scale. Soapstone lends itself easily to carving and comes in a number of colors such as soft gray, green, white, tan, black and beige, and some varieties contain delicate dendritic inclusions. Soapstone is a popular material for small carvings, sculpture, decorative objects, and architectural pieces.

Carved soapstone beaver, 2-1/2" x 1-1/2".

Black pearl soapstone sculpture, Virginia, 13" x 8".

Soapstone box.

Occurrences: Brazil, Canada, China, Egypt, India; California, South Dakota, Vermont, Virginia, USA.

Value: Virginia soapstone: $1.50 per pound.

Architectural Materials

These stones have historically been used for landscape and architectural purposes, such as for large-scale buildings, and sculptural or monumental projects. They are also used today for a variety of ornamental lapidary purposes, including smaller scale sculptures, household functional and decorative items; for beads and cabochons for jewelry making; and in the case of certain fossilized limestones, for fascinating display specimens.

Flagstone and Sandstone

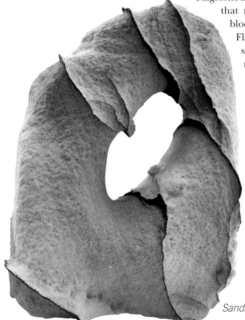

Flagstone and sandstone are both massive, compact sedimentary rocks, composed of fine to medium grains of quartz, accompanied by varying amounts of calcite, feldspar, and iron oxides. Typical colors of flagstone and sandstone are red, blue or gray, tan, and dark brown. They are often used for patios, walkways, steps, fences, construction projects, and making memorials or headstones for cemeteries. Flagstone and sandstone can occur either in flat slabs that make excellent paving stones, or thick blocks that can be cut into building stones. Flagstone and sandstone have been in use since ancient times, and many European medieval castles feature flagstone floors. Aside from architectural uses, picture sandstones are often used for small decorative or functional items, such as tabletop carvings or table coasters to set cold drinks on.

Sandstone sculpture, 5" x 4".

Occurrences: Africa, Canada, Ireland; Arizona, Colorado, Idaho, Nevada, Utah, USA.

Value: Flagstone: $.20 per pound.

Granite

Granite is a common, massive, fine to coarse grained, igneous rock composed of quartz, feldspar, and mica, with a variety of associated minerals such as hornblende, magnetite, tourmaline, epidote, and others. Granite occurs in many colors such as white, gray, pink, black, green, and many variations in between. Besides a variety of colors, granite occurs in a number of different types or patterns, including porphyry (large crystals or phenocrysts), orbicular (eye-shaped crystal clusters), and graphic (bold, unusual patterns). Granite takes a good polish and has been a popular decorative, sculptural, and building stone on a massive scale for centuries. Two types of granite, larvikite and unakite, are often used in smaller lapidary projects, such as in making spheres, eggs, carvings, cabochons, or beads. Larvikite from Norway has an iridescent sheen similar to labradorite, although it is much more coarsely grained in composition and silvery in color than the peacock colors of labradorite. Unakite is a medium-to-coarse-grained, epidote-bearing variety of granite that occurs in a mottled combination of soft green, peach, rose, and tan, with dark green and black accents.

Carved unakite cabochon.

Granite sculpture, Maine, 10" x 17".

Rough larvikite.

Occurrences: Africa, Canada, Italy, Russia; Georgia, Minnesota, Tennessee, South Dakota, Vermont, USA.

Value: Unakite: $5.00 per pound.

Marble and Limestone

Coquina polished bear,
6-1/4" x 4".

Picasso marble sphere, Utah,
3-1/2".

Basic limestone is a calcareous, compact, finely grained, opaque, sedimentary rock primarily composed of calcite, dolomite, and clay colored by the presence of limonite, hematite, carbon, bitumen, or other minerals. Limestone has been used as building material since mankind's beginnings, and was used in the building of the pyramids in ancient Egypt. Limestone is still popular today as a decorative and building material, and pisolitic (containing small spherules) or fossiliferous limestone containing small shells or shell fragments, such as coquina, is frequently used in lapidary projects such as stone boxes, vases, and sculptures. There are various forms of fossil-bearing limestone, and many are highly collectible for display, especially those containing fossils or imprints of rare and extinct creatures, marine life, and plants. Petosky stone, a fossilized coral from Michigan, is commonly used for cabochons and small carvings.

Marble is a massive, metamorphic, calcareous, recrystallized form of limestone with a hardness of 3 on the Mohs scale, translucent to opaque, fine-to-coarse grained, and occurs in colors from pure white to a variety of streaky, swirling, and dendritic patterns tinted with gray, red, pink, green, yellow, and more. Marble has been used for centuries as an important building material, but is most famously known for its lapidary application as a beautiful and prized material for statuary sculpture.

Rough Carrera marble, Italy, 7" x 3".

White marble sculpture,
Colorado, 60" x 18".

Occurrences: Greece, Italy, Scotland; Alabama, California, Georgia, Minnesota, Tennessee, Utah, USA.

Value: Carrera ordinario marble: $1.50 per pound.

Organic Materials

Besides rocks and minerals, a number of other organic types of materials are popular for lapidary use. Organic materials are those produced by biological processes, whether animal or vegetable, and can be of recent or ancient origin. To have the toughness and durability necessary for lapidary uses, these materials usually have a high percentage of mineral components in their biological composition.

Organic materials have a long history of ornamental use due to their relative softness and easy workability. Bone, ivory, and shell have been used for carving amulets, fetishes, religious totems, and works of art since the very beginning of mankind's ability to use tools. Pearls and amber have been used for hundreds of years in Asia and Europe as important trade commodities and as gemstones for royalty in many cultures. In today's market, organic materials are used extensively in jewelry making and are considered to be an essential part of the lapidary artist's repertoire.

Amber

Amber is the fossilized resin of ancient trees that existed tens of millions of years ago. Amber comes in a range of warm, beautiful colors including pale yellow, honey gold, orange or reddish brown, and can be transparent to opaque. Clear amber often has inclusions of fossilized insects that create striking and fascinating jewelry or display pieces. Amber can be easily carved and polished, and has been used throughout history to make jewelry, figurines, snuff bottles, and ornamental objects. Amber is used today primarily for bead and cabochon making for jewelry. Another resin on the market today, called copal, closely resembles amber, but is not true amber. Artificial and reconstructed amber materials are also available, so be sure to check for authenticity if you are purchasing amber.

Amber specimen, Dominican Republic, 2-1/2" x 1-1/4".

Occurrences: The Baltic, Burma, Dominican Republic, Mexico; Alaska, California, New Jersey, South Dakota, USA.

Value: $1.00 per gram.

Bone

Bone includes the many different types of calcified animal parts that are used for lapidary purposes, such as bones, hooves, horn or antlers, tusks or teeth, and claws. Elephant ivory is probably the most well known of these, and walrus, camel, boar, and cattle bone and horn are used today in place of elephant tusks for most applications. Bone can be carved, such as in the art of scrimshaw or netsuke, or cut and polished for small sculptures, beads, and cabochons. Many Native American people use antlers, teeth, and claws in their ceremonial or decorative objects, and in jewelry. Fossilized woolly mammoth or mastodon ivory is also a favorite material for carvers.

Carved ivory lion dog, China, 2" x 2-1/4".

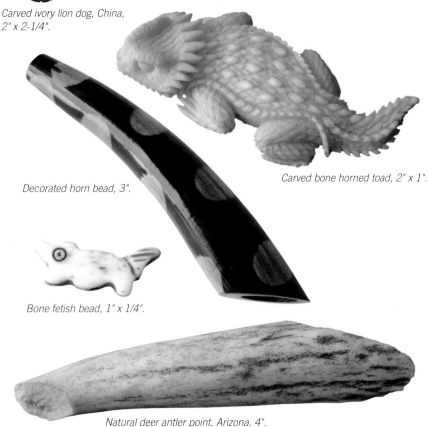

Carved bone horned toad, 2" x 1".

Decorated horn bead, 3".

Bone fetish bead, 1" x 1/4".

Natural deer antler point, Arizona. 4".

Occurrences: Africa, Asia, Canada, Russia; Alaska, Nebraska, USA.

Value: Commercially carved bone beads: $3.00 per 1" bead.

Coral

Coral is the calcareous skeletal remains of once-living colonies of marine organisms that lived in the coastal waters of the Mediterranean, Indian, and Pacific oceans. Coral is made of calcium carbonate and is relatively soft, but surprisingly durable. Coral comes in a variety of colors ranging from white to pink, red, and black. Today most coral is either bleached or dyed and is rarely of a natural color. Coral occurs in branch-like forms and can be polished and used as-is in small pieces, or cut into beads or cabochons. Inexpensive commercially dyed red coral is known as bamboo coral.

Coral bracelet with garnet and amethyst.

Occurrences: Africa, Asia, Mexico; Florida, USA.

Value: Red bamboo coral: $6.00 per 16" strand.

Pearl

Pearls are globular cysts of calcium carbonate that form within the tissues of mollusks as a protective coating as the result of an internal irritation, such as a grain of sand. Most pearls on the market today do not occur naturally, but are man-made, or cultured, by inserting an artificial irritant into the oyster to create the pearl. Cultured pearls come in many shapes and colors, and are often bleached or dyed. Natural pearls tend to be much more expensive than their cultured counterparts.

Pearls are generally a soft iridescent white with hints of pink or gray, or iridescent black with tones of green, blue or violet. Some of the common shapes of pearls are round, baroque (irregular), oval or rice, button (flat on one side), keishi (freeform), and freshwater biwa or stick. Pearls are an enduring staple of jewelry design.

Cultured pearl strand.

Stick pearl strand.

Occurrences: Australia, China, Japan, the Phillippines, Sri Lanka.

Value: Cultured freshwater white stick pearl: $12.00 per 16" strand.

Shell

A variety of colorful types of shell are used in lapidary work. Some of the most popular are abalone and paua, conch, mother-of-pearl, sea urchin, black lip oyster, spiny oyster, mussel, and nautilus. Shell is primarily composed of calcium carbonate and is easily carved into many shapes and polishes well into buttons, beads, and cabochons. Native Americans have been fashioning small shell disk beads known as heishi for ages, and heishi is still used today in modern bead stringing. Tortoiseshell is another type of shell that has been used throughout history for decorative pieces and jewelry making, but it is no longer used because of the endangered status of the turtles.

Mother of pearl carved bead, 1" x 1/2".

Natural tortoise shell, 2" x 1-3/4".

Blister pearl shell bead.

Spiny oyster shell, 3-1/2" x 3".

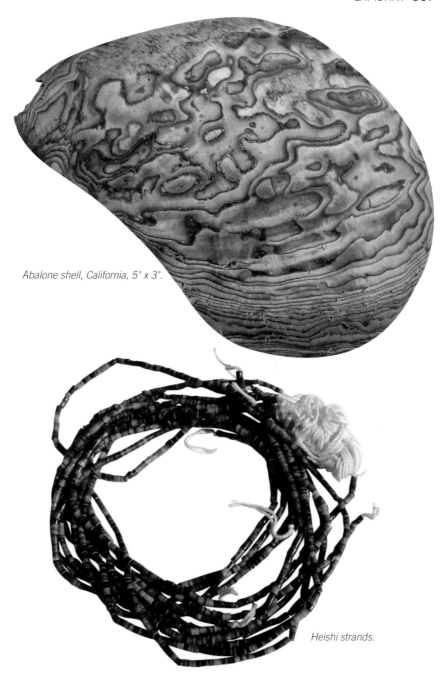

Abalone shell, California, 5" x 3".

Heishi strands.

Occurrences: Australia, Asia, Indonesia, Mexico, New Zealand; California, Florida, USA.

Value: Heishi: $5.00 per 24" strand.

Out of This World

A very popular branch of the rock and mineral collecting field is the acquisition of rocks and minerals that originate from outside of the Earth's realm, or are created on Earth by an extraterrestrial force. These collections include meteorites, which have been peppering the Earth from outer space since its earliest origins and are eagerly sought after by meteorite collecting specialists and amateurs alike; and fulgurites or tektites, both formed on Earth by external occurrences, such as lightning strikes in the case of fulgurites, or by extraterrestrial bodies in the case of tektites.

Fulgurites

Fulgurites are a natural phenomenon created in silicate sand soils by lightning strikes. They are formed when lightning strikes the dry, sandy soil with a temperature of at least 3,270 °F, instantaneously melting the silica in the sand and fusing the grains together into a glass-like tube formation. Since the electrical current travels in random patterns, fulgurites can have very interesting shapes, often showing branching or rootlike tubes. The tubes can be up to several inches in diameter, and many feet long. Their colors can range from translucent white to tan, black, or green depending on the composition of the sand they formed in. The tube's interior is normally smooth or lined with fine bubbles, and the exterior is generally porous, coated with a rough sandy crust from the surrounding soil particles. This type of fulgurite glass is called lechatelierite, which may also be formed by meteorite impacts and volcanic explosions. Fulgurites are amorphous and classified as a mineraloid. Fulgurites are sometimes referred to as petrified lightning.

The longest fulgurite ever found is approximately 17 feet long, and was found in northern Florida, USA.

Fulgurite, Utah, 4" x 1-1/2".

Occurrences: Egypt; Florida, Oregon, Texas, Utah, USA.

Value: Fulgurite specimen shown: $10.00.

Meteorites

Iron meteorites are the type most people think of when they hear the word. However, only a small portion of the meteorites that reach Earth are iron meteorites. The majority are stone or stony-irons. Stone meteorites are the most common type, but also the most precious and valuable because they are hard to distinguish from Earth rocks. They also erode more quickly than the durable irons and stony-irons. Iron meteorites are thought to originate from the metallic cores of planets or planetoids, or possibly from the explosions of supernovas.

Stony meteorite, 2" x 1".

The amount of nickel is what determines a meteorite's classification within the iron family. The combination of these two metals, iron and nickel, makes for an extremely hard material, allowing them to survive the Earth's atmosphere and fall to the ground to be picked up by some lucky collector. Meteorites are named for the locale, region, or nearby town in which the "fall" occurred, and the area where they are found is called a "strewn" field. Originally, the meteorite's metals were molten, and were then recrystallized in the high vacuum void of outer space, resulting in a crystalline structure unlike any found on Earth. Many meteorites also often contain minerals not found on Earth.

Meteorite, 2-1/2" x 2".

When a freshly cut or ground section of meteorite is etched with a mild acid, the internal crystalline structure is revealed. The Widmanstatten pattern is the unmistakable signature of an iron meteorite. Some meteorites with high nickel content will show no pattern; however, neither do stone meteorites. Often, the pattern is broken up by inclusions of various minerals, such as silicates, sulphur, carbon, and others.

Stony-irons are some of the most beautiful and rare of meteorites. There are two kinds of stony-iron meteorites: mesosiderites, and pallasites. Mesosiderites are a conglomeration of stone and metal; pallasites are composed of nickel and iron interspersed with large crystals of olivine, a yellow-green igneous rock. Pallasites are often polished in thin slices and make beautiful display pieces.

Acid-etched meteorite slice, 3-1/4" x 3".

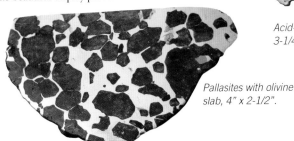

Pallasites with olivine slab, 4" x 2-1/2".

Occurrences: Africa, Australia, Argentina, Mexico; Arizona, Michigan, Kentucky, Wyoming, USA.

Value: Canyon Diablo, Arizona specimen, 25 grams: $50.00.

Tektites

Tektites are natural, dark-colored, globular silicate glass formations several inches in size formed by terrestrial rock that is melted and flung into the atmosphere by the force of an asteroid, meteor, or comet impact. Tektites are often aerodynamically shaped and are found in various areas around the world referred to as "strewn" fields. Most impact glasses show a broad range of chemical composition, reflecting the mineral content of their parent material on impact. Most tektites range in color from green to black, and are generally translucent to opaque. A beautiful translucent green form of tektite named moldavite is often used in jewelry making.

Round tektite, Vietnam, 1-1/2".

Moldavite tektite, 1-1/2" x 1".

Tektite, Indonesia, 2-3/4" x 3/4".

Occurrences: Australia, Czechoslovakia, Indonesia, Russia; Georgia, Texas, USA.

Value: Moldavite: $10.00 per gram.

Just For Fun

Sometimes people collect rock related things that fall outside the boundaries of "normal" rock and mineral collecting. These are collections that are just fun, personally interesting, or downright peculiar. I have seen all sorts of oddball collections that people have, and I even have some of my own. I have seen collections of rocks with happy faces or fanciful pictures in them; collections of rocks that are specific shapes, such as hearts, or only perfectly round rocks; rocks that have paintings on them; rocks that look like different kinds of food; other objects that look like rocks, and so forth. Some people collect pebbles as keepsakes from places they have visited for sentimental value.

My own feeling is that no matter what kinds of things you may have in your collection, however humble, goofy, or grand, the most important aspect of collecting them is that it makes you happy. So, have fun!

Bluebird painted pebble, 2" x 2".

Carved decorative stone, 3" x 3".

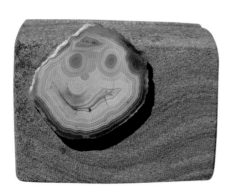

Happy face Laguna agate card holder.

Nazca Plain design stone, 1-1/2" x 3/4".

Sedona rock concert.

Welded stone Kokopelli
sculpture, 16" x 8-1/2".

Moqui ball concretion, Arizona.

Looks like a face to me,
3-1/2" x 2".

Brazillian agate guitar pick.

Stacked stone mini-temple,
12" x 10".

Soap in the likeness of opal.

1920s Vaseline glass bowl
colored with uranium.

The same bowl under UV light.

Mineral Display Specimens

Collecting mineral specimens for study or display can be a fun, rewarding, and fascinating experience. The world of minerals is full of color, beauty, and discovery. If you are a beginning collector, it is usually best to start with a general collection, then as you learn about the different aspects of mineralogy, you can narrow your focus to a particular field of study. A good way to learn about understanding and collecting minerals is to join a local mineralogy club if you can, take a class, or read as much as you can about mineralogy. Many of the excellent books about minerals that are listed in the resources section of this book are available in public libraries, and a great deal of information can be found online as well.

In this section are many, but certainly not all, of the minerals that are popular among collectors today. I have tried to include a wide spectrum of examples, but it is impossible to include every variety within the limited space of this book. Also, there is quite a bit of overlapping between mineral specimens for display and lapidary uses, so in the case of minerals that are routinely used for lapidary purposes (such as gemstones like topaz or turquoise), I am listing them in the lapidary section of the book rather than in this section, even though they are collected as mineral specimens as well.

Most minerals can be readily identified by using some simple tests and a few inexpensive pieces of equipment, such as a jeweler's loupe or ceramic streak plate. The first step in the process of identifying a mineral is to observe and assess its appearance. What is its shape and color? If it has crystals, what is their habit? Is it transparent or opaque, shiny or dull? You can also easily check a mineral's physical properties, such as streak, hardness, luster, opacity, habit, gravity (weight), cleavage, and tenacity. You can evaluate less common characteristics by taste or smell, and by other properties such as fluorescence, magnetism, or radioactivity. There are also chemical tests that can be performed, but these are best left to the professionals.

Listed on the next two pages are some of the most popular mineral characteristics that are commonly used to visually identify mineral specimens.

Crystal Habits

Habit	Description
Acicular	Needlelike or hairlike
Dendritic	Treelike or branching pattern
Equant	Having similar diameter in all directions
Prismatic	Tubular, elongated
Striated	Parallel grooves on crystal faces
Columnar	Made from slender parallel columns
Botryoidal	Bubbly or grape-like, globular
Druse	Coating or crust of fine, tightly packed crystals
Tabular	Flat, square, or rectangular planes
Fibrous	Tightly bundled fibers
Massive	Dense, interlocked crystalline grains
Stalactitic	Elongated, thin icicle shaped formations
Wheat-sheaf	Similar to a bundle of straw
Micaeous	Thin, flat sheets like pages of a book
Oolitic	Filled with small spheres
Radiating	Crystals growing outward from a center point

Mineral Identification

In this section, minerals are identified in the order of color; class; crystal system; and hardness. (It is important to note that mineral classification is an ongoing process, and mineral groups and classes are updated annually.)

Information in each of the mineral sections will correspond to the charts below for easy reference.

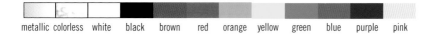

metallic colorless white black brown red orange yellow green blue purple pink

Mineral Classification

Native Elements	Includes alloys, metals, nitrides, and phosphides
Sulfides, Sulfosalts	Includes selenides, tellurides, arsenides, antimonides, and bismuthides
Halides	
Oxides, Hydroxides, Multiple Oxides	
Nitrates, Carbonates, Borates	
Sulfates	Includes chromates, molybdates, wolframates, and tungstates
Phosphates, Arsenates, Vanadates, Uranates	
Silicates	

Crystal Systems

System	Axis	Shapes
Isometric (or Cubic)	Three axes of symmetry, all at right angles to one another and all of equal length.	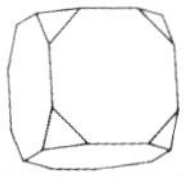
Hexagonal	Four axes of symmetry. Three of equal length lie in a plane at 120°. The fourth axis is of unequal size at right angles to the others.	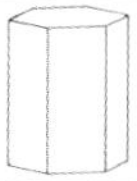
Tetragonal	Three axes of symmetry. Two axes of equal length lie in a plane at 90°. The third is of unequal size at right angles to the others.	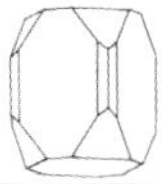
Orthorhombic	Three unequal axes, all at right angles to each other.	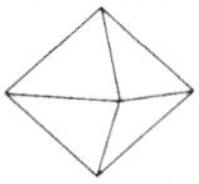
Monoclinic	Three unequal axes. Two axes are at right angles to each other on a plane. The third axis is inclined to the plane of the other two, and one twofold axis.	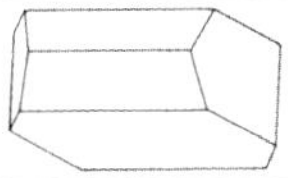
Triclinic	Three axes, all of unequal lengths and none perpendicular to the others.	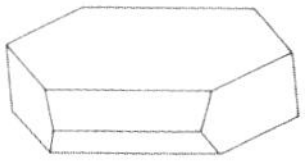

Mohs Hardness Scale

The Mohs hardness scale was developed in 1822 by Friedrich Mohs to test the hardness of minerals. The Mohs scale rates hardness from the softest, talc (at number one), to diamond (at number ten), being the hardest. You can test the hardness of a mineral yourself by using the items in the chart below to scratch the surface of the mineral you are testing. Each mineral will scratch all successive minerals below it in hardness. For example, topaz will scratch quartz, etc.

Scale	Mineral	Scratch test
1	Talc	Fingernail
2	Gypsum	Fingernail
3	Calcite	Copper penny
4	Fluorite	Knife blade
5	Apatite	Knife blade
6	Feldspar	Steel file
7	Quartz	Masonry drill bit
8	Topaz	Masonry drill bit
9	Corundum	Diamond drill bit
10	Diamond	Diamond

Mineral Values

For our purposes, mineral values will be based on an average market price for good quality specimens that a person would normally expect to pay when purchasing through a retail dealer. The price of mineral specimens is generally determined by a number of factors, including rarity of mineral type or location, appearance, color, size, and overall quality of the specimen. Any complete, well-crystallized specimen will always command top prices. Prices can vary widely for the same type of mineral specimen depending on whether its considered to be a collector-quality or museum-quality specimen. Since this is a collector's book, I will focus on collector specimens. I have also included a few rare and unusual mineral specimens for educational purposes that you would not normally encounter in the field, or readily find available for purchase, unless you are prepared to spend a very large amount of money, sometimes as much as thousands of dollars for an extraordinary museum quality specimen. Prices listed are for single specimens, except for the precious metals platinum, gold, and silver, which are bought and sold by weight.

Platinum

Platinum occurs as grains, plates, nuggets, scales, and rarely, as cubes. Platinum is a silvery, metallic gray color and does not tarnish when exposed to the atmosphere. Platinum is very heavy, ductile, and malleable, and is a good conductor of heat and electricity. Platinum is primarily used in jewelry making as a setting for precious stones in high-end jewelry pieces, but is also used in the manufacture of precision mechanical and electrical instruments and laboratory equipment. As with all the precious metals, the price of platinum fluctuates daily according to the market demand. As of this writing, platinum is $1,354.00 per troy ounce.

Color:	Metallic Gray
Group:	Native Elements
System:	Isometric
Hardness:	4-4.5

Platinum nugget.

FEATURES	
Composition	Platinum
Luster	Metallic
Opacity	Opaque
Cleavage	None
Fracture	Hackly

FEATURES	
Gravity	14-19
Environment	Basic/ultrabasic igneous rocks, placer deposits
Streak	White to gray
Tests	Insoluble in acid, except aqua regia

Occurrences: Africa, Canada, Russia, Peru; California, Oregon, North Carolina, USA.

Distinctive Field Features: Heavy weight; weak magnetism of iron-rich particles.

Value: $1,354.00 per troy ounce as of publication date.
For current value, see kitco.com/market.

Silver

Silver occurs as compact masses, dendritic branches or wires, and rarely as cube-shaped or octahedral crystals. Silver is normally a metallic silver-gray color, but tarnishes a blackish brown color over time when exposed to the atmosphere. Due to its malleability and ductility, silver has a long history of use as currency, ornamental objects, and in jewelry as settings for stones. Silver is used today in photographic processes, chemistry, and electronics because of its high conductivity, and is still used worldwide in coins, usually as an alloy with other metals. As with all the precious metals, the price of silver fluctuates daily depending on the market demand. As of this writing, silver is $17.26 per troy ounce.

Color:	Metallic Gray
Group:	Native Elements
System:	Isometric
Hardness:	2.5-3

Native silver, Michigan, 2-1/2" x 2".

FEATURES	
Composition	Silver
Luster	Metallic
Opacity	Opaque
Cleavage	None
Fracture	Hackly

FEATURES	
Gravity	10-12
Environment	Hydrothermal veins, oxidized ore deposits
Streak	Silver-white
Tests	Fusible, soluble in nitric acid

Occurrences: Australia, Canada, Mexico, Norway; Arizona, Colorado, USA.

Distinctive Field Features: Color; malleability; hardness; associated minerals.

Value: $17.26 per troy ounce as of publication date.
For current value, see kitco.com/market.

| Color: Metallic Gray |
| Group: Native Elements |
| System: Orthorhombic |
| Hardness: 2-2.5 |

Bismuth

Bismuth occurs as granular, reticulated, lamellar masses; dendritic and skeletal aggregates; and rarely, imperfect crystals that are often twinned. Bismuth is a silvery, (sometimes tinted red-pink) metallic color often coated with an iridescent film, and is frequently associated with nickel, cobalt, silver, tin, and uranium sulfides. There is also a brightly colored man-made form of bismuth with stepped crystals and a peacock-like iridescence that is often sold as decorative mineral specimens.

Bismuth, Australia, 2" x 2".

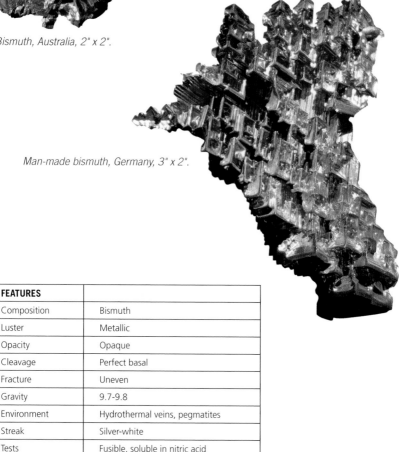

Man-made bismuth, Germany, 3" x 2".

FEATURES	
Composition	Bismuth
Luster	Metallic
Opacity	Opaque
Cleavage	Perfect basal
Fracture	Uneven
Gravity	9.7-9.8
Environment	Hydrothermal veins, pegmatites
Streak	Silver-white
Tests	Fusible, soluble in nitric acid

Occurrences: Bolivia, Canada, England, Norway; Colorado, Connecticut, South Carolina, USA.

Distinctive Field Features: Pinkish, silver-white color; broad cleavage surfaces.

Value: $6.00 - $30.00 per specimen.

Tetrahedrite
Tennanite Group

Color: Metallic Gray	
Group: Sulfosalts	
System: Isometric	
Hardness: 3-4.5	

The tetrahedrite-tennantite group is a two-member series consisting of tetrahedrite, the antimony-rich end member, and tennantite, the arsenic-rich end member. Crystals are typically tetrahedrons, often modified or twinned. They also occur as compact, granular masses. Colors can range from steel-gray to brown (depending on composition), to blackish, and occasionally to purplish-red or dark blue. The tetrahedrite-tennantite group is an important ore of copper, silver, mercury, and antimony.

Tennantite, Peru, 6" x 4".

Tetrahedrite, Connecticut, 5" x 3".

FEATURES	
Composition	Copper iron sulfides
Luster	Metallic
Opacity	Opaque
Cleavage	None
Fracture	Uneven to subconchoidal
Gravity	4.5-5.2
Environment	Hydrothermal veins
Streak	Dark gray to black, brown, or red
Tests	Fusible, soluble in nitric acid

Occurrences: Africa, Bolivia, Czechoslovakia, Peru, Sweden; Arizona, California, Montana, New Mexico, USA.

Distinctive Field Features: Tetrahedral crystals; fracture; lack of cleavage.

Value: $31.00 - $50.00+ per specimen.

Galena

| Color: Metallic Gray |
| Group: Sulfides |
| System: Isometric |
| Hardness: 2.5-2.8 |

Galena occurs as cubes and octahedral crystals, also as compact, granular masses with shiny surfaces when fresh, but tarnishing a blackish color over time when exposed to air. Color is lead gray and metallic. Galena is an important ore of lead, frequently with a by-product of silver. When galena is dissolved in hydrochloric acid, it gives off a rotten egg smell of hydrogen sulfide. Galena often occurs with sphalerite, bornite, and argentite in quartz gangue.

Galena with chalcopyrite and dolomite, Missouri, 5" x 3".

FEATURES		FEATURES	
Composition	Lead sulfide	Gravity	7.2-7.6
Luster	Metallic	Environment	Hydrothermal veins
Opacity	Opaque	Streak	Lead gray
Cleavage	Perfect cubic	Tests	Soluble in hydrochloric acid
Fracture	Subconchoidal		

Occurrences: Australia, England, Mexico; Colorado, Idaho, Missouri, Utah, USA.

Distinctive Field Features: Cubic cleavage; lead-gray color.

Value: $16.00 - $50.00 per specimen.

Molybdenite

| Color: Metallic Gray |
| Group: Sulfides |
| System: Hexagonal |
| Hardness: 1-1.5 |

Molybdenite occurs as tabular crystals with a hexagonal outline, as grains, and as bladed, foliated or finely woven masses. Molybdenite is a gray-blue color with a shiny metallic luster. Molybdenite is the primary ore of molybdenum and has many industrial uses such as a heat resistant dry lubricant and as an alloy for metallurgic purposes.

Molybdenite, Australia, 3-1/4" x 2".

FEATURES		FEATURES	
Composition	Molybdenum sulfide	Gravity	4.7
Luster	Metallic	Environment	Hydrothermal veins; granitic pegmatites
Opacity	Opaque		
Cleavage	Perfect basal	Streak	Blue-gray
Fracture	Uneven	Tests	Greasy feel, infusible

Occurrences: Australia, Bolivia, Canada, Mexico; California, Colorado, New Jersey, Washington, USA.

Distinctive Field Features: Cubic or octahedral metallic crystals; greasy feel.

Value: $16.00 - $50.00 per specimen.

Enargite

Enargite occurs mainly as lamellar aggregates or granular masses, and more rarely as tabular or elongated crystals with vertical striations on the crystal faces, often twinned. Enargite is dark gray and metallic and is associated with copper minerals such as bornite, covellite, chalcopyrite, and tetrahedrite. Enargite is an important ore of copper.

Color: Metallic Gray
Group: Sulfosalt
System: Orthorhombic
Hardness: 3

Enargite, Peru, 3" x 1-1/2".

FEATURES	
Composition	Copper arsenic sulfide
Luster	Metallic
Opacity	Opaque
Cleavage	Perfect
Fracture	Uneven

FEATURES	
Gravity	4.4-4.5
Environment	Hydrothermal veins, replacement deposits
Streak	Dark gray to black
Tests	Fuses easily, soluble in nitric acid

Occurrences: Africa, Argentina, Mexico, Peru; Alaska, California, Montana, Utah, USA.

Distinctive Field Features: Crystal shape; weight; associated minerals.

Value: $16.00 - $50.00 per specimen.

Chalcocite

Although metallic, chalcocite often occurs as granular aggregates or masses of a dull gray color, altered on the surface to a black or greenish color. It also occurs more rarely as tabular, pseudo-hexagonal, striated crystals that are frequently twinned. Chalcocite is an important ore of copper and is commonly found in conjunction with cuprite, malachite, and azurite in the reduction zone of copper deposits.

Color: Metallic Gray
Group: Sulfides
System: Orthorhombic
Hardness: 2.5-3

Chalcocite, Jerome, Arizona, 2-1/2" x 1-1/2".

FEATURES	
Composition	Copper sulfide
Luster	Metallic
Opacity	Opaque
Cleavage	Indistinct
Fracture	Conchoidal

FEATURES	
Gravity	5.5-5.8
Environment	Hydrothermal veins
Streak	Dark gray
Tests	Fusible, dissolves easily in nitric acid

Occurrences: Africa, Chile, Mexico, Peru; Arizona, Connecticut, Montana, New Mexico, USA.

Distinctive Field Features: Gray color; brittleness; association with other copper minerals.

Value: $6.00 - $30.00 per specimen.

| Color: Metallic Gray |
| Group: Sulfides |
| System: Orthorhombic |
| Hardness: 2 |

Stibnite

Stibnite occurs as prismatic or acicular crystals, elongated and striated lengthwise, sometimes bent or curved; also bladed, in radiating groups, columnar masses, and granular forms. The color is steel-gray often coated with a blackish or iridescent film. Stibnite is the most common of the antimony minerals and is frequently found with realgar, orpiment, and calcite in epithermal veins. Besides being a collectible mineral specimen in its crystal form, stibnite is used for industrial purposes such as an ingredient in alloys and in the making of fireworks. Stibnite salts are used in the rubber and textile industries and in the manufacture of medicines and glass.

Stibnite cluster, Romania, 2-1/2" x 2-3/4".

FEATURES	
Composition	Antimony sulfide
Luster	Metallic
Opacity	Opaque
Cleavage	Perfect
Fracture	Uneven to subconchoidal
Gravity	4.6-4.7
Environment	Hydrothermal veins, mineral springs deposits
Streak	Lead gray
Tests	Fusible, soluble in hydrochloric acid

Occurrences: Canada, Italy, Japan, Romania; California, Idaho, Nevada, USA.

Distinctive Field Features: Weight; crystal habit; slight flexibility.

Value: $31.00 - $50.00+ per specimen.

Arsenopyrite

Color: Metallic Gray	
Group: Sulfides	
System: Monoclinic	
Hardness: 5.5-6	

Arsenopyrite occurs as elongated, striated, prismatic crystals, with cruciform twins common; also columnar, and granular masses that are a silvery gray or gray-white color that tarnishes to a pinkish or brown hue, often with a coating of iridescence. Arsenopyrite emits a garlic odor and produces sparks when struck with a hammer. Arsenopyrite is the primary ore of arsenic, with by-products of gold, tin, silver, and cobalt. It is important to keep in mind that many minerals contain poisonous elements, and you should always wash your hands after handling them.

Arsenopyrite, Mexico,
3-1/4" x 1-1/4".

FEATURES	
Composition	Iron arsenic sulfide
Luster	Metallic
Opacity	Opaque
Cleavage	Indistinct
Fracture	Uneven
Gravity	5.9-6.2
Environment	Hydrothermal veins, metamorphic rocks
Streak	Dark gray to black
Tests	Fusible, soluble in nitric acid

Occurrences: Canada, England, Germany, Mexico; Colorado, Idaho, Maine, New York, USA.

Distinctive Field Features: Crystal habit; brittleness; smell; associated minerals.

Value: $16.00 - $50.00+ per specimen.

Color: Metallic Gray	
Group: Oxides	
System: Tetragonal	
Hardness: 6-6.5	

Pyrolusite

Pyrolusite occurs as columnar, fibrous, dendritic, concretionary aggregates or earthy masses, and very rarely as prismatic crystals. Pyrolusite is colored steel-gray to black, and the earthy varieties are quite soft and greasy, leaving a black mark or powdery residue when rubbed against a hard surface. Pyrolusite often forms beautiful dendritic patterns on the surfaces of rocks such as limestone that make attractive display pieces. Pyrolusite is one of the most abundant of the manganese minerals and is often found with barite and hematite in massive hydrothermal replacement deposits, and with calcite in epithermal veins.

Pyrolusite, Mexico, 3" x 2".

FEATURES	
Composition	Manganese oxide
Luster	Metallic to dull
Opacity	Opaque
Cleavage	Perfect
Fracture	Uneven
Gravity	4.7-5.0
Environment	Lakebed sedimentary precipitate, manganese deposits
Streak	Blue-black to black
Tests	Infusible, soluble in hydrochloric acid

Occurrences: Czechoslovakia, England, Germany, Mexico; Arizona, Arkansas, Georgia, Minnesota, USA.

Distinctive Field Features: Sooty streak; associated manganese minerals.

Value: $6.00 - $50.00 per specimen.

Franklinite

Franklinite is a member of the spinel group and occurs as octahedral or dodectahedral crystals, and as granular or massive aggregates. Franklinite has a black metallic color with a slightly reddish tint, and is associated with zincite, willemite, magnetite, rhodonite, calcite, and garnet. Franklinite is weakly magnetic, but becomes strongly magnetic if heated in a reducing flame. Franklinite itself is not fluorescent, but is often found in conjunction with associated calcite and willemite that do fluoresce in brilliant neon colors.

Color: Metallic Black
Group: Oxides
System: Isometric
Hardness: 5.5-6.5

Franklinite with green willemite and red zincite, New Jersey, 3-1/2" x 3".

FEATURES			FEATURES	
Composition	Zinc manganese iron oxide		Environment	Metamorphosed limestones and dolomites
Luster	Metallic			
Opacity	Opaque		Streak	Reddish-brown to black
Cleavage	None		Tests	Weakly magnetic, infusible, soluble in hydrochloric acid
Fracture	Uneven to subconchoidal			
Gravity	5-5.2			

Occurrences: New Jersey, USA.

Distinctive Field Features: Associated minerals; location; weak magnetism.

Value: $6.00 - $50.00+ per specimen.

Magnetite

Color: Metallic Black
Group: Oxides
System: Isometric
Hardness: 5.5-6.5

Magnetite occurs as perfect octahedral or dodecahedral crystals with striated faces, and as compact and granular masses with a bluish iridescence. The most outstanding characteristic of magnetite is its powerful magnetism, and it has also been known by the name of lodestone. Magnetite is one of the most abundant and widespread of all the oxide minerals and is found in various environments including igneous, sedimentary, and metamorphic.

Magnetite, Utah, 4-1/2" x 4".

FEATURES			FEATURES	
Composition	Iron oxide		Gravity	5.2
Luster	Metallic to dull		Environment	Igneous rocks, skarns, detrital sedimentary rocks
Opacity	Opaque			
Cleavage	None		Streak	Black
Fracture	Subconchoidal to uneven		Tests	Strongly magnetic, infusible

Occurrences: Canada, Italy, Sweden; California, New York, Utah, Vermont, USA.

Distinctive Field Features: Magnetism; streak; crystal habit.

Value: $16.00 - $50.00 per specimen.

| Color: Metallic Black |
| Group: Oxides |
| System: Hexagonal |
| Hardness: 5.5-6.5 |

Hematite

Hematite forms as tabular or rhombohedral crystals often grouped as rosettes; in massive, compact, granular masses, sometimes with an iridescent coating; in soft and earthy forms; and often in oolitic, botryoidal, reniform, or concretionary forms. Hematite occurs in a range of textures and colors from metallic steel-gray, to brownish-red, earthy red, and black. Hematite is the most important ore of iron, and the red powdery form of hematite (red ochre) has been used as a paint pigment for thousands of years. Hematite is also cut and polished as cabochons for jewelry making.

Botryoidal hematite, England, 2-1/2" x 2".

Specular hematite, England, 4" x 2-1/2".

FEATURES	
Composition	Iron oxide
Luster	Metallic to dull
Opacity	Opaque
Cleavage	None
Fracture	Conchoidal
Gravity	5.2-5.3
Environment	Igneous accessory mineral, replacement deposits
Streak	Dark brownish-red
Tests	Magnetic when heated, infusible

Occurrences: Brazil, England, Switzerland; Arizona, Michigan, New York, Utah, USA.

Distinctive Field Features: Red streak; color; hardness.

Value: $6.00 - $50.00 per specimen.

Bornite

Bornite occurs predominately as compact, granular masses, and as cubic, octahedral or dodecahedral crystals, often with rough or curved faces. Bornite is generally a reddish brown or bronze color, but when exposed to air it tarnishes to a bright iridescent blue, purple, and red color, which accounts for its common name "peacock ore." Bornite is often found in the oxidation zone of copper deposits and can be associated with malachite, chalcopyrite, and chalcocite. Bornite is one of the most important industrial copper ores.

*Bornite, Arizona,
1-1/2" x 1".*

FEATURES	
Composition	Copper iron sulfide
Luster	Metallic
Opacity	Opaque
Cleavage	Poor
Fracture	Uneven to conchoidal
Gravity	5.0-5.1
Environment	Hydrothermal veins
Streak	Gray-black
Tests	Fusible, soluble in nitric acid

Occurrences: Africa, Australia, Canada, Mexico; Alaska, Arizona, Colorado, Connecticut, Montana, USA.

Distinctive Field Features: Colorful tarnish; weight; associated copper ores.

Value: $6.00 - $50.00 per specimen.

Color: Metallic Red-Orange	
Group: Native Elements	
System: Isometric	
Hardness: 2.5-3	

Copper

Copper generally occurs as compact masses, scales, plates, lumps, and branching dendritic aggregates, more rarely as cubic or dodecahedral crystals. Copper is naturally a metallic red-orange color, but when exposed to the atmosphere it tarnishes a green, brown, or blackish color on its surface. Copper is quite malleable and ductile, and has been used since earliest times for tool-making, currency, ornamental objects, and jewelry. Copper is used today primarily for electric wiring due to its excellent conducting qualities, and as an alloy in the manufacturing of metals. Native copper pieces make striking display specimens. Copper prices fluctuate daily depending on market demand. As of this writing, the price for copper is $2.25 per pound.

Native copper splash, Michigan, 6" x 4-1/2".

Native copper on quartz, Michigan, 3-1/2" x 2".

FEATURES	
Composition	Copper
Luster	Metallic
Opacity	Opaque
Cleavage	None
Fracture	Hackly
Gravity	8.9
Environment	Reducing environments of sulfide deposits
Streak	Copper-red
Tests	Soluble in nitric acid

Occurrences: Africa, Canada, Chile, Germany, Sweden; Alaska, Arizona, Michigan, New Jersey, USA.

Distinctive Field Features: Color; luster; malleability.

Value: $1.00 - $50.00 per specimen.

Gold

Gold is one of the basic native elements, meaning that it is a singly occurring mineral on its own, without needing any other mineral to complete it, although because of the softness of pure (24k) gold, it is usually alloyed with other base metals to improve its hardness and other properties for use in jewelry and other applications. Gold occurs in numerous forms, including crystals, grains, flakes, sheets, nuggets, and wire. It can be mined by metal detecting and by panning, sluicing, or dredging in streams.

Gold nugget, California, 1/2" x 1/4".

Gold is the most malleable and ductile of all metals, and man's use of gold has a long and complex history. From gold's first discovery, it has symbolized wealth and power. Archaeological digs suggest gold was used in the Middle East with the first known civilizations. During the frontier days of the United States, gold rushes occurred in many of the Western states, the most famous occurring in California at Sutter's Mill in 1848. Elsewhere, gold rushes occurred in Australia in 1851, South Africa in 1884, and in Canada in 1897. Gold coins were widely used in the U.S. from the mid-1800s into the early 20th century. Today gold is primarily used in fine jewelry because of its beauty, workability, and resistance to tarnishing. Gold alloys are also often used in restorative dentistry, especially in tooth restorations, such as crowns and permanent bridges. Gold prices fluctuate daily with the precious metals market. Its value as of this writing is $1,114.00 per troy ounce.

Native gold, Canada, 2" x 1-1/4".

FEATURES	
Composition	Gold
Luster	Metallic
Opacity	Opaque
Cleavage	None
Fracture	Hackly
Gravity	15.6-19.3
Environment	Igneous, hydrothermal replacement deposits
Streak	Yellow
Tests	Insoluble in acids, except aqua regia: gravity

Occurrences: Africa, Canada, Mexico, Russia; Alaska, Arizona, California, Colorado, USA.

Distinctive Field Features: Gold-yellow color; weight; density.

Value: $1,114.00 per troy ounce as of publication date. For current value, see kitco.com/market.

| Color: Metallic Yellow |
| Group: Sulfides |
| System: Isometric |
| Hardness: 6-6.5 |

Pyrite

Pyrite occurs as cubic, octahedral, and pyritohedral striated crystals, commonly twinned; also as compact, granular aggregates; and as botryoidal, reniform, and stalactitic concretions. Pyrite is usually a pale to brassy yellow color, metallic and shiny, and has often been mistaken for gold, giving it the name "fool's gold." Pyrite develops a yellowish-brown or slightly iridescent tarnish over time and is frequently a replacement mineral in pseudomorphs such as pyritized fossil sand dollars or ammonites. Pyrite occurs in many different environments including all types of hydrothermal veins, mafic lavas, granite pegmatites, and many more. Pyrite is sometimes used in jewelry making as beads and faceted cabochons.

Unusual pyrite concretion, Illinois, 1-1/2" x 1-1/4".

Pyrite cluster, 4" x 3".

FEATURES	
Composition	Iron sulfide
Luster	Metallic
Opacity	Opaque
Cleavage	Indistinct
Fracture	Conchoidal to uneven
Gravity	5.0-5.2
Environment	A common accessory mineral in igneous, sedimentary, and metamorphic rocks
Streak	Greenish-black
Tests	Fuses easily, produces sparks when struck with a hammer

Occurrences: England, Germany, Italy, Spain; Arizona, Colorado, Illinois, Pennsylvania, Utah, USA.

Distinctive Field Features: Brassy yellow color; striations on crystal faces; sparks produced when struck with metal.

Value: $6.00 - $50.00 per specimen.

Chalcopyrite

Color: Metallic yellow
Group: Sulfides
System: Tetragonal
Hardness: 3.5-4

Chalcopyrite occurs as compact, microgranular, reniform or botryoidal masses; also, more rarely as pseudo-tetrahedral crystals with striated faces, sometimes twinned. Chalcopyrite is generally a dark or brassy yellow, often tarnished with an iridescent film. Chalcopyrite is frequently associated with pyrrhotite, sphalerite, pyrite, and quartz. Chalcopyrite is an important ore of copper and is quite widespread and abundant.

Chalcopyrite with quartz, Arizona, 3" x 2".

FEATURES		FEATURES	
Composition	Copper iron sulfide	Gravity	3.5-4
Luster	Metallic	Environment	Hydrothermal veins, sulfide ore deposits
Opacity	Opaque		
Cleavage	Poor	Streak	Greenish-black
Fracture	Uneven to conchoidal	Tests	Fusible, soluble in nitric acid

Occurrences: Africa, Canada, France, Mexico; Arizona, Kansas, Missouri, Oklahoma, Pennsylvania, Utah, USA.

Distinctive Field Features: Brassy color; brittleness; crystal habit.

Value: $1.00 - $50.00 per specimen.

Marcasite

Color: Metallic Yellow
Group: Sulfides
System: Orthorhombic
Hardness: 6-6.5

Marcasite occurs as flattened prismatic crystals, often twinned in the shape of "spearheads" and "cockscombs," and as radiating, nodular, massive, concretionary or stalactitic aggregates. Marcasite has a metallic, pale yellow color with a slightly greenish tinge. It oxidizes quickly when exposed to air, tarnishing a dark yellow-brown. Marcasite needs to be protected in a collection, such as in a clear plastic box, as it decomposes over time in the atmosphere and will disintegrate into a white powder if not properly preserved. Some people spray lacquer or acrylic on their specimens, but I don't recommend this, as it alters the natural appearance of the piece.

Marcasite on galena, Oklahoma, 2-1/2" x 2-1/4".

FEATURES		FEATURES	
Composition	Iron sulfide	Gravity	4.8-4.9
Luster	Metallic	Environment	Hydrothermal veins, sedimentary chemical precipitates
Opacity	Opaque		
Cleavage	Distinct	Streak	Greenish-black
Fracture	Uneven	Tests	Oxidizes quickly in air, fusible

Occurrences: Czechoslovakia, Germany, Mexico; Illinois, Kansas, Missouri, Oklahoma, USA.

Distinctive Field Features: Crystal habit; color; hardness; brittleness.

Value: $1.00 - $50.00 per specimen.

Rutile

Color: Metallic Yellow	
Group: Oxides	
System: Tetragonal	
Hardness: 6-6.5	

Rutile occurs as elongated, prismatic crystals that are often striated; very slender acicular crystals also occur as inclusions in quartz, known as rutilated quartz; and geniculated twinning is common. Rutile needles can be red, yellow, brown, or black, and transparent rutilated quartz is frequently cut and polished as cabochons for jewelry. Included rutile needles can also cause the phenomena known as "cat's eye" (chatoyancy) and "stars" (asterism) in quartz, corundum, and other mineral hosts. Rutile is an important commercial ore of titanium.

Rutile, Brazil, 1-1/4" x 1".

FEATURES	
Composition	Titanium oxide
Luster	Metallic to adamantine
Opacity	Opaque to translucent
Cleavage	Distinct
Fracture	Conchoidal to uneven

FEATURES	
Gravity	4.3
Environment	A common accessory mineral in many igneous and metamorphic rocks
Streak	Pale brown to yellowish
Tests	Insoluble, infusible

Occurrences: Australia, Brazil, Mexico, Switzerland; Arkansas, California, Georgia, Virginia, USA.

Distinctive Field Features: Crystal habit; weight; luster.

Value: $6.00 - $50.00+ per specimen.

Covellite

Color: Metallic Blue	
Group: Sulfides	
System: Hexagonal	
Hardness: 1.5-2	

Covellite occurs as foliated or platy, compact masses, and more rarely as thin, flattened, hexagonal crystals. Covellite is a deep indigo-blue color, with strong, colorful iridescence. Covellite is soft and is flexible in thin sheets, similar to mica leaves. Covellite was first discovered on Vesuvius, where it had sublimated directly from volcanic fumes. Covellite is a minor ore of copper and often occurs with chalcopyrite, pyrite, and bornite.

Covellite, Montana, 3-1/2" x 3".

FEATURES	
Composition	Copper sulfide
Luster	Submetallic to dull
Opacity	Opaque
Cleavage	Perfect basal
Fracture	Uneven

FEATURES	
Gravity	4.6-4.8
Environment	Altered hydrothermal copper veins
Streak	Dark gray to black
Tests	Fusible, soluble in hydrochloric acid

Occurrences: Bolivia, Chile, Italy, Sardinia; Colorado, Montana, Utah, USA.

Distinctive Field Features: Blue color; platy habit; association with other copper minerals.

Value: $16.00 - $50.00+ per specimen.

Halite

Color: Colorless
Group: Halides
System: Isometric
Hardness: 2.5

Halite occurs as cubic crystals, often with concave faces known as "hopper" crystals, and as crusts or granular masses. Halite comes in a wide range of colors including colorless, white, orange, yellow, red, pink, purple, blue, brown, and black. Halite is formed by precipitation in sedimentary deposits through the evaporation of saline waters, usually in a salt lake or lagoon. Halite is often found in conjunction with gypsum, dolomite, sylvite, and other evaporite minerals. Halite is also known as rock salt, and has a long and important history as a valuable trading commodity, and as a vital ingredient in the human and animal diet. When processed for human consumption, it is on our dinner table in the form of common salt.

Halite, Germany, 4" x 3".

FEATURES	
Composition	Sodium chloride
Luster	Vitreous
Opacity	Transparent to translucent
Cleavage	Perfect cubic
Fracture	Uneven to conchoidal
Gravity	2.1-2.2
Environment	Evaporite mineral in sedimentary deposits
Streak	White
Tests	Taste, soluble in water, greasy feel

Occurrences: Austria, Germany, Poland, Spain; California, Kansas, Michigan, Ohio, New York, USA.

Distinctive Field Features: Taste, moistness; crystal habit; luster.

Value: $6.00 - $30.00 per specimen.

| Color: Colorless |
| Group: Carbonates |
| System: Hexagonal |
| Hardness: 3 |

Calcite

Calcite is one of the most common of all carbonate minerals and occurs predominately in sedimentary environments as a precipitate through the evaporation of solutions rich in calcium bicarbonate. Calcite can take many forms, including rhombohedral, scalenohedral, or prismatic crystals; as compact granular masses such as onyx, limestone or marble; as concretions (stalagtites); or in fibrous forms like alabaster, and many more. Colors include colorless, gray, yellow, red, pink, orange, green, blue, brown to black. Calcite is also often fluorescent. Certain transparent crystals exhibit the quality of double refraction, or displaying a double image when an object is viewed through the crystal.

Calcite rhomb., Missouri, 2" x 1-3/4".

Besides the variety of beautiful specimen display options, calcite has many practical industrial uses including the manufacture of fertilizers, glass, and cement. Compact masses such as limestone or marble are used for sculpture and building materials.

Dogtooth calcite cluster, Mexico, 6-1/2" x 5-1/2".

Calcite crystal with chalcopyrite, Missouri, 3-1/2" x 1-1/2".

FEATURES	
Composition	Calcium carbonate
Luster	Vitreous to pearly to dull
Opacity	Transparent to translucent
Cleavage	Perfect
Fracture	Subconchoidal
Gravity	2.71
Environment	Forms in many environments
Streak	White
Tests	Effervesces in cold hydrochloric acid

Occurrences: England, Iceland, Mexico; California, Colorado, Michigan, Missouri, New York, USA.

Distinctive Field Features: Rhombohedral cleavage; hardness.

Value: $1.00 - $30.00 per specimen.

Aragonite

Aragonite occurs as elongated, prismatic crystals that are often twinned and showing pseudohexagonal forms. It also occurs as fibrous, acicular, radiating, columnar, and stalactitic aggregates. Aragonite can be colorless, white, yellow, gray, violet, blue, green, red, and brown. Aragonite is sometimes found in an interesting coral-like branching form called flos ferri or "iron flowers" that has been found in some Austrian iron mines, Mexico, and New Mexico in the United States. Aragonite is often a replacement mineral in pseudomorphs, and the inner surfaces of shells (and pearls) are composed of aragonite secreted by mollusks. Aragonite is often fluorescent.

Aragonite, Spain, 2" x 1-1/2".

FEATURES		FEATURES	
Composition	Calcium carbonate	Gravity	2.95
Luster	Vitreous, resinous	Environment	Metamorphic and sedimentary, hot springs
Opacity	Transparent to translucent		
Cleavage	Indistinct	Streak	White
Fracture	Subconchoidal	Tests	Soluble in cold hydrochloric acid, fluorescence

Occurrences: Austria, Italy, Mexico, Spain; Arizona, Colorado, New Mexico, USA.

Distinctive Field Features: Pseudohexagonal twin crystal forms; cleavage; fluorescence.

Value: $1.00 - $50.00 per specimen.

Witherite

Witherite occurs as trilling crystals resembling hexagonal bipyramids, often scepter-shaped or globular with striations parallel to the base. It also occurs in crusts with rounded surfaces and in columnar and granular masses. Witherite is generally colorless, white, gray, or yellowish-white, and commonly fluoresces blue. It is a fairly rare mineral due to its habit of altering to barite, and it is frequently associated with barite, calcite, and galena in epithermal veins.

Witherite, Illinois, 3" x 2-1/4".

FEATURES		FEATURES	
Composition	Barium carbonate	Gravity	4.3-4.4
Luster	Vitreous to resinous	Environment	Hydrothermal veins
Opacity	Transparent to translucent	Streak	White
Cleavage	Distinct	Tests	Soluble in hydrochloric acid, fluorescence
Fracture	Uneven		

Occurrences: England, Canada; Arizona, California, Illinois, USA.

Distinctive Field Features: Weight; hardness; fluorescence.

Value: $50.00+ per specimen.

Cerussite

Color: Colorless
Group: Carbonates
System: Orthorhombic
Hardness: 3-3.5

Cerussite occurs as striated flat, tabular crystals, often twinned to form reticulated lattices and star-shaped groups. It also occurs as massive, granular, compact, and stalactitic habits. It is often colorless or white, but also can be tinted gray, blue, yellow, or brown by the inclusion of other minerals, such as lead. Cerussite is often fluorescent, glowing a bright blue-green under ultraviolet light. It is a secondary lead mineral and generally forms from galena in the alteration zone of lead deposits through precipitation of waters rich in carbonic acid. Cerussite is a popular display mineral with collectors.

Cerussite, Africa, 2" x 1-1/2".

FEATURES	
Composition	Lead carbonate
Luster	Adamantine
Opacity	Transparent to translucent
Cleavage	Distinct prismatic
Fracture	Conchoidal

FEATURES	
Gravity	6.5
Environment	Oxidation zone of lead deposits
Streak	White
Tests	Soluble in nitric acid, fusible

Occurrences: Africa, Australia, Canada, Russia; Arizona, California, Colorado, New Mexico, Pennsylvania, USA.

Distinctive Field Features: Crystal habit; weight; luster; and brittleness.

Value: $31.00 - $50.00+ per specimen.

Kernite

Color: Colorless
Group: Borates
System: Monoclinic
Hardness: 2.5

Kernite occurs as slightly elongated, prismatic, striated crystals, and as cleaved masses and aggregates. Kernite is generally colorless, although it can be white or gray. Kernite is an evaporate mineral that forms in playa lake beds rich in boron, and is usually associated with minerals such as ulexite and colemanite. Kernite is a principal ore of boron, is a major source of borax, and is used in the manufacture of heat-resistant glass, enamel, soaps, and fertilizers.

Kernite, California, 6" x 4".

FEATURES	
Composition	Hydrated sodium borate
Luster	Vitreous, silky to dull
Opacity	Transparent to opaque
Cleavage	Perfect
Fracture	Splintery

FEATURES	
Gravity	1.9
Environment	Evaporate deposits, sedimentary
Streak	White
Tests	Soluble in water, fusible

Occurrences: California, USA.

Distinctive Field Features: Sweet alkaline taste; cleavage; dissolves in water.

Value: $6.00 - $30.00 per specimen.

Barite

Color: Colorless	
Group: Sulfates	
System: Orthorhombic	
Hardness: 2.5-3.5	

Barite takes a wide variety of forms and occurs as prismatic, often large, tabular crystals. It also occurs in lamellar, fibrous, granular, earthy, and compact masses, and as groups or fan-shaped plates known as "cockscomb" or sand-bearing rosettes called "desert roses." Barite can be colorless, yellow, red, blue, green, brown or black, depending on the included mineral content. Some varieties of barite are fluorescent, and barite is often associated with lead, silver, and antimony sulfides. Barite is a primary ore of barium and has many industrial uses including as a lubricant, paint pigment, and in radiography where it is used as a "barium milk shake."

Blue barite, Colorado, 3" x 2".

Tabular barite crystals, California, 3" x 2-1/4".

FEATURES	
Composition	Barium sulfate
Luster	Vitreous, pearly
Opacity	Transparent to translucent
Cleavage	Perfect
Fracture	Uneven
Gravity	4.3-4.6
Environment	Hydrothermal veins, hot springs, sedimentary
Streak	White
Tests	Insoluble, fuses with difficulty

Occurrences: Africa, England, Italy, Morocco; Colorado, Connecticut, Oklahoma, South Dakota, USA.

Distinctive Field Features: Weight; crystal habit.

Value: $1.00 - $50.00 per specimen.

| Color: Colorless |
| Group: Sulfates |
| System: Monoclinic |
| Hardness: 2 |

Gypsum

Gypsum takes many forms, occurring as tabular, bladed, and diamond-shaped crystals, often many feet long, and frequently twinned. It also occurs in fibrous form (satin spar), and in compact, granular masses (alabaster), and as rosette-shaped aggregates with included grains of sand, known as "desert roses." Gypsum varies from colorless to white, gray, yellowish, reddish, greenish, and brown. Besides being an attractive display specimen, gypsum has many industrial uses such as an ingredient in plaster of paris, flux for pottery, fertilizer. The massive variety, alabaster, is often used for sculpting and carving. Gypsum is sometimes fluorescent. Huge crystals occur in a cavern in Chihuahua, Mexico, in the aptly named "Cave of the Swords."

Gypsum "Desert Rose," Mexico, 2" x 2".

Selenite gypsum, Canada, 3" x 2-1/2".

FEATURES	
Composition	Hydrated calcium sulfate
Luster	Vitreous to silky
Opacity	Transparent to opaque
Cleavage	Perfect
Fracture	Splintery
Gravity	2.3-2.4
Environment	Evaporate in hot springs, clay beds
Streak	White
Tests	Soluble in acid and hot water, fusible

Occurrences: Canada, Italy, Mexico, Morocco; Arizona, New Mexico, New York, Utah, USA.

Distinctive Field Features: Hardness; crystal habit; flexibility.

Value: $6.00 - $50.00 per specimen.

Willemite

Color: Colorless
Group: Silicates
System: Hexagonal
Hardness: 5.5

Willemite generally occurs as compact, granular, aggregate masses; in fibrous, radiating form; and as hexagonal prismatic crystals often terminated by rhombohedra. Willemite may be colorless, white, gray, green, yellow, brown, reddish or black. Willemite is strongly fluorescent, shining bright green in ultraviolet light, and sometimes phosphorescent or triboluminescent (emitting a flash of light when struck with a metal object). The most famous occurence of willemite is in Franklin, New Jersey, where it is associated with franklinite and zincite, and this combination is a popular mineral specimen for collectors, especially for those who collect fluorescent minerals. Very rarely a willemite crystal may be faceted for jewelry making purposes.

Willemite with calcite and fluorite in daylight, New Jersey, 5" x 2".

Same specimen under UV light.

FEATURES	
Composition	Zinc silicate
Luster	Vitreous, resinous
Opacity	Transparent to translucent
Cleavage	Basal
Fracture	Uneven
Gravity	3.9-4.2
Environment	Oxidized zone of zinc deposits, metamorphics
Streak	Colorless to white
Tests	Soluble in hydrochloric acid, fluorescence

Occurrences: Africa, Canada, Greenland; Arizona, New Jersey, USA.

Distinctive Field Features: Hardness; luster; associated minerals; fluorescence.

Value: $6.00 - $50.00 per specimen.

Apophyllite

Color: Colorless
Group: Silicates
System: Tetragonal
Hardness: 4.5-5

Apophyllite occurs as cubic or tabular crystals, sometimes platy or dipyramidal, and also as lamellar, granular, and compact masses. Apophyllite is typically colorless or white, and can be tinted light shades of green, pink, and yellow. Apophyllite is often found in association with the zeolites. Apophyllite crystal specimens are an affordable and beautiful addition to any collector's mineral collection.

Apophyllite, India, 2-1/2" x 2".

FEATURES	
Composition	Hydrated potassium calcium silicate
Luster	Vitreous to pearly
Opacity	Transparent to translucent
Cleavage	Perfect basal
Fracture	Uneven

FEATURES	
Gravity	2.3-2.4
Environment	Hydrothermal, in cavities in basalt, volcanic rocks
Streak	White
Tests	Soluble in hydrochloric acid, fusible

Occurrences: Brazil, Germany, India, Mexico; Michigan, New Jersey, Virginia, USA.

Distinctive Field Features: Luster; volcanic basalts; associated zeolites.

Value: $16.00 - $50.00+ per specimen.

Danburite

Color: Colorless
Group: Silicates
System: Orthorhombic
Hardness: 7-7.3

Danburite occurs as prismatic crystals with wedge-shaped terminations, striated lengthwise. Danburite is usually colorless, but can be white, pale pink, gray, yellow, and light brown. Danburite forms in high-temperature deposits, usually in veins, where it is associated with quartz, cassiterite, fluorite, and orthoclase. It also forms in contact-metamorphosed rocks where it occurs with andradite, wollastonite, and sulfides. Danburite is often faceted as a gemstone for jewelry making and is popular for metaphysical purposes. Danburite was discovered in Danbury, Connecticut, which gives the mineral its name.

Danburite crystals, Mexico, 3-1/2" x 3".

FEATURES	
Composition	Calcium borosilicate
Luster	Vitreous
Opacity	Transparent to translucent
Cleavage	Poor
Fracture	Uneven to conchoidal

FEATURES	
Gravity	3
Environment	Hypothermal veins, contact metamorphics
Streak	Colorless
Tests	Insoluble in acid, fusible

Occurrences: Bolivia, Burma, Japan, Mexico; Connecticut, New York, USA.

Distinctive Field Features: Hardness; poor cleavage.

Value: $16.00 - $50.00 per specimen.

Natrolite

Natrolite is a member of the zeolite group and occurs as slender or acicular prismatic crystals with vertical striations. It is commonly found in radiating groups, and also in fibrous, granular, and compact masses. Natrolite is usually found lining the walls of cavities in basalts and other volcanics, and is associated with calcite and other zeolites. Natrolite may be colorless, white, gray, pink, or yellowish in color. Some natrolite will fluoresce orange in ultraviolet light.

Color: Colorless
Group: Silicates
System: Orthorhombic
Hardness: 5-5.5

Natrolite, India, 3" x 2".

FEATURES			FEATURES	
Composition	Hydrated sodium aluminum silicate		Gravity	2.20-2.26
			Environment	Vesicles in basalt, hydrothermal veins
Luster	Vitreous to pearly, silky			
Opacity	Transparent to translucent		Streak	White
Cleavage	Perfect		Tests	Soluble in strong acids, fusible
Fracture	Uneven			

Occurrences: Brazil, Canada, India, Russia; California, Colorado, New Jersey, USA.

Distinctive Field Features: Crystal habit; hardness; cleavage.

Value: $16.00 - $50.00+ per specimen.

Hemimorphite

Hemimorphite occurs as thin tabular, bladed or platy crystals with vertical striations, and with different terminations at either end (hemimorphic). It also occurs as fibrous, radiating crusts, and as botryoidal, stalactitic, compact granular, and earthy masses. Hemimorphite can be colorless, white, yellowish, blue-green, or brown. Hemimorphite is commonly associated with smithsonite, cerussite, anglesite, sphalerite, and galena. Some hemimorphite will fluoresce a pale orange in ultraviolet light. Brightly colored botryoidal plates of blue-green hemimorphite make beautiful display pieces.

Color: Colorless
Group: Silicates
System: Orthorhombic
Hardness: 4.5-5

Hemimorphite, Mexico, 3" x 3".

FEATURES			FEATURES	
Composition	Hydrated zinc silicate		Gravity	3.4-3.5
Luster	Vitreous to silky		Environment	Oxidation zones of zinc deposits
Opacity	Transparent to translucent		Streak	Colorless
Cleavage	Perfect		Tests	Soluble in strong acids, fuses with difficulty
Fracture	Uneven to conchoidal			

Occurrences: China, England, Mexico, Russia; Colorado, Missouri, Montana, New Jersey, Pennsylvania, USA.

Distinctive Field Features: Radiating aggregates; weight; color.

Value: $6.00 - $50.00+ per specimen.

| Color: Colorless |
| Group: Silicates |
| System: Monoclinic |
| Hardness: 5-5.5 |

Datolite

Datolite occurs as short, prismatic to blunt wedge-shaped complex crystals, as granular aggregates, and as porcelaneous botryoidal crusts and nodular masses. Datolite is generally colorless, white, pale green, or yellow. Datolite crystals are usually found as a secondary mineral in cavities in basalts and in hydrothermal deposits, where they are associated with zeolites, prehnite, and calcite. It is only in the Portage Lake lava series, which forms the Keweenaw Penninsula, that the porcelaneous or cryptocrystalline form occurs. The nodules are cauliflower shaped, and are usually cut and polished as collector specimens. The smaller ones may be used to cut cabochons for jewelry. The datolite nodules are most commonly colored pink or reddish by hematite, but may also be colored green by native copper, and more rarely, by native silver.

Datolite crystals, New Jersey, no longer available from this location, 4-1/2" x 3-1/2".

FEATURES	
Composition	Hydrous calcium borosilicate
Luster	Vitreous
Opacity	Transparent to translucent
Cleavage	None
Fracture	Uneven to conchoidal
Gravity	2.9-3.0
Environment	Basalts, hydrothermal deposits
Streak	Colorless
Tests	Fusible, soluble in acids

Occurrences: Canada, Germany, Mexico; Massachusetts, Michigan, New Jersey, USA.

Distinctive Field Features: Glassy; wedge-shaped crystals; associated minerals.

Value: $16.00 - $50.00 per specimen.

Dolomite

Dolomite occurs as rhombohedral crystals with curved "saddle" faces in aggregates; also as compact, granular masses. Dolomite can be white, colorless, pink, gray, green, or brown, and develops in a variety of environments, occurring with calcite, gypsum, fluorite, barite, and galena, just to name a few. Dolomite has many commercial uses in the chemical industry, in metallurgic processing, and as a building material.

Color: White	
Group: Carbonates	
System: Hexagonal	
Hardness: 3.5-4	

Dolomite, Romania, 3" x 2".

FEATURES	
Composition	Copper iron sulfide
Luster	Metallic
Opacity	Opaque
Cleavage	Poor
Fracture	Uneven to conchoidal

FEATURES	
Gravity	3.5-4
Environment	Hydrothermal veins, sulfide ore deposits
Streak	Greenish-black
Tests	Fusible, soluble in nitric acid

Occurrences: Canada, Italy, Mexico, Switzerland; California, Iowa, Michigan, Missouri, New York, USA.

Distinctive Field Features: Pearly luster; curved faces on crystals.

Value: $1.00 - $30.00 per specimen.

Strontianite

Strontianite occurs as prismatic, acicular needles, often in bundles or intergrown; also as fibrous, columnar, divergent, compact and granular growths. Strontianite is generally white or colorless, but may have a yellowish, gray, green, pink or brownish tint. Strontianite is an ore of strontium and is used in making fireworks, in glass-making, and in the sugar processing industry.

Color: White	
Group: Carbonates	
System: Orthorhombic	
Hardness: 3.5-4	

Strontianite, Illinois, 2-1/2" x 2".

FEATURES	
Composition	Strontium carbonate
Luster	Vitreous to resinous
Opacity	Transparent to translucent
Cleavage	Perfect prsimatic
Fracture	Uneven
Gravity	3.7

FEATURES	
Environment	Hydrothermal veins, clays and limestones
Streak	White
Tests	Soluble in hydrochloric acid, fusible

Occurrences: Canada, Germany, Mexico, Spain; California, Pennsylvania, Washington, USA.

Distinctive Field Features: Hardness; difficult to distinguish from similar minerals in the field without tests.

Value: $6.00 - $50.00 per specimen.

Colemanite

Color: White	
Group: Borates	
System: Monoclinic	
Hardness: 4-4.5	

Colemanite occurs as short, prismatic dipyramidal crystals; also as cleavable, granular, compact, masses and crusts or druzy coatings in geodes. Colemanite is usually white, and may be tinted pink, yellow or gray by impurities, and occasionally may be fluorescent. Colemanite has many important and wide-ranging commercial uses including as an ingredient in strong metal alloys, rocket fuel, heat-resistant glass, steel paints, and in the pharmaceutical and cosmetic industries. Colemanite is commonly associated with ulexite and borax.

Colemanite, California, 4" x 2-1/2".

FEATURES		FEATURES	
Composition	Hydrated calcium borate	Gravity	2.4
Luster	Vitreous	Environment	Evaporite deposits, clays
Opacity	Transparent to translucent	Streak	White
Cleavage	Perfect	Tests	Soluble in hydrochloric acid, fusible
Fracture	Uneven toc onchoidal		

Occurrences: Argentina, Chile, Turkey; California, Nevada, USA.

Distinctive Field Features: Crystal habit; cleavage; hardness; associated minerals.

Value: $1.00 - $30.00 per specimen.

Borax

Color: White	
Group: Borates	
System: Monoclinic	
Hardness: 2-2.5	

Borax occurs as short, prismatic crystals, sometimes flattened; also as compact, earthy masses and crusts. Borax is usually white, colorless, or gray, and may be tinted green or blue. Borax forms in evaporated deposits in the muds of saline lakebeds, and is often found in conjunction with kernite, ulexite, and halite. Borax is the principal ore of boric acid, and is used commercially as a flux, cleaning agent, and water softener. One of the most popular and famous collecting locations for borax in the United States is found in the Death Valley area of California.

Borax, California, 4" x 3-1/2".

FEATURES		FEATURES	
Composition	Hydrated sodium borate	Gravity	1.7
Luster	Vitreous to earthy	Environment	Evaporite deposits
Opacity	Transparent to opaque	Streak	White
Cleavage	Perfect	Tests	Soluble in water, fusible
Fracture	Conchoidal		

Occurrences: Iceland, Germany, Mexico; Colorado, Michigan, New York, USA.

Distinctive Field Features: Sweet alkaline taste; greasy feel; dissolves in water.

Value: $1.00 - $30.00 per specimen.

Ulexite

Ulexite occurs as silky, hair-like parallel fibers in rounded or lens-like crystal masses (prismatic crystals are rare); also as crusts and tufts, similar to cotton balls. Occasionally chatoyant, ulexite is usually white or colorless and frequently occurs with halite, kernite, colemanite, gypsum, or glauberite in borax deposits and evaporite salt beds. Ulexite was the precursor to the invention of today's modern fiber optics by exhibiting the ability to transmit light along and through its fibers; thus, it is also known by the name "TV rock."

Color: White
Group: Borates
System: Triclinic
Hardness: 1

Ulexite, California, 2" x 1-1/2".

FEATURES	
Composition	Hydrated sodium calcium borate
Luster	Vitreous to silky
Opacity	Transparent to translucent
Cleavage	Perfect
Fracture	Uneven

FEATURES	
Gravity	1.9
Environment	Evaporite deposits
Streak	White
Tests	Soluble in hot water, fusible

Occurrences: Argentina, Chile, Peru; California, Nevada, USA.

Distinctive Field Features: Crystal habit; hardness; associated minerals.

Value: $1.00 - $30.00 per specimen.

Glauberite

Glauberite occurs as prismatic, tabular, or dipyramidal crystals, sometimes with striated and rounded faces; and also as compact masses and crusts. Glauberite is usually white, colorless, pale yellow, tan, or gray, and will alter to gypsum over time when exposed to oxygen. Glauberite may occasionally phosphoresce. One of the most famous places in the United States for collecting excellent glauberite specimens is located near Camp Verde, Arizona.

Color: White
Group: Sulfates
System: Monoclinic
Hardness: 2.5-3

Glauberite, Arizona, 4" x 3".

FEATURES	
Composition	Sodium calcium sulfate
Luster	Vitreous to greasy
Opacity	Transparent to semi-opaque
Cleavage	Perfect
Fracture	Conchoidal

FEATURES	
Gravity	2.8
Environment	Evaporite deposits
Streak	White
Tests	Soluble in hydrochloric acid, fusible

Occurrences: Africa, Austria, Chile, India, Spain; Arizona, California, New Jersey, USA.

Distinctive Field Features: Salty, bitter taste; crystal habit.

Value: $1.00 - $30.00 per specimen.

Analcime

Color: White	
Group: Silicates	
System: Isometric	
Hardness: 5-5.5	

Analcime occurs as shiny trapezohedral or modified trapezohedral cubes; also as granular, compact aggregates, often lining cavities within basaltic lavas. Analcime is usually white, colorless, gray, or pink, and may have a yellow or greenish tint. When analcime is rubbed or heated, it becomes slightly charged with electricity (piezoelectric). Analcime is a member of the zeolite group and is often associated with other zeolites, and prehnite, and calcite in volcanic basalts.

Analcime, Oregon, 7" x 4".

FEATURES	
Composition	Hydrated sodium aluminum silicate
Luster	Vitreous
Opacity	Transparent to translucent
Cleavage	Poor
Fracture	Subconchoidal

FEATURES	
Gravity	2.2-2.3
Environment	Igneous, intrusive volcanics
Streak	White
Tests	Soluble in acids, fusible

Occurrences: Austria, Canada, Italy; California, Colorado, Michigan, New Jersey, Oregon, USA.

Distinctive Field Features: Shiny crystals lining cavities; associated minerals.

Value: $6.00 - $50.00 per specimen.

Thomsonite

Color: White	
Group: Silicates	
System: Orthorhombic	
Hardness: 5-5.5	

Thomsonite is a member of the zeolite group and occurs typically as radiating balls or globular aggregates, and more rarely as acicular prismatic crystals. Thomsonite is generally white or colorless, often tinted pink, green, yellow, or brown from other mineral impurities. Thomsonite is a secondary mineral deposited in volcanic basaltic cavities by hydrothermal fluids. Thomsonite is often associated with calcite, prehnite, and other zeolite minerals. Thomsonite is sometimes cut and polished as unusual cabochons for jewelry making.

Thomsonite, New Jersey, 5" x 2".

FEATURES	
Composition	Hydratedsodium calcium aluminum silicate
Luster	Vitreous to pearly
Opacity	Transparent to translucent
Cleavage	Perfect
Fracture	Uneven to subconchoidal

FEATURES	
Gravity	2.25-2.40
Environment	Cavities in basaltic volcanics
Streak	Colorless
Tests	Soluble in hydrochloric acid, fusible

Occurrences: Canada, Germany, India, Scotland; Colorado, Minnesota, New Jersey, Oregon, USA.

Distinctive Field Features: Crystal habit; found in basaltic cavities; associated minerals.

Value: $6.00 - $50.00+ per specimen.

Orthoclase

Color:	White
Group:	Silicates
System:	Monoclinic
Hardness:	6-6.5

Orthoclase is a member of the K-feldspar group and occurs as prismatic, columnar, or tabular crystals, often twinned as penetration twins or contact twins. It also occurs as lamellar, compact, and granular masses. Colors include white, colorless, gray, yellowish, green, pink, and brown. The feldspar group represents varieties of a single mineral species. All feldspars are aluminum silicates of soda, potash, or lime (with a few exceptions), and all are closely related in structure and composition. The feldspars include orthoclase, microcline, and the plagioclase group of albite, oligloclase, andesine, labradorite, bytownite, and anorthite. Besides quartz, the feldspars are one of the most abundant minerals on Earth, and are the principal constituents of most igneous and plutonic rocks. Some of the best common orthoclase crystals can be found in phenocrysts within porphytitic granitic rock formations. Adularia, one of the varieties of orthoclase, displays adularescence (a bluish sheen that appears when the stone is rotated), and is commonly cut as a cabochon for jewelry making under the name of moonstone. Another variety, sanidine, has crystals that can be very glassy and may also be cut as gemstones when transparent.

Orthoclase (var. adularia with chlorite), Switzerland, 1" x 3/4".

Microcline feldspar, Colorado, 5" x 3".

Orthoclase (var. albite), Colorado, 4" x 3".

FEATURES	
Composition	Potassium aluminum silicate
Luster	Vitreous to pearly
Opacity	Transparent to translucent
Cleavage	Perfect
Fracture	Uneven to conchoidal
Gravity	2.55-2.63
Environment	Igneous, plutonic, and metamorphic rocks
Streak	White
Tests	Soluble only in hydrofluoric acid, fuses with difficulty

Occurrences: Burma, Italy, Madagascar, Spain; California, Colorado, Nevada, New Mexico, USA.

Distinctive Field Features: Blocky cleavage; twinned crystals.

Value: $1.00 - $50.00 per specimen.

| Color: White |
| Group: Silicates |
| System: Triclinic |
| Hardness: 6 |

Plagioclase

Plagioclase is a member of the feldspar group. Freestanding, tabular (often twinned), crystals, except for albite and anorthite, are not very common. Plagioclase members are usually found as compact and granular masses, often with parallel or criss-cross twinning striations, and as phenocrysts. Colors include white, colorless, gray, yellowish, green, pink, and brown. The feldspar group of minerals are composed of a variety of related mineral species in a series determined by a gradual shift in mineral composition. The plagioclase group of feldspars includes albite, oligoclase, andesine, labradorite, bytownite, and anorthite. A few of the minerals in this group display some phenomenal physical characteristics, such as the beautiful peacock iridescence found in labradorite and bytownite, the adularescence that is seen in the albite moonstone, and the schiller effect found in the oligoclase sunstone, which has an orange-brown background color often enhanced by small hematite crystals that give it an additional sparkle. All of these stones are frequently cut and polished as cabochons and beads for jewelry making.

Labradorite, Canada, 2" x 2".

Sunstone crystal, Oregon, 1" x 1-1/2".

FEATURES	
Composition	Sodium calcium aluminum silicate
Luster	Vitreous to pearly
Opacity	Transparent to translucent
Cleavage	Perfect
Fracture	Uneven to conchoidal
Gravity	2.6-2.8
Environment	Igneous, plutonic, and metamorphic rocks
Streak	White
Tests	Soluble only in hydrofluoric acid, fuses with difficulty

Occurrences: Canada, Finland, Labrador, Madagascar, Norway; California, North Carolina, Oregon, Virginia, USA.

Distinctive Field Features: Repeated twinning; parallel lines on cleavage faces; hardness; weight.

Value: $16.00 - $50.00+ per specimen.

Scolecite

Scolecite is a member of the zeolite group (a group of related hydrous tectosilicate minerals). It occurs as prismatic, slender, striated crystals often grouped in radiating, fibrous masses. Scolecite is generally white, colorless, pink, or a pale yellowish color, and is primarily found with other zeolites in cavities or vesicles within basaltic volcanic formations. Scolecite makes a beautiful display specimen, and all members of the zeolite group are popular among mineral collectors.

Color: White	
Group: Silicates	
System: Monoclinic	
Hardness: 5-5.5	

Scolecite, India, 6" x 4".

FEATURES		FEATURES	
Composition	Hydrated calcium aluminum silicate	Fracture	Uneven
		Gravity	2.26-2.4
Luster	Vitreous to silky	Environment	Cavities in basaltic volcanics
Opacity	Transparent to translucent	Streak	Colorless
Cleavage	Perfect	Tests	Soluble in acid, fusible

Occurrences: Brazil, Iceland, India, Scotland; California, Colorado, New Jersey, USA.

Distinctive Field Features: Crystal habit; hardness; associated minerals.

Value: $16.00 - $50.00+ per specimen.

Heulandite

Heulandite is a member of the zeolite family and occurs as elongated tabular crystals (coffin-shaped), often in parallel aggregates. It also occurs as radiating, foliated, globular, and granular masses. Colors range from white to colorless, gray, yellow, greenish, reddish-orange, pink, and brown. Heulandite is frequently found within cavities in volcanic rocks, associated with calcite and other zeolites, and in veins in schists and gneiss.

Color: White	
Group: Silicates	
System: Monoclinic	
Hardness: 3.5-4	

Heulandite, India, 2-1/4" x 1-1/2".

FEATURES		FEATURES	
Composition	Hydrated sodium calcium aluminum silicate	Gravity	2.2
		Environment	Cavities in basaltic volcanics
Luster	Vitreous to pearly	Streak	White
Opacity	Transparent to translucent	Tests	Soluble in hydrochloric acid, fusible
Cleavage	Perfect		
Fracture	Uneven		

Occurrences: Australia, Iceland, Nova Scotia; New Jersey, Oregon, Washington, USA.

Distinctive Field Features: Crystal habit; associated minerals.

Value: $16.00 - $50.00+ per specimen.

Spodumene

Color: White	
Group: Silicates	
System: Monoclinic	
Hardness: 6.5-7	

Spodumene, 2" x 1".

Spodumene occurs as prismatic crystals, often vertically striated and flattened, sometimes very large in size; also columnar, and as cleavable masses. Spodumene is found in a variety of colors including white, yellowish, gray, or a greenish color. Certain colors, when transparent, are cut into gemstones such as hiddenite (the emerald green variety) and kunzite (the pink-lilac variety). Spodumene is a trichroic mineral, which means it changes color depending on the angle at which it is viewed. Spodumene occurs in lithium-bearing pegmatites and is frequently associated with quartz, feldspars, lepidolite, beryl, and tourmaline.

FEATURES	
Composition	Lithium aluminum silicate
Luster	Vitreous
Opacity	Transparent to semi-opaque
Cleavage	Perfect
Fracture	Uneven

FEATURES	
Gravity	3.1-3.2
Environment	Granitic pegmatites
Streak	White
Tests	Insoluble, fusible

Occurrences: Brazil, Canada, Madagascar, Mexico; California, Maine, North Carolina, South Dakota, USA.

Distinctive Field Features: Crystal habit; tough splintery fracture; associated minerals.

Value: $16.00 - $50.00+ per specimen.

Stilbite

Color: White	
Group: Silicates	
System: Monoclinic	
Hardness: 3.5-4	

Stilbite, India, 4" x 2-1/2".

Stilbite is a member of the zeolite group and occurs as intergrown tabular crystals, as pseudo-orthorhombic and cruciform twins in aggregates, as bladed, wheat-sheaf formations, and in radiating and globular masses. Stilbite is generally white, gray, yellow and reddish-brown, and is found within cavities in basaltic rocks, associated with calcite and other zeolites.

FEATURES	
Composition	Hydrated sodium calcium aluminum silicate
Luster	Vitreous to pearly
Opacity	Transparent to translucent
Cleavage	Perfect
Fracture	Uneven

FEATURES	
Gravity	2.1-2.2
Environment	Cavities in basaltic volcanics
Streak	White
Tests	Soluble in hydrochloric acid, fusible

Occurrences: Australia, Brazil, Iceland, India; Oregon, New Jersey, USA.

Distinctive Field Features: Wheat-sheaf formations; associated minerals.

Value: $6.00 - $50.00+ per specimen.

Pectolite

Color:	White
Group:	Silicates
System:	Triclinic
Hardness:	5

Pectolite generally occurs as aggregates of acicular needles in fibrous, radiating, botryoidal, compact masses. Pectolite is commonly white, light gray, or colorless, and is often found within cavities in basalts associated with zeolites, calcite, and prehnite; as fillings in fractures in serpentinites; and in contact metamorphosed limestones.

Avoid handling pectolite whenever possible, as its needles easily separate and penetrate the skin like fiberglass and are uncomfortable and difficult to remove. Pectolite may fluoresce in ultraviolet light.

A single occurence of a lovely, light blue variety of massive pectolite is found only in the Dominican Republic. It is sold as a gem material under the trade name of "Larimar" and is used for cutting cabochons in jewelry making.

Pectolite, New Jersey, 5" x 4".

FEATURES	
Composition	Hydrous sodium calcium silicate
Luster	Vitreous to silky
Opacity	Transparent to translucent
Cleavage	Perfect
Fracture	Uneven
Gravity	2.7-2.9
Environment	Cavities in basaltic volcanics
Streak	White
Tests	Soluble in hydrochloric acid, fusible

Occurrences: Canada, Czechoslovakia, Italy, Russia; Arkansas, California, Michigan, New Jersey, USA.

Distinctive Field Features: Radiating fibrous, botryoidal habit; association with zeolites.

Value: $6.00 - $50.00 per specimen.

| Color: White |
| Group: Silicates |
| System: Monoclinic |
| Hardness: 2-2.5 |

Muscovite

Muscovite is a member of the mica group, a group of minerals that are similar in chemical composition, structure, and physical properties. The mica group includes muscovite, biotite, phlogopite, and lepidolite. Muscovite occurs as tabular, commonly twinned, pseudo-hexagonal crystals, often with deep striations on the prism faces. It also occurs as foliated, scaly, lamellar masses. Muscovite has a perfect cleavage, which allows fine, thin, flexible sheets to be peeled away in layers from the main body of the specimen. Muscovite is usually white (sometimes with a silvery sheen), gray, yellow, pinkish, green or brown. Fuchsite is a variety of muscovite that is colored green by chromium, and another variety, alurgite, is colored red by inclusions of manganese and iron. Muscovite is one of the most common rock-forming minerals, and is an important component of granite and some schists. Before the prominence of modern day glass-making, large sheets of muscovite were once used as window panes and lamp shades.

Fuchsite, Brazil, 2" x 1-1/2".

Phlogopite, New Jersey, 3" x 1-1/2".

Muscovite with tourmaline, South Dakota, 5" x 4-1/4".

FEATURES	
Composition	Hydrous potassium aluminum silicate
Luster	Vitreous to pearly
Opacity	Transparent to translucent
Cleavage	Perfect basal
Fracture	Uneven
Gravity	2.77-2.88
Environment	Granitic pegmatites, schist, and gneiss
Streak	Colorless
Tests	Insoluble, fuses with difficulty

Occurrences: Brazil, Canada, India, Russia; Colorado, North Carolina, South Dakota, Virginia, USA.

Distinctive Field Features: Thin, flexible cleavage flakes; color; associated minerals.

Value: $6.00 - $50.00 per specimen.

Cassiterite

Cassiterite occurs as short, prismatic, and bipyramidal crystals, also as massive, granular, disseminated, and reniform with radiating fibrous structure. Cassiterite typically ranges from black to brownish-black to brown, but may also be colorless, gray, or pale yellow. Cassiterite is an important ore of tin, and is frequently found in pegmatites, and in sedimentary river and marine placers. Cassiterite also forms in granular, banded fibrous masses that resemble pieces of wood.

Color: Black
Group: Oxides
System: Tetragonal
Hardness: 6-7

Cassiterite, Bolivia, 3" x 2-1/2".

FEATURES			FEATURES	
Composition	Tin oxide		Gravity	6.8-7.1
Luster	Adamantine to dull		Environment	Hydrothermal veins, pegmatites, and greisens
Opacity	Transparent to semi-opaque			
Cleavage	Poor		Streak	White to light brown
Fracture	Subconchoidal to uneven		Tests	Insoluble, infusible

Occurrences: China, Bolivia, England, Russia; California, Maine, South Dakota, Virginia, USA.

Distinctive Field Features: Weight; hardness.

Value: $16.00 - $50.00 per specimen.

Romanechite
(Psilomelane)

Romanechite occurs as botryoidal, stalactitic, dendritic, crusts and masses; also in earthy or powdery forms, never as crystals. Romanechite is black to steel gray and often forms as a dendritic coating on the fracture planes of quartz and limestones, creating an interesting branching pattern that make attractive display pieces. Romanechite is a fairly widespread mineral, but good specimen collecting locations are limited. A highly desirable form of botryoidal romanechite called "Crown of Silver" is mined in Mexico and is eagerly sought by lapidaries for cabochon cutting.

Color: Black
Group: Oxides
System: Orthorhombic
Hardness: 5-7

Romanechite with calcite, 5-1/2" x 2-1/4".

FEATURES			FEATURES	
Composition	Hydrous barium manganese oxide		Gravity	3.7-4.7
			Environment	Manganese oxidation zones, silicate deposits
Luster	Submetallic to dull			
Opacity	Opaque		Streak	Black to brown
Cleavage	None		Tests	Soluble in hydrochloric acid, infusible
Fracture	Uneven			

Occurrences: Brazil, Mexico, Morocco, Russia; Arizona, New Mexico, Virginia, USA.

Distinctive Field Features: Massive or dendritic habit; associated manganese minerals.

Value: $1.00 - $50.00 per specimen.

| Color: Black |
| Group: Silicates |
| System: Monoclinic |
| Hardness: 2.5-3 |

Biotite

Biotite is a member of the mica group and occurs most commonly as disseminated, platy aggregates; in granular form; and as tabular, sometimes barrel-shaped, pseudo-hexagonal crystals. Biotite ranges in color from black or dark brown to reddish-brown and brownish-green. Biotite cleaves easily into small, flexible transparent or translucent sheets, and is distinguished from the other micas by its dark color. Biotite is one of the main rock-forming minerals of igneous and metamorphic rocks, and is a common mineral of pegmatites. Biotite is also often found in dark volcanic rocks as larger crystals known as porphyry phenocrysts.

Biotite, Colorado, 2" x 2-1/4".

FEATURES	
Composition	Hydrous potassium aluminum silicate
Luster	Vitreous
Opacity	Transparent to opaque
Cleavage	Perfect basal
Fracture	Uneven
Gravity	2.8-3.4
Environment	Igneous rocks, pegmatites, metamorphics
Streak	Colorless
Tests	Soluble in sulfuric acid, fuses with difficulty

Occurrences: Brazil, Canada, Greenland, Italy; Arizona, Colorado, North Carolina, Utah, USA.

Distinctive Field Features: Color; platy aggregates.

Value: $1.00 - $30.00 per specimen.

Goethite/Limonite

Color:	Brown
Group:	Hydroxides
System:	Orthorhombic
Hardness:	5-5.5

Goethite occurs rarely as prismatic, vertically striated crystals; more commonly as tabular, acicular, felted, botryoidal, stalactitic, oolitic or pisolitic aggregates; also as amorphous, porous, earthy masses. Goethite ranges in color from blackish brown to brownish-yellow, and is an important constituent of limonite, a secondary mineral that forms from the alteration of iron-bearing minerals, especially sulfides such as pyrite, marcasite, and arsenopyrite. Pseudomorphs after pyrite are common. Goethite is an important iron ore, and the ochres of goethite and limonite have been used as paint pigments since man's earliest beginnings.

Goethite penetration twin, Utah, 1-3/4" x 2-1/2".

Limonite, South Dakota, 2-1/4" x 1-1/2".

FEATURES	
Composition	Iron hydroxide
Luster	Adamantine, submetallic to dull
Opacity	Opaque
Cleavage	Perfect
Fracture	Uneven
Gravity	3.3-4.3
Environment	Oxidation zone of iron-rich deposits
Streak	Blackish-brown to yellowish brown
Tests	Magnetic when heated, soluble in hydrochloric acid

Occurrences: England, France, Germany; Colorado, Michigan, Minnesota, New Mexico, USA.

Distinctive Field Features: Streak color; silky, fibrous structure.

Value: $1.00 - $30.00 per specimen.

Color: Brown
Group: Tungstates
System: Monoclinic
Hardness: 5-5.5

Wolframite Group

This is a series of three members consisting of ferberite (the iron-rich member), wolframite (the iron-manganese rich intermediate member), and hübnerite (the manganese-rich end member). All members can occur as tabular crystals with vertically striated faces, and twinning is common. Members can also occur as bladed and granular masses. Colors range from reddish-brown to brownish-black. Ferberite can be weakly magnetic, and members of this group are frequently associated with cassiterite, arsenopyrite, hematite, fluorite, feldspar, and quartz. The ferberite-hübnerite group is a primary ore of tungsten used commercially as a filament in light bulbs and as a carbide in the manufacture of drilling equipment.

*Ferberite, Russia,
3-1/2" x 2-1/4".*

Wolframite, Kazakhstan, 3" x 3".

*Hübnerite, Colorado,
3" x 2-1/2".*

FEATURES	
Composition	Iron manganese tungstates
Luster	Submetallic to resinous
Opacity	Transparent to semi-opaque
Cleavage	Perfect
Fracture	Uneven
Gravity	7.1-7.5
Environment	Hydrothermal veins, granitic pegmatites
Streak	Reddish-brown to black
Tests	Insoluble in acid, fuses slowly

Occurrences: Australia, China, Canada, Portugal; Colorado, Nevada, New Mexico, South Dakota, USA.

Distinctive Field Features: Crystal habit; weight; color.

Value: $6.00 - $50.00 per specimen.

Descloizite

This is a two-member series consisting of the more common member descloizite (the zinc-rich end member), and mottramite (the copper-rich end member). Descloizite occurs as pyramidal, tabular, or prismatic crystals with uneven faces; as crusts of small, plumose crystal groupings; and as fibrous, botryoidal, and stalactitic masses. Colors run from reddish-brown to black in descloizite, and brownish to olive green in mottramite. Both descloizite and mottramite are secondary minerals occurring in the alteration zone of hydrothermal replacement deposits, and are frequently associated with vanadanite, cerussite, wulfenite, and pyromorphite.

Color: Brown	
Group: Vanadates	
System: Orthorhombic	
Hardness: 3.5	

Descloizite, Arizona, 3" x 2-1/2".

FEATURES		FEATURES	
Composition	Hydrous lead zinc vanadate	Environment	Oxidation zone of lead, zinc, and copper deposits
Luster	Vitreous to greasy		
Opacity	Transparent to translucent	Streak	Orange to reddish-brown, greenish (mottramite)
Cleavage	None		
Fracture	Uneven	Tests	Soluble in acid, fusible
Gravity	5.9-6.2		

Occurrences: Africa, Argentina, England; Arizona, New Mexico, USA.

Distinctive Field Features: Crystal habit; associated minerals.

Value: $6.00 - $50.00 per specimen.

Vesuvianite

Also known as idocrase, vesuvianite occurs as short, prismatic, pyramidal crystals with a square cross-section. It also occurs as columnar, granular, and compact masses. Vesuvianite typically ranges in color from brown to olive green, but also can occur in blue (cyprine), purple, and yellow. Massive, translucent green vesuvianite is called californite, and is often sold as "California jade" for lapidary purposes. When vesuvianite is transparent enough, it is commonly faceted as a gemstone for jewelry making. Vesuvianite is frequently associated with various garnets, wollastonite, diopside, and calcite. Vesuvianite is named after Mount Vesuvius, where it was first discovered.

Color: Brown	
Group: Silicates	
System: Tetragonal	
Hardness: 6.5	

Vesuvianite, Italy, 1" x 3/4".

FEATURES		FEATURES	
Composition	Hydrous calcium magnesium aluminum silicate	Gravity	3.3-3.45
		Environment	Contact metamorphic skarns, serpentines
Luster	Vitreous to resinous		
Opacity	Transparent to opaque	Streak	White
Cleavage	Poor	Tests	Insoluble in acid, fusible
Fracture	Uneven to conchoidal		

Occurrences: Canada, Italy, Mexico, Pakistan; Arkansas, California, Montana, New Jersey, USA.

Distinctive Field Features: Crystal habit; color; associated minerals.

Value: $6.00 - $50.00 per specimen.

Staurolite

Color: Brown
Group: Silicates
System: Orthorhombic
Hardness: 7-7.5

Staurolite occurs as short, prismatic crystals; as cruciform twins, often with a rough surface; as granules; and often as parallel intergrowths with kyanite. Colors are dark brown, reddish brown, yellowish brown, and brownish black. Staurolite is associated with garnet, kyanite, and the micas in regional metamorphic rocks. It can often be collected in alluvial sands due to its ability to withstand erosion because of its hardness. Staurolite is most well known and collected for its cross-shaped form, and is popular as a good luck charm. Staurolite is also known as a "fairy cross."

Staurolite, New Mexico, 1-1/4" x 1".

FEATURES		FEATURES	
Composition	Hydrous iron magnesium aluminum silicate	Gravity	3.7-3.8
Luster	Vitreous to dull	Environment	Metamorphic schists and gneisses
Opacity	Semi-opaque to opaque	Streak	White
Cleavage	Poor	Tests	Infusible, insoluble
Fracture	Uneven to subconchoidal		

Occurrences: Italy, Scotland, Switzerland; California, Georgia, Maine, New Hampshire, New Mexico, USA.

Distinctive Field Features: Crystal habit.

Value: $6.00 - $50.00 per specimen.

Titanite (Sphene)

Color: Brown
Group: Silicates
System: Monoclinic
Hardness: 5-5.5

Titanite occurs as prismatic, short, wedge-shaped, flattened crystals or as tabular, platy crystals. Contact or penetration twins are common in both crystal forms. Titanite also occurs as granular aggregates. Colors vary from dark brown to black, gray, or yellow-green, and rarely as colorless or pink. Some varieties may display trichroism. Transparent, strongly colored crystals are faceted as brilliant gemstones for jewelry making. Titanite occurs as small crystals in granite, granodiorite, diorite, and monzonite of plutonic rocks, and in granite and nepheline syenite pegmatites.

Titanite, Colorado, 1-1/4" x 1".

FEATURES		FEATURES	
Composition	Calcium titanium silicate	Gravity	3.4-3.5
Luster	Adamantine to resinous	Environment	Metamorphic rocks, marble, schist, gneiss
Opacity	Transparent to translucent		
Cleavage	Distinct	Streak	White
Fracture	Conchoidal	Tests	Soluble in sulfuric acid, fusible

Occurrences: Brazil, Canada, Italy, Mexico, Switzerland; Montana, New York, Pennsylvania, USA.

Distinctive Field Features: Crystal habit; luster; and color.

Value: $16.00 - $50.00+ per specimen.

Sphalerite

Color: Red	
Group: Sulfides	
System: Isometric	
Hardness: 3.5-4	

Sphalerite occurs as tetrahedral or pseudo-octahedral crystals with rounded faces; twins with striated faces are common. It also occurs as botryoidal, granular, and cleavage masses. Sphalerite's colors range from red to reddish-brown, yellow, green, black, and gray. Sphalerite shares many environments with galena, and occurs with fluorite and cerussite in sedimentary (limestone) deposits; with arsenopyrite and quartz in hypothermal and mesothermal veins; and with pyrite and chalcopyrite in disseminated hydrothermal replacement deposits. Sphalerite is the primary ore of zinc and is occasionally faceted as a rare gemstone if sufficiently transparent. Some sphalerite is fluorescent and triboluminescent, emitting flashes of orange light when lightly rubbed with a hard object, such as a knife blade.

"Ruby Jack" sphalerite, Missouri, 4" x 2-1/2".

FEATURES	
Composition	Zinc iron sulfide
Luster	Resinous to adamantine, submetallic
Opacity	Transparent to translucent
Cleavage	Perfect
Fracture	Conchoidal
Gravity	3.9-4.2
Environment	Hydrothermal veins, skarns, sedimentary deposits
Streak	Light brown, reddish
Tests	Soluble in hydrochloric acid

Occurrences: Canada, Hungary, Mexico, Yugoslavia; Kansas, Missouri, New Jersey, Oklahoma, USA.

Distinctive Field Features: Color; cleavage; associated with galena, fluorite, and pyrite.

Value: $16.00 - $50.00+ per specimen.

220 MINERALS

| Color: Red |
| Group: Sulfides |
| System: Hexagonal |
| Hardness: 2-2.5 |

Cinnabar

Cinnabar occurs as thick, tabular, rhombohedral crystals, commonly twinned; also as masses, granular, and earthy crustations. Cinnabar is most recognized by its bright red color, but it also can be a brownish or purplish red hue. Cinnabar is the chief ore of mercury and is deposited by hot ascending solutions near the surface of the Earth, and is frequently associated with native mercury, stibnite, realagar, orpiment, barite, opal, and quartz. When handling potentially toxic minerals, it is always a good idea to wash your hands after coming in contact with them.

Cinnabar, Russia, 2-1/4" x 2".

FEATURES	
Composition	Mercury sulfide
Luster	Adamantine to dull
Opacity	Transparent to opaque
Cleavage	Perfect
Fracture	Uneven to subconchoidal
Gravity	8.0-8.2
Environment	Hydrothermal deposits, hot springs
Streak	Scarlet red
Tests	Insoluble in acids, unaffected by atmosphere

Occurrences: China, Italy, Spain; Arkansas, California, Nevada, Oregon, Texas, USA.

Distinctive Field Features: Bright red color; hardness; weight.

Value: $16.00 - $50.00+ per specimen.

Cuprite

Cuprite occurs as octahedral, cubic, dodecahedral crystals; in compact, granular, crust, and massive forms; and as fine, acicular needles, often as parallel growths in cavities in limonite (chalcotrichite). Cuprite is usually a ruby-red color, but may also appear reddish-black. Cuprite is a secondary copper mineral and forms in the zone of alteration in disseminated hydrothermal replacement deposits, where it is associated with native copper, malachite, azurite, and limonite. Very rarely crystals have been faceted as exotic gemstones, and when massive cuprite with chrysocolla has sufficient silica content, it is marketed as a lapidary material under the trade name "Sonoran Sunrise."

Cuprite (var. chalcotrichite), Arizona, 3" x 2-1/4".

FEATURES	
Composition	Copper oxide
Luster	Adamantine to dull, submetallic
Opacity	Translucent to semi-opaque
Cleavage	Poor
Fracture	Uneven
Gravity	6.1
Environment	Oxidation zone of copper deposits
Streak	Brownish red
Tests	Fuses easily, soluble in acid

Occurrences: Africa, Bolivia, Chile, France; Arizona, New Mexico, Utah, USA.

Distinctive Field Features: Crystal shape; hardness; associated copper minerals.

Value: $6.00 - $50.00+ per specimen.

Crocoite

Color: Red
Group: Chromates
System: Monoclinic
Hardness: 2.5-3

Crocoite occurs as prismatic crystals, often striated lengthwise (commonly poorly terminated with pitted depressions) in aggregates; and also can be massive in form. Crocoite is usually a bright orange-red, and can also be pinkish-orange, yellow, orange, or red in color. Crocoite forms primarily in oxidized lead veins as a secondary mineral, and is associated with wulfenite, cerussite, and vanadanite. Crocoite was the original source for the extraction of the mineral chromium, and today it is a rare and spectacular display specimen eagerly sought after by mineral collectors.

Crocoite, Australia, 3" x 2".

FEATURES	
Composition	Lead chromate
Luster	Adamantine to vitreous
Opacity	Translucent
Cleavage	Poor
Fracture	Uneven to conchoidal

FEATURES	
Gravity	5.9-6.1
Environment	Hydrothermal replacement deposits
Streak	Orange-yellow
Tests	Fuses easily, soluble in acid

Occurrences: Australia, Brazil, Russia; Arizona, California, Pennsylvania, USA.

Distinctive Field Features: Bright red-orange color; crystal habit.

Value: $31.00 - $50.00+ per specimen.

Vanadinite

Color: Red
Group: Vanadates
System: Hexagonal
Hardness: 3

Vanadanite occurs as small hexagonal crystals, sometimes barrel-shaped and as cavernous masses; also as compact, fibrous, radiating masses or crusts. Vanadanite can range in color from bright red and orange-red to brownish-red, brown, and yellow. Vanadanite is a secondary mineral formed by the alteration of lead ores in massive hydrothermal replacement deposits, and is commonly associated with descloizite, wulfenite, cerussite, galena, barite, and other secondary ore minerals. Vanadanite crystals may darken and dull on exposure to light, so keep them in a protected area if possible.

Vanadanite, Arizona, 3-1/2" x 2-1/2".

FEATURES	
Composition	Lead vanadate chloride
Luster	Adamantine to resinous
Opacity	Transparent to translucent
Cleavage	None
Fracture	Uneven to conchoidal

FEATURES	
Gravity	6.8-7.1
Environment	Oxidation zone of lead deposits
Streak	White, pale yellow
Tests	Fuses easily, soluble in acid

Occurrences: Africa, Argentina, Mexico, Morocco; Arizona, New Mexico, USA.

Distinctive Field Features: Color; weight; mineral associations.

Value: $6.00 - $50.00 per specimen.

Realgar

Color: Orange
Group: Sulfides
System: Monoclinic
Hardness: 1.5-2

Realgar occurs as stubby, prismatic crystals, and as granular, compact, earthy aggregates and crusts. Realgar is commonly orange-red, but may also be scarlet red or orange, and may turn yellow and disintegrate over time on exposure to light. Realgar forms in low-temperature hydrothermal veins, and is associated with orpiment, cinnabar, stibnite, silver, tin, lead, and calcite. Realgar is an ore of arsenic, so be sure to wash your hands after handling it. Aside from its use as a mineral specimen, realgar is used commercially in the manufacture of paint products and fireworks.

Realgar, Nevada, 3" x 2".

FEATURES	
Composition	Arsenic sulfide
Luster	Resinous, adamantine to dull
Opacity	Translucent to transparent
Cleavage	Good
Fracture	Conchoidal
Gravity	3.5-3.6
Environment	Hydrothermal veins, hot springs
Streak	Orange-yellow
Tests	Fuses easily, dissolves in aqua regia

Occurrences: Romania, Switzerland, Turkey; California, Nevada, Utah, Washington, USA.

Distinctive Field Features: Color; hardness; weight; prismatic crystals.

Value: $1.00 - $15.00 per specimen.

Color: Orange	
Group: Oxides	
System: Hexagonal	
Hardness: 4-4.5	

Zincite

Zincite usually occurs in granular or lamellar masses, and much more rarely as pyramidal hemimorphic crystals. Zincite is typically red-orange in color, but may also be deep red, orange-yellow, or brown. Zincite is a rare mineral and forms commonly in contact metamorphic rocks, most specifically (and famously) at the Franklin, New Jersey, deposit where it is associated with magnetite, franklinite, green willemite, and calcite. Good zincite crystals are quite rare, and are highly prized by collectors and mineralogists.

Zincite crystal,
New Jersey, 3/4" x 1/4".

Zincite (red crystals),
New Jersey, 3-1/2" x 3".

FEATURES	
Composition	Zinc manganese oxide
Luster	Adamantine to subadamantine
Opacity	Transparent to translucent
Cleavage	Perfect
Fracture	Conchoidal
Gravity	5.4-5.7
Environment	Contact metamorphic rocks
Streak	Orange-yellow
Tests	Soluble in hydrochloric acid, infusible

Occurrences: Australia, Poland, Spain; New Jersey, USA.

Distinctive Field Features: Vivid color; locality; association with willemite and franklinite.

Value: $16.00 - $50.00+ per specimen.

Chabazite

Color: Orange
Group: Silicates
System: Hexagonal
Hardness: 4-5

Chabazite is a member of the zeolite group and occurs as pseudo-cubic, rhombohedral crystals, often as penetration twins. Some crystals may show a crackled appearance just under the shiny surface of the faces. Chabazite can be orange-pink, pink, red, yellow, white, greenish or colorless. Chabazite usually forms within cavities of basaltic volcanic rocks by chemical deposition, and is often associated with calcite and other zeolite minerals.

Chabazite, Nova Scotia, Canada, 3" x 2-1/4".

FEATURES	
Composition	Hydrated calcium aluminum silicate
Luster	Vitreous
Opacity	Transparent to translucent
Cleavage	Good rhombohedral
Fracture	Uneven
Gravity	2.0-2.2
Environment	Volcanic and intrusive igneous rocks
Streak	White
Tests	Fuses easily, soluble in hydrochloric acid

Occurrences: Australia, Canada, Italy, Scotland; New Jersey, Oregon, USA.

Distinctive Field Features: Rhombohedral crystals; luster; association with other zeolites.

Value: $1.00 - $15.00 per specimen.

Color: Yellow
Group: Native Elements
System: Orthorhombic
Hardness: 1.5-2.5

Sulfur

Sulfur occurs as dipyramidal, sometimes tabular, crystals; as fibrous, compact, stalactitic, and earthy masses; and as granular aggregates and crusts. Sulfur is usually a bright lemon-yellow, but can be greenish or reddish yellow, brown, black, or gray, depending on the mineral impurities. Sulfur commonly forms as a sublimation deposit from gases in volcanic rocks, and is associated with cinnabar and stibnite. Sulfur has many important industrial uses including the manufacture of explosives, sulfuric acid, fungicides, and in the vulcanization of rubber. Sulfur is a poor conductor of electricity, and if rubbed, will become negatively charged. Specimens should be kept out of sunlight and handled as little as possible, as even the warmth of a hand may cause the crystals to expand and crack.

Sulfur crystal, Italy, 1-1/2" x 1-1/2".

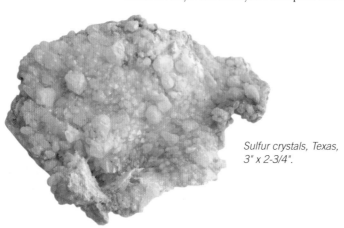

Sulfur crystals, Texas, 3" x 2-3/4".

FEATURES	
Composition	Sulfur
Luster	Resinous to greasy
Opacity	Transparent to translucent
Cleavage	Poor
Fracture	Uneven to conchoidal
Gravity	2.0-2.1
Environment	Evaporite deposits, volcanics
Streak	White
Tests	Fusible, giving off sulfur dioxide

Occurrences: France, Italy, Russia, Sicily; California, Louisiana, Texas, Utah, USA.

Distinctive Field Features: Bright yellow color; hardness.

Value: $6.00 - $50.00 per specimen.

Orpiment

Orpiment occurs as small prismatic crystals in compact masses characterized by flexible, micaeous flakes, and as foliated, granular, and earthy encrustations. Orpiment is usually lemon yellow to golden yellow, or orange yellow. Orpiment is associated with realgar, cinnabar, arsenic, and calcite in low-temperature hydrothermal veins. Orpiment needs to be protected in a collection, as it tends to disintegrate over time when exposed to light and air. Also, orpiment is toxic, so be sure to wash your hands after contact with it.

Color:	Yellow
Group:	Sulfides
System:	Monoclinic
Hardness:	1.5-2

Orpiment with realgar, Nevada,
3-1/2" x 2-1/4".

FEATURES	
Composition	Arsenic sulfide
Luster	Resinous, pearly
Opacity	Transparent to translucent
Cleavage	Perfect
Fracture	Uneven

FEATURES	
Gravity	3.4-3.5
Environment	Hydrothermal veins, hot springs
Streak	Yellow
Tests	Fusible, soluble in nitric acid

Occurrences: China, Peru, Romania, Russia, Turkey; Nevada, Utah, USA.

Distinctive Field Features: Color; cleavage; associated minerals.

Value: $16.00 - $50.00 per specimen.

Siderite

Siderite occurs as rhombohedral crystals with curved faces, sometimes scalenohedrons, also as cleavable, granular aggregates, and compact, botryoidal, fibrous masses. Siderite ranges from pale yellow to reddish-brown, dark brown, gray and almost black. Siderite occurs in sedimentary formations, ore veins, and pegmatites, and is often associated with calcite, barite, galena, pyrite, and sphalerite. Siderite is an ore of iron and easily alters to limonite pseudomorphs, which preserve the shape of the original crystal.

Color:	Yellow
Group:	Carbonates
System:	Hexagonal
Hardness:	3.5-4

Siderite crystals, Colorado, 4" x 3".

FEATURES	
Composition	Iron carbonate
Luster	Vitreous, pearly to dull
Opacity	Transparent to translucent
Cleavage	Perfect rhombohedral
Fracture	Uneven to conchoidal
Gravity	3.8-3.9

FEATURES	
Environment	Hydrothermal veins, sedimentary
Streak	White
Tests	Soluble in hot hydrochloric acid, nearly infusible

Occurrences: Brazil, Canada, England, Greenland, Peru; Arizona, Colorado, Connecticut, Vermont, USA.

Distinctive Field Features: Rhombohedral cleavage; curved faces; color.

Value: $6.00 - $50.00 per specimen.

Scheelite

Color: Yellow	
Group: Sulfates	
System: Tetragonal	
Hardness: 4.5-5	

Scheelite occurs as dipyramidal, pseudo-octahedral crystals, sometimes tabular, striated on some faces, also as granular, compact crusts. It is yellow, orange-yellow, white, gray, greenish, reddish, brownish, purplish, and colorless. Scheelite is an important ore of tungsten and forms in hydrothermal veins, pegmatites, and some contact metamorphic rocks. It is fluorescent in short-wave ultraviolet light, giving off a pale blue light. Occasionally fine, transparent crystals have been faceted as gemstones for jewelry making.

Scheelite, China, 2-1/2" x 2-1/2".

FEATURES		FEATURES	
Composition	Calcium tungstate	Gravity	5.9-6.1
Luster	Vitreous to adamantine	Environment	Pegmatites, hydrothermal veins
Opacity	Transparent to translucent	Streak	White
Cleavage	Distinct	Tests	Soluble in acid, fuses with difficulty
Fracture	Uneven to conchoidal		

Occurrences: Brazil, Canada, China, Mexico; Arizona, California, Idaho, Nevada, Utah, USA.

Distinctive Field Features: Weight; crystal habit; fluorescence.

Value: $16.00 - $50.00 per specimen.

Wulfenite

Color: Yellow	
Group: Molybdates	
System: Tetragonal	
Hardness: 2.75-3	

Wulfenite occurs as prismatic, pyramidal, and square-shaped, tabular (often thin) crystals. It also occurs as massive, granular, or earthy aggregates. Wulfenites colors range from bright yellow-orange to reddish-orange, brown, greenish-brown, white, or yellowish-gray. Wulfenite is a secondary ore of molybdenum that forms in the oxidation zones of lead deposits, often as pseuodmorphs of cerrusite. Barite, molybdenite, and sphalerite are common associations. The brilliant colors and tabular crystal habit makes wulfenite one of the most easily recognizable and showy minerals in the field of mineral collecting.

Wulfenite, Arizona, 5" x 3".

FEATURES		FEATURES	
Composition	Lead molybdate	Gravity	6.5-7
Luster	Resinous to adamantine	Environment	Oxidation zone of lead deposits
Opacity	Transparent to translucent	Streak	White
Cleavage	Distinct	Tests	Soluble in acid, fusible
Fracture	Subconchoidal		

Occurrences: Africa, China, Iran, Mexico, Morocco; Arizona, New Mexico, Pennsylvania, USA.

Distinctive Field Features: Color; crystal habit.

Value: $16.00 - $50.00 per specimen.

Autunite

Autunite occurs as tabular, micaceous lamellae with a square outline, often intergrown into fan-shaped aggregates and crusts. Autunite is bright lemon-yellow or yellow-green, and also fluoresces brilliant yellow-green under ultraviolet light. Autunite is an important ore of uranium, highly radioactive, and was the most widely used source of uranium during World War II. Autunite is an unstable mineral and will decompose over time, so collectors often use spray lacquer or other sealants to seal and preserve their specimens.

Color: Yellow/Green
Group: Phosphates
System: Tetragonal
Hardness: 2-2.5

Autunite, Washington, 2" x 1-1/2".

FEATURES		FEATURES	
Composition	Hydrated copper uranium phosphate	Gravity	3.1-3.2
Luster	Vitreous to pearly	Environment	Alteration zone of uranium minerals
Opacity	Transparent to translucent	Streak	Yellow
Cleavage	Perfect basal	Tests	Fusible, radioactive, fluorescent
Fracture	Uneven		

Occurrences: Australia, France, Portugal; Arizona, New Mexico, North Carolina, Washington, USA.

Distinctive Field Features: Vivid color; crystal habit; fluorescence.

Value: $16.00 - $50.00 per specimen.

Mimetite

Mimetite occurs as pseudohexagonal, prismatic, slender to thick needles, sometimes with curved faces or barrel-shaped (campylite) in aggregate groups. Other habits include reniform, mammilary crusts. Mimetite ranges in color from yellow to orange, brown, white, greenish, and colorless. Mimetite is a secondary ore of lead and is associated with galena, arsenopyrite, vanadanite, and barite.

Color: Yellow
Group: Arsenates
System: Monoclinic
Hardness: 3.5

Mammilary mimetite, Mexico, 2" x 1-1/4".

FEATURES		FEATURES	
Composition	Lead arsenate chloride	Gravity	7.0-7.3
Luster	Resinous to adamantine	Environment	Oxidation zone of lead ore deposits
Opacity	Transparent to translucent		
Cleavage	Poor	Streak	White
Fracture	Subconchoidal to uneven	Tests	Soluble in acid, fusible

Occurrences: Africa, Australia, England, Mexico; Arizona, Pennsylvania, Utah, USA.

Distinctive Field Features: Color; crystal habit; associated minerals.

Value: $16.00 - $50.00 per specimen.

| Color: Yellow |
| Group: Silicates |
| System: Monoclinic |
| Hardness: 2.5-4 |

Chrysotile

Chrysotile occurs in fibrous masses and is a member of the serpentine group. Fibrous chrysotile is also known by the name asbestos, and colors ranges from yellow to olive-green, blackish-green, brown, and whitish-gray. Chrysotile forms by metamorphic alteration of ultramafic rocks in a low-grade environment rich in water, and some yellow varieties exhibit fluorescence, giving off a cream-yellow color. Chrysotile fibers are elastic and so flexible that they can actually be woven, and asbestos has many important industrial applications including uses as brake linings, electrical insulation, and fireproof fabrics. Asbestos mining, once a major industry because of asbestos's excellent insulation properties, fell by the wayside in the 1950s and 1960s when it was discovered to be hazardous to the lungs.

Chrysotile, Canada, 5" x 3".

FEATURES	
Composition	Hydrous magnesium silicate
Luster	Silky to greasy
Opacity	Translucent to opaque
Cleavage	None
Fracture	Uneven
Gravity	2.55
Environment	Serpentinites
Streak	White
Tests	Infusible, soluble in strong acids

Occurrences: Canada, Italy, Russia; Arizona, California, New Jersey, Vermont, USA.

Distinctive Field Features: Fibrous habit; hardness.

Value: $6.00 - $50.00 per specimen.

Pyrophyllite

Color: Yellow
Group: Silicates
System: Monoclinic
Hardness: 1-2

Pyrophyllite usually occurs as foliated, fibrous, radiating, compact masses, and rarely as distinct crystals. Pyrophyllite is typically yellow, green, gray, white, and greenish-brown. Pyrophyllite forms primarily in metamorphic schists with quartz, albite, andalusite, and muscovite. It also forms with barite and gypsum in hydrothermal replacement deposits. In small sections, pyrophyllite is flexible, but not quite elastic. Pyrophyllite has numerous commercial uses such as a dry lubricant and electrical insulation, and in the making of soap, fabric and rubber. Agalmatolite, a fine-grained, compact variety, is used for carvings and ornamental purposes.

Pyrophyllite, California, 4" x 3".

FEATURES	
Composition	Hydrous aluminum silicate
Luster	Pearly to greasy
Opacity	Translucent to opaque
Cleavage	Perfect
Fracture	Uneven
Gravity	2.8
Environment	Metamorphic, hydrothermal replacements
Streak	White
Tests	Infusible, almost insoluble

Occurrences: Africa, China, Russia; Arkansas, California, Georgia, South Carolina, USA.

Distinctive Field Features: Greasy feel; hardness; micaceous habit.

Value: $6.00 - $50.00 per specimen.

| Color: Green |
| Group: Carbonates |
| System: Monoclinic |
| Hardness: 4.5 |

Rosasite

Rosasite occurs as groups of acicular, radiating crystals in spherules or ball shapes, and as crusts. It is a minor ore of copper and is generally green to blue-green in color. Rosasite forms in the oxidation zones of copper, zinc, and lead ore deposits. Associated minerals are siderite, malachite, greenockite, brochantite, and aurichalcite. Rosasite is a colorful and attractive addition to any mineral collection.

Rosasite, Arizona, 4" x 3".

FEATURES	
Composition	Hydrous copper zinc carbonate
Luster	Vitreous to silky
Opacity	Transparent to translucent
Cleavage	Distinct/Good
Fracture	None
Gravity	4.0-4.2
Environment	Oxidation zone of zinc/copper/lead deposits
Streak	Light blue
Tests	Soluble in acid, fusible

Occurrences: Africa, Italy, Mexico, Morocco; Arizona, New Mexico, Utah, USA.

Distinctive Field Features: Color; associated minerals.

Value: $6.00 - $50.00 per specimen.

Malachite

Color: Green
Group: Carbonates
System: Monoclinic
Hardness: 3.5-4

Malachite is a secondary ore of copper and occasionally occurs as small, prismatic crystals, but more commonly as fibrous, stalactitic, radiating, botryoidal or reniform masses and crusts, and as concretionary, banded masses. Malachite is a rich emerald-green color, and is found in the alteration zone of copper deposits, along with associated minerals such as native copper, azurite, limonite, chalcopyrite, and cuprite. When malachite is massive and compact, and cut and polished across its concentric banding, it exhibits beautiful undulating patterns that are highly desirable for display, decorative objects, carving and sculpture, and beads and cabochons for jewelry making.

Malachite, Africa, 4" x 2-1/2".

FEATURES	
Composition	Hydrous copper carbonate
Luster	Metallic
Opacity	Adamantine to silky
Cleavage	Perfect
Fracture	Uneven to conchoidal
Gravity	4.0
Environment	Oxidation zone of copper ores
Streak	Light green
Tests	Soluble in hydrochloric acid, fusible

Occurrences: Africa, Australia, Mexico, Russia; Arizona, Nevada, Utah, USA.

Distinctive Field Features: Color; concentric banding; associated minerals.

Value: $6.00 - $50.00 per specimen.

Brochantite

Color: Green	
Group: Sulfates	
System: Monoclinic	
Hardness: 3.5-4	

Brochantite occurs as small, prismatic or tabular crystals, and as druzy coatings, fibrous, granular, or felted crusts. Brochantite is a bright emerald-green to a blackish-green color, and is an important ore of copper. It forms most frequently in the alteration zone of copper deposits, and is associated with malachite, azurite, cerussite, and chalcopyrite. Brochantite appears similar to malachite but is much rarer.

Brochantite, Mexico, 3-1/2" x 1-1/2".

FEATURES		FEATURES	
Composition	Hydrous copper sulfate	Gravity	3.97
Luster	Vitreous	Environment	Oxidation zone of copper deposits
Opacity	Transparent to translucent		
Cleavage	Perfect	Streak	Light green
Fracture	Conchoidal to uneven	Tests	Soluble in acid, fusible

Occurrences: Africa, Chile, Mexico, Romania; Arizona, California, Idaho, New Mexico, Utah, USA.

Distinctive Field Features: Color; crystal habit; associated minerals.

Value: $1.00 - $50.00 per specimen.

Pyromorphite

Color: Green	
Group: Phosphates	
System: Hexagonal	
Hardness: 3.5-4	

Pyromorphite occurs as short, prismatic, barrel-shaped crystals that are often hollow, and as parallel aggregates, reniform masses and crusts. Pyromorphite ranges in color from dark green to yellow-green, yellow, brown, and light gray. Pyromorphite is found in the alteration zone of lead deposits, and is associated with barite, vanadanite, and limonite. Pyromorphite is a relatively rare mineral and is highly prized by collectors and museums.

Pyromorphite, China, 3-1/2" x 2".

FEATURES		FEATURES	
Composition	Lead phosphate chloride	Gravity	6.7
Luster	Resinous to adamantine	Environment	Oxidation zone of lead deposits
Opacity	Translucent	Streak	White
Cleavage	None	Tests	Soluble in acid, fusible
Fracture	Uneven to subconchoidal		

Occurrences: Canada, China, Mexico, Spain; Idaho, North Carolina, Pennsylvania, USA.

Distinctive Field Features: Hollow crystals; luster; associated minerals.

Value: $16.00 - $50.00+ per specimen.

Torbernite

Color: Green	
Group: Phosphates	
System: Tetragonal	
Hardness: 2-2.5	

Torbernite occurs as square-shaped, tabular crystals, and as lamellar, scaly aggregates or crusts. It occurs in a variety of shades of green, from emerald and grass-green, to apple-green and yellow-green. Torbernite is a secondary uranium mineral and is associated with autunite in the alteration zone of hydrothermal veins and pegmatites that contain uraninite and copper sulfides. Torbernite is a radioactive mineral, but not fluorescent in ultraviolet light. Over time, torbernite dehydrates and becomes the mineral known as metatorbernite.

Torbernite, Africa, 3-1/2" x 2".

FEATURES	
Composition	Hydrated copper uranium phosphate
Luster	Vitreous to pearly
Opacity	Transparent to translucent
Cleavage	Perfect
Fracture	Uneven
Gravity	3.22
Environment	Alteration zone of uraninite, pegmatites
Streak	Pale green
Tests	Soluble in strong acid, fusible, radioactive

Occurrences: Africa, Australia, Czechoslovakia, Mexico; Connecticut, North Carolina, South Dakota, USA.

Distinctive Field Features: Square crystal shape; color.

Value: $16.00 - $50.00+ per specimen.

Color: Green	
Group: Phosphates	
System: Orthorhombic	
Hardness: 3.5-4	

Wavellite

Wavellite occurs as spherulitic, fibrous, radiating aggregates, and occasionally as fine, acicular crystals. Wavellite also forms as botryoidal crusts and in a stalactitic habit. Wavellite's colors include green to light green, yellowish, white, gray, and brownish hues. Wavellite is a secondary mineral that forms as coatings in fissures of rocks within low-temperature hydrothermal deposits rich in aluminum, and is associated with turquoise, quartz, and limonite. It also occurs in hornfels of metamorphic rocks, associated with quartz and muscovite.

Wavellite, Arkansas, 6" x 4".

FEATURES	
Composition	Hydrated aluminum phosphate
Luster	Vitreous to pearly
Opacity	Translucent
Cleavage	Perfect
Fracture	Uneven to subconchoidal
Gravity	2.3-2.4
Environment	Low-temperature hydrothermal deposits, contact metamorphics
Streak	White
Tests	Soluble in nitric acid, infusible

Occurrences: Brazil, Bolivia, Germany; Arkansas, Colorado, Pennsylvania, USA.

Distinctive Field Features: Radiating, fibrous, spherical shape; color.

Value: $6.00 - $50.00 per specimen.

Conichalcite

Color: Green	
Group: Arsenates	
System: Orthorhombic	
Hardness: 4.5	

Conichalcite occurs as short, prismatic crystals in reniform or botryoidal crusts and masses with a radial fibrous structure. Conichalcite ranges in color from a vivid grass-green to yellow-green. Conichalcite is a secondary copper mineral and develops in the zone of alteration of copper deposits and is associated with other copper minerals, including olivenite, linarite, clinoclase, and malachite. Conichalcite is primarily of interest to collectors and has no commercial applications.

Conichalcite, Mexico, 3-1/2" x 2-1/2".

FEATURES	
Composition	Hydrous calcium copper arsenate
Luster	Vitreous to greasy
Opacity	Translucent
Cleavage	None
Fracture	Uneven
Gravity	4.3
Environment	Oxidation zone of copper deposits
Streak	Green
Tests	Soluble in acid, fusible

Occurrences: Africa, Mexico; Arizona, Nevada, Utah, USA.

Distinctive Field Features: Color; associated minerals.

Value: $6.00 - $50.00 per specimen.

Color: Green	
Group: Silicates	
System: Hexagonal	
Hardness: 5	

Dioptase

Dioptase occurs as short, prismatic crystals with rhonbohedral terminations. Other habits include granular aggregates and masses. It is a beautiful emerald green to a deep aqua color, and makes striking display pieces. Dioptase forms in the oxidized zone of copper ores, often within cavities and hollow pockets in the surrounding rock and is commonly associated with limonite, chrysocolla, and cerussite. Dioptase has a distinctive blue cast to its color, and once seen, it is easily recognized again in the field. Dioptase is sometimes faceted as a valuable gemstone for jewelry making if the crystal is sufficiently clear.

Dioptase, Africa, 1-1/2" x 1".

FEATURES	
Composition	Hydrous copper silicate
Luster	Vitreous
Opacity	Transparent to translucent
Cleavage	Perfect
Fracture	Uneven to conchoidal
Gravity	3.3
Environment	Oxidation zone of copper deposits
Streak	Pale greenish-blue
Tests	Soluble in acid and ammonia, infusible

Occurrences: Africa, Kazakhstan, Mexico; Arizona, New Mexico, USA.

Distinctive Field Features: Color; hardness.

Value: $16.00 - $50.00+ per specimen.

Olivine

Color: Green-Yellow	
Group: Silicates	
System: Orthorhombic	
Hardness: 6.5-7	

Olivine is the name for a series of minerals of varying compositions, consisting of forsterite (magnesium rich), chrysolite (magnesium iron rich), and fayalite (iron rich) that when combined, form the magnesium iron silicate commonly called olivine. Olivine occurs as stubby, often wedge-shaped, prismatic crystals, and as rounded grains, and granular masses. Olivine ranges in color from yellow-green to grass and olive green, to yellowish-brown, brown, and white. Olivine is a common rock-forming mineral, and forsterites are typical of ultramafic and mafic igneous rocks, dunites, and contact metamorphosed limestones. Forsterites rich in nickel are often found in meteorites. Fayalites are rare and occur as a minor component of granites, and in pockets of rhyolites and pegmatites. Many minerals are formed by the alteration of olivine, including serpentine, and the gem variety of olivine, peridot, is very popular as a faceted gemstone.

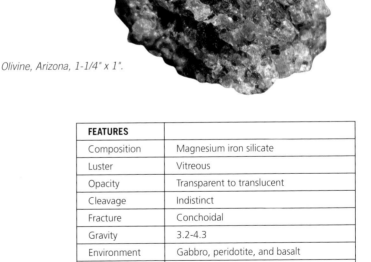

Olivine, Arizona, 1-1/4" x 1".

FEATURES	
Composition	Magnesium iron silicate
Luster	Vitreous
Opacity	Transparent to translucent
Cleavage	Indistinct
Fracture	Conchoidal
Gravity	3.2-4.3
Environment	Gabbro, peridotite, and basalt
Streak	Colorless
Tests	Soluble in hydrochloric acid, infusible

Occurrences: Burma, Hawaii, Pakistan, Russia; Arizona, California, North Carolina, USA.

Distinctive Field Features: Color; hardness; locality.

Value: $16.00 - $50.00+ per specimen.

| Color: Green |
| Group: Silicates |
| System: Orthorhombic |
| Hardness: 6-6.5 |

Prehnite

Prehnite occurs primarily as botryoidal, reniform masses with ridged surfaces, and more rarely as prismatic, tabular, or pyramidal crystals. Prehnite is usually green in color, but may also be yellow, gray, white, or colorless. Prehnite forms as a hydrothermal mineral alteration in the cavities of volcanic basalts, and in some metamorphic rocks, and is associated with the zeolites, calcite, and pectolite. Prehnite may lose some of its color over time when exposed to light and air, so it's a good idea to keep it in a protected location. Prehnite has no industrial uses and is mainly of interest to collectors as display specimens, or as a minor gemstone in jewelry making.

Prehnite, New Jersey, 6" x 4".

FEATURES	
Composition	Hydrous calcium aluminum silicate
Luster	Vitreous to waxy
Opacity	Transparent to translucent
Cleavage	Distinct
Fracture	Uneven
Gravity	2.9-3.0
Environment	Basaltic volcanic rocks
Streak	Colorless
Tests	Soluble in hydrochloric acid, fusible

Occurrences: Canada, France, India; Connecticut, Massachusetts, Michigan, New Jersey, USA.

Distinctive Field Features: Botryoidal formation; color; associated minerals.

Value: $16.00 - $50.00 per specimen.

Epidote

Color: Green
Group: Silicates
System: Monoclinic
Hardness: 6-7

Epidote occurs as prismatic, slender, grooved crystals, and as fibrous, radiating aggregates. Other habits include tabular crystals, wheat-sheaf formations, and granular masses. Epidote's color ranges from yellowish-green to greenish-black. Epidote is a common constituent of rocks, and forms in regional and contact metamorphics, granite pegmatites, and in the cavities of basaltic volcanic rocks. Epidote is often associated with the zeolites, calcite, albite, and actinolite. The name epidote is also used in reference to a group of complex related minerals including zoisite, clinozoisite, piedmontite, and alanite. Epidote is occasionally faceted as a gemstone if sufficiently transparent.

Epidote, Mexico, 3" x 2".

FEATURES	
Composition	Hydrous calcium aluminum iron silicate
Luster	Vitreous
Opacity	Transparent to translucent
Cleavage	Perfect
Fracture	Uneven
Gravity	3.3-3.5
Environment	Metamorphic and igneous rocks
Streak	Colorless to gray
Tests	Insoluble, fusible

Occurrences: Austria, Brazil, Mexico, Pakistan; Alaska, California, Colorado, Idaho, USA.

Distinctive Field Features: Color; crystal habit.

Value: $16.00 - $50.00 per specimen.

| Color: Green |
| Group: Silicates |
| System: Monoclinic |
| Hardness: 5-6 |

Actinolite

Actinolite occurs as elongated, columnar, bladed, or acicular, prismatic crystals in aggregates. Other habits include radiating, fibrous, felted, and granular masses. Actinolite is normally dark to light green in color, and occasionally occurs in shades of grayish-green to nearly black. Actinolite is common in metamorphosed limestones, gneisses, schists, serpentines, and granites, and is associated with albite, chlorite, and epidote in regional metamorphics, and with barite and anhydrite in hydrothermal replacement deposits. When actinolite is massive and combined with tremolite, it is commonly known as nephrite jade and used extensively as an ornamental stone in jewelry making and for sculpture.

Actinolite, California, 5" x 4-1/2".

FEATURES	
Composition	Hydrous calcium magnesium iron silicate
Luster	Vitreous
Opacity	Transparent to translucent
Cleavage	Perfect
Fracture	Uneven to subconchoidal
Gravity	3.0-3.5
Environment	Metamorphics, schists, amphibolites
Streak	Colorless
Tests	Insoluble, fusible

Occurrences: Canada, Finland, New Zealand; Alaska, California, Vermont, Wyoming, USA.

Distinctive Field Features: Crystal habit; color.

Value: $6.00 - $50.00 per specimen.

Smithsonite

Color:	Blue
Group:	Carbonates
System:	Hexagonal
Hardness:	5.5

Smithsonite generally occurs as thick, radiating botryoidal crusts with a crystalline surface, and as earthy masses or indistinct, rounded, rhombohedral or scalenohedral crystals. Depending on the impurities present, smithsonite has a broad range of colors including sky blue to blue-green, yellow, pink, violet, brown, and white. Smithsonite is a secondary mineral and forms as a precipitate in the oxidized zone of hydrothermal replacement deposits where it is associated with hemimorphite, cerussite, malachite, pyromorphite, anglesite, and galena. Many varieties of smithsonite show a pinkish fluorescence when exposed to ultraviolet light. Smithsonite is an ore of zinc and is used occasionally as a lapidary material.

Pink-violet smithsonite,
New Mexico, 2-3/4" x 1-1/2".

Smithsonite,
New Mexico,
4-1/2" x 2-3/4".

FEATURES	
Composition	Zinc carbonate
Luster	Vitreous to pearly
Opacity	Translucent
Cleavage	Perfect rhombohedral
Fracture	Subconchoidal to uneven
Gravity	4.3-4.5
Environment	Oxidation zone of sulfide deposits
Streak	White
Tests	Soluble in hydrochloric acid, infusible

Occurrences: Africa, Mexico, Russia, Turkey; Arkansas, Colorado, New Mexico, USA.

Distinctive Field Features: Botryoidal habit; weight; associated minerals.

Value: $16.00 - $50.00+ per specimen.

| Color: Blue |
| Group: Carbonates |
| System: Monoclinic |
| Hardness: 3.5-4 |

Azurite

Azurite occurs as tabular crystals, and as fine needles or hairs in radiating groups, rosettes, or aggregates. It also may be botryoidal or stalactitic, and forms as earthy masses or crusts. Azurite is a deep azure blue color, hence its name. Azurite is a secondary copper mineral and develops in the zone of alteration in copper deposits, where it is closely associated with malachite (azurite will alter over time into malachite), limonite, chrysocolla, chalcocite, and calcite. Azurite is not only a beautiful display specimen, but is also sometimes used in jewelry making if the stone has sufficient hardness, and even then, it is susceptible to breaking. When azurite is combined with chrysocolla, is acquires greater hardness due to the associated silica content, and can be then successfully carved and polished as an ornamental stone. Azurite has also historically been ground into a powder and used as a paint pigment.

Azurite, Arizona, 2-1/4" x 1-1/2".

FEATURES	
Composition	Hydrous copper carbonate
Luster	Vitreous to dull
Opacity	Transparent to opaque
Cleavage	Perfect
Fracture	Conchoidal
Gravity	3.7-3.8
Environment	Oxidized zone of copper deposits
Streak	Pale blue
Tests	Soluble in hydrochloric acid, fusible

Occurrences: Africa, Australia, Mexico, Romania; Arizona, Utah, USA.

Distinctive Field Features: Color; associated minerals.

Value: $6.00 - $50.00 per specimen.

Aurichalcite

Color: Blue	
Group: Carbonates	
System: Monoclinic	
Hardness: 2-2.5	

Aurichalcite occurs most commonly as crusts of tufted, mammillary balls of small, fine, acicular crystals or scales, and very rarely as isolated crystals. It is a beautiful sky blue to blue-green color, and makes a handsome display specimen. Aurichalcite is a minor ore of zinc, and forms in the oxidation zone of zinc and copper sulfide deposits. It is associated with limonite, malachite, azurite, and calcite.

Aurichalcite, Nevada, 2-3/4" x 2".

FEATURES	
Composition	Hydrous zinc copper carbonate
Luster	Silky to pearly
Opacity	Translucent
Cleavage	Perfect
Fracture	Uneven
Gravity	3.6-4.0
Environment	Oxidation zone of sulfide deposits
Streak	Pale blue-green
Tests	Soluble in hydrochloric acid, infusible

Occurrences: Africa, China, Mexico, Russia; Arizona, New Mexico, USA.

Distinctive Field Features: Crystal habit; color; associated minerals.

Value: $6.00 - $50.00 per specimen.

| Color: Blue |
| Group: Sulfates |
| System: Orthorhombic |
| Hardness: 3-3.5 |

Celestite

Celestite occurs as prismatic or tabular crystals, and also as radiating, nodular, granular, and compact masses. Celestite varies in color from light blue to yellowish, greenish, reddish, brown, white or colorless. Celestite develops as an accessory mineral of ore veins that formed from warm solutions, and is usually found in sedimentary rocks, especially in the cavities of sandstone or limestone. Celestite is usually associated with fluorite, calcite, gypsum, dolomite, galena, and sphalerite. Some varieties of celestite are fluorescent under ultraviolet light, and the name celestite (also known as celestine), comes from the Latin word *caelestis* meaning "of the sky" due to its color. Celestite is a major ore of strontium and has many industrial uses, including the manufacture of fireworks and flares, paints, rubber products, specialty glass, and ceramic glazes.

Celestite, Utah, 4" x 2-1/2".

FEATURES	
Composition	Strontium sulfate
Luster	Vitreous to pearly
Opacity	Transparent to translucent
Cleavage	Perfect
Fracture	Uneven
Gravity	3.9-4.0
Environment	Evaporite deposits, sedimentary
Streak	White
Tests	Soluble in acid with difficulty, fusible

Occurrences: Canada, Madagascar, Mexico; California, Colorado, Ohio, New York, Texas, USA.

Distinctive Field Features: Color; weight; associated minerals.

Value: $6.00 - $50.00+ per specimen.

Linarite

Color: Blue
Group: Sulfates
System: Monoclinic
Hardness: 2.5

Linarite occurs as elongated prismatic crystals, often tabular, and also in clusters or crusts of randomly oriented crystals. Linarite typically is a bright blue to azure blue color, and forms in the oxidation zone of lead and copper ore deposits. Linarite is sometimes confused with azurite, which it resembles, but it is more rare, softer, and heavier than azurite. Linarite is associated with cerussite, malachite, brochantite, and smithsonite.

Linarite, New Mexico, 4" x 2-1/2".

FEATURES	
Composition	Hydrous lead copper sulfate
Luster	Virteous to subadamantine
Opacity	Transparent to translucent
Cleavage	Perfect
Fracture	Conchoidal
Gravity	5.35
Environment	Oxidation zone of lead and copper deposits
Streak	Light blue
Tests	Soluble in nitric acid, fusible

Occurrences: Africa, Argentina, England, Spain; Arizona, California, Idaho, Nevada, New Mexico, Utah, USA.

Distinctive Field Features: Color; weight; hardness.

Value: $6.00 - $50.00 per specimen.

| Color: Blue |
| Group: Sulfates |
| System: Triclinic |
| Hardness: 2.5 |

Chalcanthite

Chalcanthite usually occurs as botryoidal crusts or stalactitic masses, and as short, prismatic or tabular crystals. Chalcanthite can also form occasionally in fibrous veins, and sometimes displays the habit of curved crystals known as "ram's horns." Chalcanthite is primarily sky blue, but may also be dark blue or greenish-blue. Chalcanthite develops in the alteration zone of copper-iron hydrothermal replacement deposits, associated with aragonite and calcite, and also forms on damp mine timbers and walls. Chalcanthite is a mineral that must be preserved, as it loses water fairly quickly and will disintegrate to a powder if not protected and sealed. Chalcanthite crystals can be home grown using prepared chalcanthite salts and is fun for new mineral collectors to experiment with.

Chalcanthite, Arizona, 3/4" x 1/2".

FEATURES	
Composition	Hydrated copper sulfate
Luster	Vitreous to resinous
Opacity	Transparent to translucent
Cleavage	Indistinct
Fracture	Conchoidal
Gravity	2.28-2.3
Environment	Oxidation zone of copper deposits
Streak	Colorless
Tests	Soluble in water, infusible

Occurrences: Chile, Mexico, Spain; Arizona, Nevada, Tennessee, Utah, USA.

Distinctive Field Features: Dissolves in water; color; sweet taste (taste with discretion, as it is poisonous!).

Value: $6.00 - $50.00 per specimen.

Lazulite

Color: Blue	
Group: Phosphates	
System: Monoclinic	
Hardness: 5-6	

Lazulite occurs as wedge-shaped, tabular, or bipyramidal crystals, frequently embedded in matrix, and as granular, compact masses. Lazulite is a bright blue to light blue, deep blue, or greenish-blue color. Lazulite occurs in pegmatite dikes, metamorphic rocks, quartz veins in metamorphic formations, and in some hydrothermal replacement deposits. Lazulite is associated with quartz, muscovite, andalusite, corundum, hematite, and rutile. Lazulite is occasionally cut as a semi-precious gemstone.

Lazulite, Austria, 3-1/2" x 3".

FEATURES	
Composition	Hydrous magnesium aluminum phosphate
Luster	Vitreous to dull
Opacity	Translucent to opaque
Cleavage	Poor prismatic
Fracture	Uneven
Gravity	3.0-3.1
Environment	Pegmatites, metamorphics
Streak	White
Tests	Soluble in hot acids with difficulty, infusible

Occurrences: Austria, Brazil, Canada, Switzerland; California, Georgia, USA.

Distinctive Field Features: Color; crystal habit.

Value: $6.00 - $50.00 per specimen.

Color: Blue	
Group: Phosphates	
System: Monoclinic	
Hardness: 1.5-2	

Vivianite

Vivianite occurs as prismatic or tabular crystals, and earthy masses. Vivianite also forms in cleavable, flexible flakes, and radiating, fibrous crusts or aggregates. Vivianite is usually nearly colorless when fresh, but turns dark blue with exposure to light, and may also be blue-green, green or violet in color. Vivianite is a secondary mineral in ore veins, iron-manganese rich phosphate pegmatites, and in sedimentary clays as a concretion. Vivianite is associated with muscovite, sphalerite, and quartz, and is often found in conjunction with fossils from sedimentary rocks. Vivianite is a delicate mineral and requires a dark, protected environment, as it tends to dry out and cleave apart over time.

Vivianite, Bolivia, 2" x 1".

FEATURES	
Composition	Hydrated iron phosphate
Luster	Vitreous to pearly
Opacity	Transparent to translucent
Cleavage	Perfect
Fracture	Uneven
Gravity	2.6-2.7
Environment	Oxidation zone of sulfide deposits
Streak	Colorless to bluish-white
Tests	Soluble in acid, fusible

Occurrences: Bolivia, Mexico; Colorado, Idaho, New Jersey, Utah, USA.

Distinctive Field Features: Color; micaceous crystal habit.

Value: $16.00 - $50.00+ per specimen.

Microcline

Color: Blue	
Group: Silicates	
System: Triclinic	
Hardness: 6-6.5	

Microcline is a common, rock-forming member of the K-feldspars group and occurs as prismatic crystals that are frequently twinned, and often quite large. Microcline also forms as compact, granular masses and disseminated grains. Microcline ranges in color from white to pink, reddish, brown, gray, yellowish, and blue-green. The blue-green color is recognized as its own variety, known as amazonite. Microcline is usually found in granitic pegmatites, and metamorphic or plutonic rocks. Microcline is often associated with quartz and albite, and the blue-green variety, amazonite, is used extensively as a lapidary material in the making of cabochons and beads.

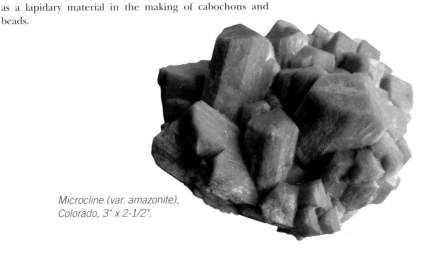

Microcline (var. amazonite), Colorado, 3" x 2-1/2".

FEATURES	
Composition	Potassium aluminum silicate
Luster	Vitreous
Opacity	Transparent to translucent
Cleavage	Good
Fracture	Uneven
Gravity	2.5-2.6
Environment	Granitic pegmatites, metamorphics
Streak	White
Tests	Soluble in hydrofluoric acid, infusible

Occurrences: Brazil, India, Madagascar, Russia; California, Colorado, New Mexico, Virginia, USA.

Distinctive Field Features: Twinned crystals; cleavage; hardness.

Value: $16.00 - $50.00 per specimen.

| Color: Blue |
| Group: Silicates |
| System: Triclinic |
| Hardness: 5-7 |

Kyanite

Kyanite generally occurs as elongated, bladed crystals, rarely terminated, and often embedded, as aggregates. Kyanite is usually blue, but may be white, gray, green, yellow, pink, or nearly black. Kyanite has a hardness of 4-5 along its cleavage planes, and 6-7 across its cleavage planes. Kyanite is formed from regional metamorphism and is associated with quartz, biotite, and almandine in schist and gneiss, and is sometimes found intergrown with staurolite. Kyanite has many commercial uses including the manufacture of ceramics, spark plugs, electrical insulators, and acid-resistant products. Kyanite is also used as a lapidary material as-is for wire-wrapping, and is popular as a healing tool in the metaphysical community.

Kyanite, Brazil, 2-1/4" x 2".

FEATURES	
Composition	Aluminum silicate
Luster	Vitreous to pearly
Opacity	Transparent to translucent
Cleavage	Perfect
Fracture	Splintery
Gravity	3.5-3.7
Environment	Metamorphics
Streak	Colorless
Tests	Insoluble in acid, infusible

Occurrences: Africa, Brazil, Switzerland; California, Georgia, North Carolina, Virginia, USA.

Distinctive Field Features: Color; hardness; crystal habit.

Value: $1.00 - $50.00 per specimen.

Fluorite

Color: Violet
Group: Halides
System: Isometric
Hardness: 4

Fluorite occurs as cubes, octahedrons, and dodecahedrons, often twinned. It also occurs in columnar, granular, and compact masses. The colors in fluorite are extremely variable (allochromatic) and include purple, pink, green, yellow, blue, and colorless, and are often combined together in banded zones that make for beautiful collector specimens. Fluorite is a fairly common mineral, and besides its lapidary uses as a carving, bead, and cabochon material, it has many industrial uses including as a flux in the metal industry and in the manufacture of steel and hydrofluoric acid. Fluorite is also often highly fluorescent in colors of blue or violet, and is a popular addition to fluorescent collections.

Blue fluorite crystals, New Mexico, 3" x 2".

Purple fluorite, 3" x 2-1/4".

FEATURES	
Composition	Calcium fluoride
Luster	Vitreous
Opacity	Transparent to translucent
Cleavage	Perfect octahedron
Fracture	Uneven
Gravity	3.0-3.2
Environment	Hydrothermal replacement deposits
Streak	White
Tests	Fuses fairly easily, fluorescent

Occurrences: Brazil, Canada, England, Germany, Norway; Colorado, Illinois, Kentucky, Ohio, USA.

Distinctive Field Features: Perfect octahedral cleavage; cubes.

Value: $16.00 - $50.00+ per specimen.

| Color: Violet |
| Group: Phosphates |
| System: Orthorhombic |
| Hardness: 4-4.5 |

Purpurite

Purpurite is an alteration product of lithiophylite in complex granitic pegmatites. Purpurite occurs as crusts of a reddish-purple, violet, or dark pink color with a brownish black surface alteration in compact, granular masses. Purpurite is mainly of interest to scientists and collectors, and is often artificially colored bright purple through acid treatment. Purpurite is brittle and has a slightly powdery consistency that may rub off if the piece is lightly abraded.

Purpurite, South Dakota, 3" x 1-3/4".

FEATURES	
Composition	Manganese iron phosphate
Luster	Dull, earthy
Opacity	Translucent to opaque
Cleavage	Distinct/good
Fracture	Uneven
Gravity	3.4
Environment	Granitic pegmatites
Streak	Dark red
Tests	Fuses easily, dissolves in acid

Occurrences: Australia, France, Portugal; California, North Carolina, South Dakota, USA.

Distinctive Field Features: Color; association with lithiophylite in complex granitic pegmatites.

Value: $16.00 - $50.00+ per specimen.

Lepidolite

Color: Violet
Group: Silicates
System: Monoclinic
Hardness: 2.5-4

Lepidolite is a member of the mica group and occurs rarely as tabular, pseudo-hexagonal crystals. It also occurs as medium to fine-grained, platy aggregates. Colors include lavender or lilac, pink, gray, white, and colorless. Lepidolite most often forms in lithium-bearing pegmatites, and is frequently associated with spodumene, tourmaline, and amblygonite. Because of its lithium content, lepidolite is often used in metaphysical practice as a calming mineral for the mind and spirit when kept in close proximity to a person's body.

Lepidolite, Brazil, 4" x 2-1/2".

FEATURES	
Composition	Hydrous potassium lithium aluminum silicate
Luster	Pearly
Opacity	Transparent to translucent
Cleavage	Perfect, one direction
Fracture	Elastic
Gravity	2.8-2.9
Environment	Lithium bearing pegmatites
Streak	Colorless
Tests	Fuses easily, insoluble in acid

Occurrences: Australia, Brazil, Canada, Madagascar; California, Connecticut, Maine, South Dakota, USA.

Distinctive Field Features: Found in granite pegmatites; lilac color; platy or scaly surfaces.

Value: $6.00 - $30.00 per specimen.

| Color: Violet |
| Group: Silicates |
| System: Monoclinic |
| Hardness: 2-2.5 |

Clinochlore
(var. kammererite)

Kammererite, is the chromium rich variety of clinochlore. Clinochlore is a member of the chlorite mineral group and occurs as lamellar, pseudo-hexagonal crystals, and fine-grained masses. Most chlorites have a green color due to components of iron and magnesium, but kammererite has small amounts of chromium in its structure, and it is the chromium that colors the crystals of kammererite to the unusual violet, lavender, and magenta red that it is known for. Chromium is a very powerful coloring agent and is responsible for creating strong colors in many different minerals. The magenta red color of kammererite is similar to the slightly more purple color of erythrite, which is colored by another strong coloring agent, cobalt. Erythrite's crystals are also similar to kammererite in that they are usually thin platy crystal aggregates. Erythrite's crystals are more pointed and have acute angles that are lacking on kammererite's crystals.

Clinochlore (var. kammererite), Turkey, 2" x 1-3/4".

FEATURES	
Composition	Hydrous magnesium iron chromium silicate
Luster	Vitreous to pearly
Opacity	Translucent
Cleavage	Perfect
Fracture	Uneven
Gravity	2.6-2.8
Environment	Chlorite and talc schists
Streak	White
Tests	Soluble in acid, does not fuse

Occurrences: Finland, Turkey; California, Pennsylvania, USA.

Distinctive Field Features: Vivid color; crystal habit.

Value: $50.00+ per specimen.

Rhodochrosite

Color:	Pink
Group:	Carbonates
System:	Hexagonal
Hardness:	3.5-4.5

Rhodochrosite is an ore of manganese and occurs as pink rhombohedral, scalenohedral, prismatic, or tabular crystals. It also occurs in granular, concretionary, mammilary, reniform, or stalactic masses. Colors range from hot pink to reddish pink, to pale pink, with off-white, and orangy-tan accents. Rhodochrosite is often associated with copper, silver, and lead sulfides, and other manganese minerals. Massive rhodochrosite frequently exhibits a crystalline, banded, wavy pattern that makes attractive cabochons and carved decorative items. Pink rhodochrosite crystal clusters make beautiful display specimens.

Rhodochrosite crystals, Colorado, 2" x 1-1/2".

FEATURES	
Composition	Manganese carbonate
Luster	Vitreous to pearly
Opacity	Transparent to translucent
Cleavage	Perfect
Fracture	Uneven

FEATURES	
Gravity	3.4-3.6
Environment	Hydrothermal veins
Streak	White
Tests	Soluble when heated

Occurrences: Africa, Argentina, Romania; Colorado, Maine, Montana, USA.

Distinctive Field Features: Color; rhombohedral cleavage.

Value: $16.00 - $50.00+ per specimen.

Erythrite

Color:	Pink
Group:	Arsenates
System:	Monoclinic
Hardness:	1.5-2.5

Erythrite occurs as small, striated acicular and prismatic crystals in radiating aggregates, earthy masses, and reniform or gobular shapes with druzy crusts. Colors can run from deep purple-red to pink to blue-pink. Erythrite is a secondary mineral and forms by the alteration of arsenides and sulfides of cobalt and nickel. Because of its bright color, it is an excellent guide to locating cobalt-bearing mineral deposits.

Erythrite, Mexico, 1-1/4" x 3/4".

FEATURES	
Composition	Hydrated cobalt arsenate
Luster	Vitreous to pearly
Opacity	Translucent to transparent
Cleavage	Perfect
Fracture	Uneven

FEATURES	
Gravity	3.06
Environment	Alteration product of cobalt minerals
Streak	Red to pink
Tests	Fuses easily, dissolves in acid

Occurrences: Canada, Germany, Morocco; Idaho, USA.

Distinctive Field Features: Vivid purple-red color; forms thin crusts.

Value: $31.00 - $50.00+ per specimen.

Color: Pink	
Group: Carbonates	
System: Trigonal	
Hardness: 4	

Sphaerocobaltite

Sphaerocobaltite is a rare and colorful mineral, occurring as rhombohedrons and scalahedrons. It also occurs as small spherical masses with a crystalline surface and concentric, radiated structure, as globular and stalactitic masses, and as crusts on matrix. Associated minerals are calcite, malachite, cobaltite, and dolomite. Sphaerocobaltite is a carbonate of cobalt with a small percentage of calcite that creates a beautiful, distinctive, hot pink color highly desirable to collectors.

It can be easy to confuse sphaerocobaltite with two other carbonates—rhodochrosite and stichtite—because all three are described as red to pink minerals. However, in comparison, the color difference is obvious, as sphaerocobaltite has a more "hot pink" color than the redder pink of rhodochrosite or the more purple-pink of stichtite.

Sphaerocobaltite on dolomite, Africa, 3-1/2" x 2-1/4".

FEATURES	
Composition	Cobalt carbonate with calcium
Luster	Vitreous
Opacity	Transparent to translucent
Cleavage	Perfect
Fracture	Uneven
Gravity	4.2
Environment	Secondary cobalt ore locations
Streak	Pale pink
Tests	Effervesces easily with dilute acids

Occurrences: Africa, Germany, Morocco, Mexico.

Distinctive Field Features: Bright color; associations with cobalt ore deposits.

Value: $50.00+ per specimen.

Glossary

Acicular: An aggregate of long, slender, crystals (i.e. natrolite). This term is also used to describe the crystal habit of single long, thin, slender crystals.

Adamantine (luster): Transparent minerals with a very high luster are said to have an adamantine luster. (Translucent to nearly opaque minerals with a very high luster are said to have a submetallic luster.)

Adularescence: An effect seen on certain minerals that causes it to display a billowy, rounded, ghost-like reflection with a bluish-whitish color emanating from the surface when the mineral is cut into a cabochon. It is caused by structural anomalies or build up of water in the mineral. The minerals most famous for exhibiting adularescence are opal and moonstone, and the name is derived from adularia, of which moonstone is a variety.

Aggregate: A grouping of crystals. Aggregates are defined by the ways crystals are clustered together.

Amorphous: Without a crystalline shape.

Aqueous: Formed from precipitating hard water. Stalagmites and stalactites are common examples.

Asterism: Effect exhibited on some minerals (usually only in polished cabochons) causing it to reflect a billowy, star-like formation of concentrated light that moves around when the mineral is rotated. Asterism is caused by dense inclusions of tiny, parallel, slender, fibers in the mineral that cause the light to reflect in such an interesting manner. Minerals that display asterism may exhibit four, six, and sometimes twelve-rayed "stars," depending on the inclusions, size, and facet mode. Some specimens may display much stronger asterism than others, and some specimens may have areas where the inclusions are not present, leaving holes or empty areas in the star.

Aventurescence: The effect caused by small inclusions of a mineral with a highly reflective surface (commonly hematite, pyrite, or goethite) that create a glistening effect, as if it is pasted with glitter, when rotated or looked at from different positions. The name is derived from aventurine, a green variety of quartz that exhibits this effect.

Axis: Imaginary line drawn through the center of an object, either horizontally or vertically. In the case of minerals, it is used to determine if and how mineral has symmetry. The horizontal axis is known as the x axis, the vertical axis, the y axis. Axis lines are usually drawn as dotted lines.

Banding: The presence of color zoning lines, or "bands," in some minerals.

Bladed: Crystal habit describing flat, elongated, "knife-like" crystals (i.e. kyanite).

Botryoidal: Aggregate resembling a cluster of grapes. Also known as globular. Rounded agglomerations of botryoidal aggregates are smaller than reniform agglomerations and considerably smaller than mammilary agglomerations.

Boule: Synthetic gems created from molten liquids placed in tear shaped molds to crystallize, leaving them with a tear-like form. Mostly applied to synthetic rubies and sapphires.

Cabochon: Gemstone without facets that is highly polished, domed, and has smooth, rounded edges.

Carat: Weight measurement used in reference to gemstones in regard to their evaluation. A carat is .2 grams (or 200 milligrams), and this weight is used worldwide, even in the U.S., where the metric system isn't used. A point is the weight used only in reference to very small, precious gemstones, and represents 1/100th of a carat. The abbreviation for carat is Ct. and for point is Pt. The term carat in regard to gemstones should not be confused with the term carat in regard to gold. When referring to gold, it means the content of gold a gold ornament contains. Because of the confusion, the term carat in regard to gold has been changed to karat.

Cat's eye: A mineral with dense inclusions of tiny, parallel, slender, fibers that may cause it to exhibit chatoyancy. The most notable cat's eye mineral is chrysoberyl cat's eye, which is known simply as cat's eye.

Chatoyancy: A phenomenon of certain cat's eye minerals that cause it to exhibit a concentrated narrow band of reflected light across the center of the mineral. Chatoyancy is usually only seen on polished cabochons.

Cleavage: The splitting or tendency of a crystal to split along definite crystalline planes to produce smooth surfaces.

Cluster: Dense agglomeration of crystals.

Columnar: Aggregate defining a mineral that has parallel, slender, compact, adjoining crystals.

Conchoidal: Mineral fracture in which the indentation resembles a shell.

Crazing: Condition in opal that causes it to form small, internal cracks, and in some severe cases will eventually disintegrate the opal.

Crystal system: The primary method of classification of crystals. The crystal system classifies crystals in six groups: isometric, tetragonal, hexagonal (which includes trigonal), orthorhombic, monoclinic, and triclinic.

Crystalline: Having a crystal structure; composed of visible crystals.

Dichroism: Literally means "two colors." A mineral that exhibits one color when viewed from one angle but a different color when viewed from a different angle is said to display dichroism.

Double refraction: Phenomenon exhibited on all non-opaque minerals except for amorphous ones and ones that crystallize in the isometric system. A light ray enters the crystal and splits into two rays, making anything observed through the crystal appear as double. The double refraction on most minerals is so weak that it cannot be observed without special instruments. However, in some minerals, such as the Iceland spar variety of calcite, it is strongly seen. The double refraction is different in every mineral and, thus, can be used to identify gems. Double refraction is measured with a refractometer.

Doubly terminated: Exhibiting a pointed crystal figure on both bases.

Dull (luster): The luster of minerals with little reflectiveness.

Earthy (luster): Luster describing minerals that are microcrystalline or amorphous and have nonreflective surfaces.

Elongated: Describing a crystal with a lengthened side, meaning that one side is far longer in one direction.

Environment: Area or region conducive for the development of a mineral. Certain minerals only develop in certain environments.

Even (fracture): Mineral fracture forming a smooth, flat surface.

Facet: A singular flat surface displayed in a gem. It may grow naturally but is usually hand cut. This definition includes the meaning of a specific cut for gems.

Feldspar: Group of minerals that are aluminum silicates containing potassium, sodium, and/or calcium. Some minerals in this group are wrongly classified as other minerals in this group. This is the most abundant group of minerals on the earth, and the building block of many rocks.

Fibrous: Aggregate describing a mineral constructed of fine, usually parallel threads. Some fibrous minerals contain cloth-like flexibility, meaning they can be bent and feel like cotton.

Flame test: Complex, scientific test conducted to identify a mineral. A small fragment of a mineral is placed on the end of a platinum wire and held in a flame. Different metals present in the mineral change the color of the flame.

Form: The setting of all the crystal faces and the structure of a mineral.

Fossil: Animal or plant remains of a previous age embedded and preserved in rock.

Fracture: The characteristic way a mineral breaks when placed under stress, aside from cleavage.

Geode: Hollow rock filled or partially filled with crystals.

Globular: The term globular is used as a synonym of botryoidal, but sometimes describes any rounded agglomeration, such as botryoidal, reniform, and mammilary.

Group: The classification order of minerals based on their chemical structure.

Habit: The attributes of the appearance of a crystal or aggregate.

Hackly (fracture): Type of fracture resembling broken metal, exhibiting sharp, jagged surfaces. This fracture is sometimes also known as a "jagged" fracture.

Igneous rock: A type of rock from volcanic origins. Igneous rock can be glassy, crystalline, or both.

Inclusion: A crystal or fragment of another substance enclosed in a crystal or rock.

Iridescence: Light effect causing a mineral to display a play of colors on an apparently plain surface. Iridescence is also the result of mild tarnishing of a few metallic lustered minerals, such as chalcopyrite and hematite.

Japanese twin: Form of contact twinning in which two single quartz crystals are joined by their base at an angle near 90 degrees.

Karat: Unit of measurement describing the content of gold in an ornament. The karat unit measures the percentage of gold in metallic objects made of gold (mainly jewelry). Since pure gold bends easily, it is mixed with tougher metals when made into ornaments to form a tougher, although impurer, gold. The abbreviation of karat is k. or kt.

Labradorescence: Effect that causes dark, metallic-like color shimmers, commonly blue and green, to be displayed on a few minerals. The name is derived from labradorite, a mineral that produces the best example of this effect.

Lenticular: Lens shaped. When applied to minerals, it refers to concretions or nodules that have a flattened, lens-like shape.

Luster: The way in which a mineral shines due to reflected light.

Mammilary: Aggregate describing smooth, rounded, agglomerations.

Massive: Term used to describe a rock or mineral that has no definitive shape.

Metal: Any of a category of electropositive elements or combinations of them in the form of minerals that exhibit a metallic luster, malleability, ductility, and conductivity.

Metallic (luster): Exhibiting the luster of a metal, which is opaque and highly reflective.

Metamorphic: Mineral environment in which the minerals are secondary in origin, forming from alteration through heat and pressure.

Microcrystalline: Composed of tiny crystals that can only be seen with a microscope.

Micromount: A mineral specimen that is not more 1/10 of an inch (15 -27 mm.) in size.

Native Elements: Group of minerals containing naturally occurring minerals with a molecular structure of only one element, such as copper, gold, and diamond.

Non-crystalline: Not containing any crystals; amorphous.

Occurrence: The area where a particular mineral is found.

Oolitic: Aggregate composed of very small, spherical particles.

Optical properties: Physical properties of a mineral or gem that have to do with optics, such as dispersion, absorption spectra, refractive index, asterism, and dichroism, to name a few.

Ore: Material that has a valuable constituent, usually a precious metal, that makes it profitable for extraction.

Oxidation: The process of undergoing a chemical change through exposure to oxygen.

Paramorph: A pseudomorph involving two minerals with an identical composition but different crystal structures. The original mineral forms, but conditions then cause it to become unstable, so it transforms into the other mineral with the same chemical structure while retaining the original crystal shape.

Pearly (luster): Exhibiting a shimmering luster similar to the inside of a mollusk shell or pearl.

Phosphorescence: The ability of some fluorescent minerals to continue glowing for several seconds after an ultraviolet source has been removed.

Pisolitic: Aggregate composed of small, spherical particles, larger in size than oolitic minerals.

Placer deposit: Area in a stream or river where heavy material settles after being carried downstream in the current of the river or stream.

Pleochroism: The effect present in a mineral exhibiting two or more separate colors when viewed at different angles. Pleochroism and dichroism are similar, but dichroism refers only to two colors, but pleochroism can be more than two.

Porphry: Igneous rock containing large, noticeable crystals, usually feldspars.

Prismatic: Crystal habit describing a crystal with four or more sides similar in length and width. Prismatic crystals are usually elongated in one direction.

Radiating: Aggregate composed of tiny, slender crystals compacted together radiating from a central point. The radiation can be flat or three dimensional. If three dimensional, this aggregate commonly occurs with circular, ball-like masses, and is known as spherulitic.

Refraction: The splitting of white light into the colors of the spectrum.

Refractive index: The amount of refraction that takes place in a particular substance, which is directly related to the speed of light passing through that substance. The higher the refractive index, the greater the amount of dispersion, which increases the brilliance of a material. The refractive indices of gems are measured with a refractometer.

Reniform: Aggregate describing smooth, rounded, kidney-like agglomerations.

Resinous (luster): Luster describing yellow, dark orange, or brown minerals with slightly high refractive indices; having a honey-like sheen, but not necessarily the same color.

Reticulated: Aggregate composed of long crystals in a net-like form in which all the crystals crisscross each other.

Rough: Rocks as found in the field. In regard to gemstones, it refers to unfaceted material.

Schiller: Color reflections or color "flashes" present in a mineral.

Sedimentary rock: Rock formed by the weathering of substances; forming layers from accumulation of minerals and organic substances.

Semi-precious stone: Gem or gemstone used in jewelry that lacks in one or more property such as luster, hardness, or rarity that would make it a precious gemstone.

Silky (luster): Luster of minerals that have a very fine fibrous structure, causing it to display optical properties similar to silk cloth.

Specific gravity: The weight ratio of a mineral due to the density of the atomical arrangement and the heaviness of the elements it contains.

Spherulitic: Aggregate consisting of rounded, ball-like structures composed of radiating crystals.

Splintery (fracture): Fracture forming elongated splinters. All fibrous minerals fall into this category.

Stalactites: Icicle-like formations on the roof of caverns created when mineral-rich water drips down from the roof and the dissolved mineral accumulates into the icicle-like formation. May be confused with stalagmites, which are tall-domed formations on the bottom of caverns built up from the mineral-rich water depositing the dissolved mineral on the floor.

Staurolite twin: Form of penetration twinning in which two monoclinic crystals form interpenetrating twins at 90 degrees, forming a cross.

Streak: The color of a mineral's powder. A streak can be tested by rubbing a mineral against a hard, white, unglazed porcelain object (streak plate). The streak that remains is the color of the streak of the mineral.

Striations: Tiny, parallel lines or grooves seen on some crystal faces.

Structure: The form of a mineral based on the way its molecules are arranged.

Submetallic (luster): Luster of opaque to nearly opaque minerals with very good reflective properties.

Synthetic gem: Manmade gem created by using molten chemicals to solidify and form the gem.

Tabular: Crystal habit describing a flat, tough, usually four-sided crystal.

Tarnish: Oxidation occuring in some minerals that causes them to discolor when placed in certain environments.

Transparent: An object that is able to transmit light, and can clearly be seen through as if there is nothing interfering.

Translucent: Describing something that is able to transmit light, but not completely. Objects can be seen through a translucent object, but they will be unclear.

Twinning: Tendency of some crystals to intergrow in a distinct way or form specific, repeated patterns.

Uneven (fracture): Fracture that leaves a rough or irregular surface.

Vein: A long, narrow section of a mineral, usually in fibrous form, embedded in native host rock. Usually caused by magma filling open spaces or cracks in the rock with the mineral.

Vitreous (luster): Luster describing minerals with reflective properties similar to that of glass.

Waxy (luster): Luster of a mineral in which it appears to be coated by a layer of wax.

Wheat sheaf: Aggregate of compact bundles of crystals, slightly radiating and thicker at the top and the bottom than in the center. Appears in the shape of an hourglass.

Widmanstaetten lines: Etched crystal faces that are seen on some polished meteorites.

Wiry: Aggregate composed of long, slender, curvy, interwoven wires.

Resources

Magazines

Colored Stone: www.colored-stone.com

Fossil News - Journal of Avocational Paleontology: www.fossilnews.com

Geological Society of America: http://geology.gsapubs.org

Mineralogical Record: www.minrec.org

www.Rockhounds.com (online magazine)

Rock & Gem: www.rockngem.com

Rocks & Minerals: www.rocksandminerals.org

Books

A Color Atlas of Meteorites in Thin Section by Dante S. Lauretta and Marvin Killgore

Agates I & II by Johann Zenz

American Lapidary - Designing The Carved Gemstone by Henry Hunt

Ancient Forests: A Closer Look at Fossil Wood by Frank J. Daniels & Richard D. Dayvault

Audubon Field Guide to North American Fossils by Ida Thompson

Collecting Fluorescent Minerals by Stuart Schneider

Discovering Fossils by Frank A. Garcia & Donald S. Miller

Facet Cutters Handbook by Edward Soukup

Field Collecting Gemstones & Minerals by John Sinkankas

Flintknapping - Making and Understanding Stone Tools by John C. Whittaker

Gem Cutting, A Lapidary's Manual by John Sinkankas

Geodes - Nature's Treasures by Brad Cross & June Culp Zeitner

Gem Identification Made Easy : A Hands-On Guide to More Confident Buying & Selling by Antoinette L. Matlins & A.C. Bonanno

Gemstones of North America by John Sinkankas

Gem Trail Guide Series (by region)

Gem Tumbling and Baroque Jewelry Making by Arthur Earl Victor and Lila Mae Victor

Gemstones of the World by Walter Schumann

Gold Prospectors Handbook by Jack Black

How To Find Gold by James Klein and Jerry Keene

Master Gemcutting Tips by Gerald L. Wykoff

Petrified Wood: The World of Fossilized Wood, Cones, Ferns, and Cycads by Frank J. Daniels

Roadside Geology Series (by region)

Smithsonian Eyewitness Fossils

Smithsonian Handbook of Gemstones

The Art of Collecting Meteorites by Kevin Kichinka

The Art of Flint Knapping by D.C. Waldorf

Gem & Mineral Dealers

www.danweinrich.com

www.excaliburmineral.com

www.gemrockauctions.com

www.johnbetts-fineminerals.com

www.meteorite.com

millsgeological.homestead.com/
www.ramseyssedona.com
www.thegemshop.com
www.themineralgallery.com

Lapidary Materials & Supplies
www.riogrande.com
www.acelapidary.com
www.diamondpacific.com
www.greatrough.com
www.kingsleynorth.com
Jim & Ellen's Rock Shop, Cottonwood, AZ 928-649-1938
Tom's Hidden Valley Treasures, Cornville, AZ 928-634-4698

Topographic Maps & GPS Supplies
www.garmin.com
www.topomaps.usgs.gov/

Gem & Mineral Shows
Martin Zinn Expositions: www.mzexpos.com/
Quartzsite PowWow Gem & Mineral Show: www.qiaaz.org/PowWow.htm
Tucson Gem & Mineral Show: www.tgms.org or www.colored-stone.com/tsg/

Gem & Mineral Organizations/Clubs
American Federation of Mineralogical Societies: www.amfed.org
Fluorescent Mineral Society: www.uvminerals.org
Gem and Mineral Federation of Canada: www.gmfc.ca
Geological Society of America: www.geosociety.org
Mineralogical Society of America: www.minsocam.org

Gem & Mineral Museums
Arizona Mining and Mineral Museum: www.admmr.state.az.us
Smithsonian Museum of Natural History Mineral Sciences Collections
www.mineralsciences.si.edu/collections.htm
Mineral Museums Worldwide: www.agiweb.org/smmp/IMA-CM/museums.htm

Private Collections
www.achate.at/
www.agategrrrl.com
www.agateswithinclusions.com
www.gemartcenter.com
www.quartzpage.de/index.html

General Interest
Brazilgemtours.com
Claracohan.com
Kateallisonphotography.com

Bibliography

American Geological Institute. *Dictionary of Geological Terms*. Garden City, N.Y.: Dolphin Books, 1962.

Arem, J. *Color Encyclopedia of Gemstones*. New York: Van Nostrand Reinhold Co., 1987.

Chesterman, C.W. *Audubon Society Field Guide to North American Rocks and Minerals*. New York: Alfred A. Knopf, 1993.

Cipriani, C. and A. Borelli. *Guide to Gems and Precious Stones*. New York: Simon & Schuster, 1986.

Dake, H.C., F. Fleener, and B.H. Wilson. *Quartz Family Minerals*. New York: McGraw-Hill, 1938.

Emmons, C. and M. Fenton. *Geology Principles and Processes*. New York: McGraw-Hill, 1955.

Ford, W.E. *A Textbook of Mineralogy*. New York: John Wiley & Sons, 1966.

Gleason, S. *Ultraviolet Guide to Minerals*. North Clarendon, Vermont: Charles E. Tuttle Co., 1972.

Leiper, H. *Agates of North America*. Salida, Colorado: Lapidary Journal, 1966.

Mottana, A., R. Crespi and G. Liborio. *Guide to Rocks and Minerals*. New York:Simon & Schuster, 1978.

Nininger, H.H. *A Comet Strikes the Earth*. El Centro, California: Desert Press, 1953.

Pearl, R.M. *Successful Mineral Collecting & Prospecting*. New York: Bonanza Books, 1961.

Pellant, C. *Rocks & Minerals*. New York: Dorling Kindersley, 1992.

Pough, F. H. *A Field Guide to Rocks & Minerals*. New York: Houghton Mifflin, 1983.

Quick, L. *The Book of Agates*. Philadelphia: Chilton Books, 1963.

Ransom, J. *Gems and Minerals of America*. New York: Harper & Row, 1975.

Sanborn, W.B. *Handbook of Crystal & Mineral Collecting*. Baldwin Park, California: Gembooks, 1966.

Schumann, W. *Gemstones of the World*. New York: Sterling, 1977.

Sinkankas, J. *Gem Cutting: A Lapidary's Manual*. New York: Van Nostrand Reinhold Co., 1988.

———. *Gemstones & Minerals*. New York: D. Van Nostrand Co., 1961.

Zeitner, J.C. *Gem & Lapidary Materials*. Tucson, Arizona: Geoscience Press, 1996.

Zenz, J. *Agates I & II*. Haltern, Germany: Bode Publishing, 2005, 2009.

Photo Credits

Credits list photos in left-to-right, top-to-bottom order, with photographer listed first, followed by collection owner.

Pg. 32
M. Nelson, Patti Polk
M. Nelson, Patti Polk
M. Nelson, Patti Polk
M. Nelson, Tom's Hidden
 Valley Treasures

Pg. 33
M. Nelson, Patti Polk
M. Nelson, Patti Polk
M. Nelson, Patti Polk

Pg. 34
M. Nelson, Patti Polk
M. Nelson, Tom's Hidden
 Valley Treasures
M. Nelson, Patti Polk
M. Nelson, Ramsey's Rocks
 & Minerals

Pg. 35
M. Nelson, Ramsey's Rocks
 & Minerals
M. Nelson, Patti Polk
M. Nelson, Patti Polk
M. Nelson, Patti Polk

Pg. 36
M. Nelson, Patti Polk
M. Nelson, Patti Polk

Pg. 37
M. Nelson, Ramsey's Rocks
 & Minerals
M. Nelson, Ramsey's Rocks
 & Minerals

Pg. 38
M. Nelson, Patti Polk
M. Nelson, Patti Polk
M. Nelson, Jason Badgley
M. Nelson, Jim & Ellen's
 Rock Shop

Pg. 39
M. Nelson, Ramsey's Rocks
 & Minerals
M. Nelson, Patti Polk
M. Nelson, Patti Polk

Pg. 43
M. Nelson, Patti Polk
M. Nelson, Patti Polk
M. Nelson, Patti Polk
M. Nelson, Patti Polk
M. Nelson, Patti Polk

Pg. 44
M. Nelson, Patti Polk
M. Nelson, Patti Polk
M. Nelson, Patti Polk

Pg. 45
M. Nelson, Tom's Hidden
 Valley Treasures
M. Nelson, Patti Polk
M. Nelson, Patti Polk
M. Nelson, Tom's Hidden
 Valley Treasures

Pg. 46
M. Nelson, Tom's Hidden
 Valley Treasures
M. Nelson, Tom's Hidden
 Valley Treasures

Pg. 47
M. Nelson, Patti Polk
M. Nelson, Patti Polk
M. Nelson, Tom's Hidden
 Valley Treasures

Pg. 48
M. Nelson, Patti Polk
M. Nelson, Patti Polk
M. Nelson, Jason Badgley
M. Nelson, Patti Polk

Pg. 49
M. Nelson, Patti Polk
M. Nelson, Jason Badgley
M. Nelson, Patti Polk

Pg. 50
M. Nelson, Patti Polk
M. Nelson Tom's Hidden
 Valley Treasures
M. Nelson, Patti Polk

Pg. 52
M. Nelson, Patti Polk
M. Nelson, Patti Polk
M. Nelson, Patti Polk
M. Nelson, Patti Polk
M. Nelson, Jason Badgley

Pg. 53
M. Nelson, Jason Badgley
M. Nelson, Patti Polk
M. Nelson, Jason Badgley
M. Nelson, Patti Polk
M. Nelson, Patti Polk
M. Nelson, Patti Polk

Pg. 54
M. Nelson, Jim & Ellen's
 Rock Shop
M. Nelson, Patti Polk
M. Nelson, Patti Polk
M. Nelson, Patti Polk

Pg. 55
M. Nelson, Patti Polk
M. Nelson, Jason Badgley
Gene Mueller, Gene
 Mueller
M. Nelson, Patti Polk

Pg. 56
M. Nelson, Patti Polk
M. Nelson, Patti Polk
M. Nelson, Jason Badgley
M. Nelson, Jason Badgley
M. Nelson, Patti Polk
M. Nelson, Patti Polk

Pg. 57
M. Nelson, Jason Badgley
M. Nelson, Patti Polk
M. Nelson, Patti Polk
M. Nelson, Jason Badgley

Pg. 58
Pat McMahan, Pat McMahan
M. Nelson, Patti Polk
M. Nelson, Patti Polk

Pg. 59
M. Nelson, Jason Badgley
M. Nelson, Patti Polk
M. Nelson, Patti Polk

Pg. 60
M. Nelson, Jason Badgley
M. Nelson, Patti Polk

Pg. 61
Pat McMahan, Pat McMahan
M. Nelson, Patti Polk
M. Nelson, Jason Badgley
M. Nelson, Patti Polk
M. Nelson, Jason Badgley

Pg. 62
M. Nelson, Patti Polk
M. Nelson, Jason Badgley
M. Nelson, Jason Badgley
Gene Mueller, Gene
 Mueller

Pg. 63
M. Nelson, Jason Badgley
M. Nelson, Jason Badgley
M. Nelson, Patti Polk
Gene Mueller, Gene
 Mueller

Pg. 64
Gene Mueller, Gene
 Mueller
M. Nelson, Jason Badgley
M. Nelson, Jason Badgley

M. Nelson, Patti Polk

Pg. 65
M. Nelson, Patti Polk
M. Nelson, Patti Polk
M. Nelson, Patti Polk

Pg. 66
M. Nelson, Patti Polk
M. Nelson, Patti Polk
M. Nelson, Pat McMahan
M. Nelson, Patti Polk

Pg. 67
M. Nelson Jason Badgley
M. Nelson, Patti Polk
M. Nelson Jason Badgley

Pg. 68
M. Nelson Jason Badgley
M. Nelson, Patti Polk
M. Nelson Jason Badgley

Pg. 69
M. Nelson Jason Badgley
M. Nelson Patti Polk
M. Nelson Patti Polk

Pg. 70
M. Nelson Jason Badgley
M. Nelson Patti Polk
M. Nelson Patti Polk

Pg. 71
M. Nelson, Jason Badgley
M. Nelson Patti Polk
Pat McMahan, Pat McMahan
M. Nelson, Jason Badgley

Pg. 72
M. Nelson, Jason Badgley
M. Nelson Patti Polk
M. Nelson, Jason Badgley
M. Nelson, Jason Badgley

Pg. 73
M. Nelson, Jason Badgley
M. Nelson, Jason Badgley
M. Nelson, Jason Badgley
M. Nelson, Patti Polk

Pg. 74
M. Nelson, Jason Badgley
M. Nelson, Jason Badgley
M. Nelson, Jason Badgley
M. Nelson, Patti Polk
M. Nelson, Patti Polk

Pg. 75
M. Nelson, Jason Badgley
M. Nelson, Patti Polk

M. Nelson, Jason Badgley
M. Nelson, Jason Badgley

Pg. 76
M. Nelson, Patti Polk
M. Nelson, Patti Polk
M. Nelson, Patti Polk

Pg. 77
M. Nelson, Patti Polk
Pat McMahan, Pat McMahan
M. Nelson, Patti Polk

Pg. 78
M. Nelson, Patti Polk
M. Nelson, Patti Polk

Pg. 79
M. Nelson, Jason Badgley
M. Nelson, Patti Polk

Pg. 60
M. Nelson, Patti Polk
M. Nelson, Patti Polk
M. Nelson, Patti Polk

Pg. 81
M. Nelson, Patti Polk
M. Nelson, Patti Polk
M. Nelson, Patti Polk
M. Nelson, Patti Polk
M. Nelson, Jason Badgley

Pg. 82
M. Nelson, Jason Badgley
M. Nelson, Patti Polk
M. Nelson, Jason Badgley
M. Nelson, Jason Badgley

Pg. 83
Pat McMahan, Pat McMahan
Gene Mueller, Gene
  Mueller
M. Nelson, Patti Polk

Pg. 84
M. Nelson, Patti Polk
M. Nelson, Jason Badgley

Pg. 85
M. Nelson, Patti Polk
M. Nelson, Jason Badgley

Pg. 86
M. Nelson, Patti Polk
M. Nelson, Jason Badgley
M. Nelson, Patti Polk

Pg. 87
M. Nelson, Patti Polk
M. Nelson, Tom's Hidden
  Valley Treasures

Pg. 88
M. Nelson, Jason Badgley
Pat McMahan, Pat McMahan
M. Nelson, Jason Badgley
M. Nelson, Patti Polk

Pg. 89
M. Nelson, Patti Polk
M. Nelson, Patti Polk

M. Nelson, Patti Polk

Pg. 91
M. Nelson, Patti Polk
Gene Mueller, Gene
  Mueller
M. Nelson, Patti Polk
M. Nelson, Harry Brown

Pg. 92
M. Nelson, Patti Polk
Kate Gaines, Barbara Grill
M. Nelson, Patti Polk
M. Nelson, Patti Polk

Pg. 93
M. Nelson, Patti Polk
M. Nelson, Harry Brown
M. Nelson, Patti Polk

Pg. 94
M. Nelson, Patti Polk
M. Nelson, Patti Polk
M. Nelson, Harry Brown
M. Nelson, Ramsey's Rocks
  & Minerals
M. Nelson, Patti Polk

Pg. 95
M. Nelson, Patti Pollk
M. Nelson, Jason Badgley
M. Nelson, Patti Pollk

Pg. 96
M. Nelson, Patti Polk
M. Nelson, Jason Badgley
M. Nelson, Patti Polk

Pg. 97
M. Nelson, Patti Polk
M. Nelson, Patti Polk
Gene Mueller, Gene
  Mueller
M. Nelson, Patti Polk
Pat McMahan, Pat McMahan

Pg. 98
M. Nelson, Patti Polk
M. Nelson, Patti Polk
M. Nelson, Jim & Ellen's
  Rock Shop
M. Nelson, Patti Polk
M. Nelson, Patti Polk

Pg. 99
Gene Mueller, Gene
  Mueller
M. Nelson, Patti Polk
M. Nelson, Patti Polk
M. Nelson, Jim & Ellen's
  Rock Shop

Pg. 100
M. Nelson Jason Badgley
M. Nelson, Jim & Ellen's
  Rock Shop
M. Nelson Jason Badgley
M. Nelson, Jason Badgley
M. Nelson, Jim & Ellen's
  Rock Shop
Gene Mueller, Gene
  Mueller

Pg. 101
M. Nelson, Jason Badgley
M. Nelson, Patti Polk
M. Nelson, Patti Polk

Pg. 103
M. Nelson, Nancy Bihler
M. Nelson, Patti Polk
M. Nelson, Jason Badgley
M. Nelson, Harry Brown
M. Nelson, Patti Polk

Pg. 104
M. Nelson, Patti Polk
M. Nelson, Nancy Bihler
M. Nelson, Nancy Bihler
Kate Gaines, Barbara Grill

Pg. 105
M. Nelson, Nancy Bihler
M. Nelson, Nancy Bihler
M. Nelson, Patti Polk
M. Nelson, Patti Polk
M. Nelson, Patti Polk

Pg. 106
M. Nelson, Nancy Bihler
M. Nelson, Nancy Bihler
M. Nelson, Patti Polk
M. Nelson, Jason Badgley

Pg. 107
M. Nelson, Patti Polk
M. Nelson, Patti Polk
M. Nelson, Patti Polk

Pg. 108
Jim Mills, Jim Mills
M. Nelson, Nancy Bihler

Pg. 109
M. Nelson, Nancy Bihler
Val Latham, Val Latham
M. Nelson, Patti Polk

Pg. 110
Jim Mills, Jim Mills
Jim Mills, Jim Mills
M. Nelson, Patti Polk
Jim Mills, Jim Mills

Pg. 111
Jim Mills, Jim Mills
Jim Mills, Jim Mills
Jim Mills, Jim Mills
Kate Gaines, Barbara Grill

Pg. 112
Jim Mills, Jim Mills
M. Nelson, Patti Polk
M. Nelson, Patti Polk
M. Nelson, Jason Badgley

Pg. 114
M. Nelson, Patti Polk
M. Nelson, Ramsey's Rocks
  & Minerals
M. Nelson, Patti Polk
M. Nelson, Jason Badgley
M. Nelson, Tom's Hidden
  Valley Treasures

Pg. 115
M. Nelson, Patti Polk
M. Nelson, Patti Polk
M. Nelson, Patti Polk
Pat McMahan, Pat McMahan
M. Nelson, Patti Polk
M. Nelson, Nancy Bihler

Pg. 116
M. Nelson, Patti Polk
M. Nelson, Dick Moore
M. Nelson, Nancy Bihler.

Pg. 117
M. J. Colella, Helen
  Serras-Herman
M. Nelson, Patti Polk
M. Nelson, Patti Polk

Pg. 118
M. Nelson, Nancy Bihler
M. Nelson, Nancy Bihler
M. Nelson, Ramsey's Rocks
  & Minerals
M. Nelson, Patti Polk

Pg. 119
M. Nelson, Dick Moore
M. Nelson, Patti Polk

Pg. 120
M. Nelson, Patti Polk
M. Nelson, Nancy Bihler

Pg. 121
M. Nelson, Patti Polk
M. Nelson, Jason Badgley

Pg. 122
Kate Gaines, Barbara Grill
M. Nelson, Patti Polk
Kate Gaines, Barbara Grill

Pg. 123
M. Nelson, Ramsey's Rocks
  & Minerals
M. Nelson, Patti Polk

Pg. 124
M. Nelson, Ramsey's Rocks
  & Minerals
M. Nelson, Dick Moore
M. Nelson, Ramsey's Rocks
  & Minerals

Pg. 125
M. Nelson, Patti Polk
M. Nelson, Patti Polk
M. Nelson, Patti Polk

Pg. 126
M. Nelson, Patti Polk
M. Nelson, Nancy Bihler
M. Nelson, Patti Polk
M. Nelson, Jason Badgley

Pg. 127
M. Nelson, Dick Moore
M. Nelson, Ramsey's Rocks
  & Minerals

Pg. 128
M. Nelson, Ramsey's Rocks
& Minerals
M. Nelson, Patti Polk
M. Nelson, Dick Moore

Pg. 129
M. Nelson, Patti Polk
M. Nelson, Patti Polk

Pg. 130
M. Nelson, Harry Brown
M. Nelson, Ramsey's Rocks
& Minerals

Pg. 131
Pat McMahan, Pat McMahan
Pat McMahan, Pat McMahan
M. Nelson, Patti Polk

Pg. 133
Glenn Worthington, Glenn
Worthington

Pg. 134
M. Nelson, Patti Polk
M. Nelson, Ramsey's Rocks
& Minerals
M. Nelson, Harry Brown
M. Nelson, Harry Brown

Pg. 135
M. Nelson, Patti Polk
M. Nelson, Patti Polk
M. Nelson, Ramsey's Rocks
& Minerals

Pg. 136
M. J. Colella, Helen
Serras-Herman
M. Nelson, Patti Polk
M. Nelson, Ramsey's Rocks
& Minerals

Pg. 137
M. Nelson, Patti Polk
Jeff Weissman, Excalibur
Mineral Company

Pg. 138
Jeff Weissman, Excalibur
Mineral Company
M. Nelson, Patti Polk

Pg. 139
M. Nelson, Dick Moore
M. Nelson, Patti Polk
M. Nelson, Dick Moore
M. Nelson, Dick Moore
M. Nelson, Harry Brown
M. Nelson, Dick Moore

Pg. 140
M. Nelson, Ramsey's Rocks
& Minerals
M. Nelson, Patti Polk

Pg. 141
M. Nelson, Ramsey's Rocks
& Minerals
M. Nelson, Patti Polk
M. Nelson, Ramsey's Rocks

& Minerals
Kate Gaines, Barbara Grill

Pg. 142
M. Nelson, Ramsey's Rocks
& Minerals
M. Nelson, Dick Moore

Pg. 143
Bob Jones, California
Federation of Mineralogical
Societies
M. Nelson, Harry Brown

Pg. 144
M. Nelson, Ramsey's Rocks
& Minerals
Jeff Weissman, Excalibur
Mineral Company
M. Nelson, Ramsey's Rocks
& Minerals
M. Nelson, Jason Badgley

Pg. 145
M. Nelson, Dick Moore
M. Nelson, Harry Brown
M. Nelson, Harry Brown

Pg. 146
M. Nelson, Patti Polk

Pg. 147
M. Nelson, Patti Polk
M. Nelson, Patti Polk
M. Nelson, Patti Polk

Pg. 148
M. Nelson, Jim & Ellen's
Rock Shop
M. Nelson, Jim & Ellen's
Rock Shop

Pg. 149
M. Nelson, Tom's Hidden
Valley Treasures
M. Nelson, Patti Polk

Pg. 150
M. Nelson, Patti Polk
M. Nelson, Jason Badgley
M. Nelson, Jason Badgley

Pg. 151
M. Nelson, Patti Polk
M. Nelson, Nancy Bihler
M. Nelson, Ramsey's Rocks
& Minerals
M. Nelson, Tom's Hidden
Valley Treasures

Pg. 152
Kate Gaines, Barbara Grill
M. Nelson, Patti Polk

Pg. 153
Clara Cohan, Clara Cohan
M. Nelson, Patti Polk
M. Nelson, Jim & Ellen's
Rock Shop
M. Nelson, Tom's Hidden
Valley Treasures

Pg. 154
M. Nelson, Patti Polk
M. Nelson, Ramsey's Rocks
& Minerals
M. Nelson, Tom's Hidden
Valley Treasures

Pg. 155
M. Nelson, Ramsey's Rocks
& Minerals
M. Nelson, Jason Badgley
M. Nelson, Tom's Hidden
Valley Treasures

Pg. 156
M. Nelson, Ramsey's Rocks
& Minerals
Pat McMahan, Pat McMahan

Pg. 157
M. Nelson, Ramsey's Rocks
& Minerals
M. Nelson, Ramsey's Rocks
& Minerals

Pg. 158
M. Nelson, Ramsey's Rocks
& Minerals
M. Nelson, Patti Polk
M. Nelson, Tom's Hidden
Valley Treasures

Pg. 159
M. Nelson, Patti Polk
Clara Cohan, Patti Polk
M. Nelson, Patti Polk

Pg. 160
M. Nelson, Ramsey's Rocks
& Minerals

Pg. 161
M. Nelson, Patti Polk
Clara Cohan, Clara Cohan
M. Nelson, Patti Polk

Pg. 162
M. Nelson, Nancy Bihler
M. Nelson, Nancy Bihler
Clara Cohan, Clara Cohan
Kate Gaines, Barbara Grill

Pg. 163
M. Nelson, Patti Polk
M. Nelson, Ramsey's Rocks
& Minerals

Pg. 164
M. Nelson, Ramsey's Rocks
& Minerals
M. Nelson, Patti Polk
M. Nelson, Patti Polk
M. Nelson, Patti Polk

Pg. 165
M. Nelson, Patti Polk
M. Nelson, Ramsey's Rocks
& Minerals
M. Nelson, Patti Polk

Pg. 166
M. Nelson, Patti Polk

M. Nelson, Patti Polk
M. Nelson, Patti Polk
M. Nelson, Tom's Hidden
Valley Treasures

Pg. 167
M. Nelson, Patti Polk
M. Nelson, Patti Polk

Pg. 168
M. Nelson, Ramsey's Rocks
& Minerals

Pg. 169
M. Nelson, Ramsey's Rocks
& Minerals
M. Nelson, Harry Brown
M. Nelson, Ramsey's Rocks
& Minerals
M. Nelson, Ramsey's Rocks
& Minerals

Pg. 170
M. Nelson, Harry Brown
M. Nelson, Ramsey's Rocks
& Minerals
M. Nelson, Ramsey's Rocks
& Minerals

Pg. 171
M. Nelson, Patti Polk
M. Nelson, Patti Polk
M. Nelson, Ramsey's Rocks
& Minerals
M. Nelson, Patti Polk

Pg. 172
M. Nelson, Jim & Ellen's
Rock Shop
M. Nelson, Ramsey's Rocks
& Minerals
M. Nelson, Patti Polk
M. Nelson, Ramsey's Rocks
& Minerals
M. Nelson, Patti Polk
M. Nelson, Patti Polk
M. Nelson, Patti Polk
M. Nelson, Patti Polk
M. Nelson, Patti Polk

Pg. 173
M. Nelson, Dick Moore

Pg. 176
M. Nelson, Dick Moore

Pg. 177
Bob Jones, University of
Arizona, Tucson
M. Nelson, Harry Brown

Pg. 178
M. Nelson, Dick Moore
M. Nelson, Dick Moore

Pg. 179
M. Nelson, Dick Moore
M. Nelson, Dick Moore

Pg. 180
M. Nelson, Dick Moore
M. Nelson, Dick Moore

Pg. 181
M. Nelson, Dick Moore
M. Nelson, Dick Moore

Pg. 182
M. Nelson, Dick Moore

Pg. 183
M. Nelson, Dick Moore

Pg. 184
M. Nelson, Dick Moore

Pg. 185
M. Nelson, Dick Moore
M. Nelson, Dick Moore

Pg. 186
M. Nelson, Nancy Bihler
M. Nelson, Dick Moore

Pg. 187
M. Nelson, Harry Brown

Pg. 188
M. Nelson, Harry Brown
M. Nelson, Harry Brown

Pg. 189
M. Nelson, Ramsey's Rocks
& Minerals
M. Nelson, Dick Moore

Pg. 190
M. Nelson, Dick Moore
M. Nelson, Patti Polk

Pg. 191
M. Nelson, Dick Moore
M. Nelson, Dick Moore

Pg. 192
M. Nelson, Dick Moore
M. Nelson, Harry Brown

Pg. 193
M. Nelson, Dick Moore

Pg. 194
M. Nelson, Harry Brown
M. Nelson, Nancy Bihler
M. Nelson, Dick Moore

Pg. 195
M. Nelson, Dick Moore
M. Nelson, Dick Moore

Pg. 196
M. Nelson, Dick Moore
M. Nelson, Dick Moore

Pg. 197
M. Nelson, Dick Moore
M. Nelson, Dick Moore

Pg. 198
M. Nelson, Ramsey's Rocks
& Minerals
M. Nelson, Dick Moore

Pg. 199
M. Nelson, Jim & Ellen's
Rock Shop

M. Nelson, Jim & Ellen's
Rock Shop

Pg. 200
M. Nelson, Dick Moore
M. Nelson, Dick Moore

Pg. 201
M. Nelson, Dick Moore
M. Nelson, Dick Moore

Pg. 202
M. Nelson, Dick Moore

Pg. 203
M. Nelson, Dick Moore
M. Nelson, Dick Moore

Pg. 204
M. Nelson, Dick Moore
M. Nelson, Dick Moore

Pg. 205
M. Nelson, Jim & Ellen's
Rock Shop
M. Nelson, Harry Brown

Pg. 206
M. Nelson, Dick Moore
M. Nelson, Dick Moore

Pg. 207
M. Nelson, Harry Brown
M. Nelson, Dick Moore
M. Nelson, Dick Moore

Pg. 208
M. Nelson, Jason Badgley
M. Nelson, Patti Polk

Pg. 209
M. Nelson, Dick Moore
M. Nelson, Dick Moore

Pg. 210
M. Nelson, Jim & Ellen's
Rock Shop
M. Nelson, Dick Moore

Pg. 211
M. Nelson, Dick Moore

Pg. 212
M. Nelson, Ramsey's Rocks
& Minerals
M. Nelson, Dick Moore
M. Nelson, Dick Moore

Pg. 213
M. Nelson, Dick Moore
M. Nelson, Dick Moore

Pg. 214
M. Nelson, Dick Moore

Pg. 215
M. Nelson, Dick Moore
M. Nelson, Harry Brown

Pg. 216
M. Nelson, Dick Moore
M. Nelson, Dick Moore

M. Nelson, Dick Moore

Pg. 217
M. Nelson, Dick Moore
M. Nelson, Harry Brown

Pg. 218
M. Nelson, Dick Moore
M. Nelson, Dick Moore

Pg. 219
M. Nelson, Dick Moore

Pg. 220
M. Nelson, Dick Moore

Pg. 221
M. Nelson, Dick Moore

Pg. 222
M. Nelson, Dick Moore
M. Nelson, Patti Polk

Pg. 223
M. Nelson, Dick Moore

Pg. 224
M. Nelson, Patti Polk
M. Nelson, Dick Moore

Pg. 225
M. Nelson, Dick Moore

Pg. 226
M. Nelson, Dick Moore
M. Nelson, Tom's Hidden
Valley Treasures

Pg. 227
M. Nelson, Dick Moore
M. Nelson, Dick Moore

Pg. 228
M. Nelson, Dick Moore
M. Nelson, Dick Moore

Pg. 229
M. Nelson, Dick Moore
M. Nelson, Dick Moore

Pg. 230
M. Nelson, Dick Moore

Pg. 231
M. Nelson, Dick Moore

Pg. 232
M. Nelson, Dick Moore

Pg. 233
M. Nelson, Dick Moore

Pg. 234
M. Nelson, Harry Brown
M. Nelson, Dick Moore

Pg. 235
M. Nelson, Dick Moore

Pg. 236
M. Nelson, Dick Moore

Pg. 237
M. Nelson, Dick Moore

Pg. 238
M. Nelson, Dick Moore

Pg. 239
M. Nelson, Harry Brown

Pg. 240
M. Nelson, Dick Moore

Pg. 241
M. Nelson, Patti Polk

Pg. 242
M. Nelson, Dick Moore

Pg. 243
M. Nelson, Tom's Hidden
Valley Treasures
M. Nelson, Dick Moore

Pg. 244
M. Nelson, Tom's Hidden
Valley Treasures

Pg. 245
M. Nelson, Dick Moore

Pg. 246
M. Nelson, Dick Moore

Pg. 247
M. Nelson, Dick Moore

Pg. 248
M. Nelson, Harry Brown

Pg. 249
M. Nelson, Dick Moore

Pg. 250
M. Nelson, Dick Moore

Pg. 251
M. Nelson, Dick Moore

Pg. 252
M. Nelson, Tom's Hidden
Valley Treasures

Pg. 253
M. Nelson, Dick Moore
M. Nelson, Harry Brown

Pg. 254
M. Nelson, Dick Moore

Pg. 255
M. Nelson, Dick Moore

Pg. 256
M. Nelson, Dick Moore

Pg. 257
M. Nelson, Dick Moore
M. Nelson, Harry Brown

Pg. 258
M. Nelson, Dick Moore

Index

A

actinolite, 242
agate, 51, 150-151
agate
  banded, 52-53
  bouquet, 61
  brecciated, 54
  dendritic, 55-56
  dot and eye,
  57-59
  fire, 45
  flame, 60
  flower, 61
  fortification,
  62-64
  iris, 82
  lace, 65-66
  lattice, 65-66
  moss, 67-70
  plume, 71-73
  pseudomorphic,
  83-84
  sagenite, 74-75
  snowflake, 76
  tube, 77-80
  waterline, 81
alabaster, 152
alexandrite, 135
amber, 163
amethyst quartz,
  38, 140
analcime, 206
apatite, 145
apophyllite, 200
aquamarine, 136
arsenopyrite, 183
aurichalcite, 245
autunite, 229
aventurine quartz,
  37
azurite, 244

B

banded agate,
  52-53
benitoite, 143
beryl, 136
biotite, 214
bismuth, 178
black chalcedony,
  44
blue chalcedony, 48
blue quartz, 38
bone, 164
borax, 204
bornite, 187
bouquet agate, 61
brecciated agate, 54
brochantite, 234

C

calcite onyx, 153
carnelian, 45
cassiterite, 213
catlinite, 153
celestite, 246
chabazite, 225
chalcanthite, 248
chalcedony, 43
chalcedony
  black, 44
  blue, 48
  pink, 50
  purple, 49
chalcedony rose, 44
chalcocite, 181
chrysoberyl, 135
chrysocolla, 47, 151
chrysoprase, 46
chrysotile, 230
cinnabar, 220
citrine quartz, 36,
  140
classification,
  mineral, 174

clinochlore, 256
colemanite, 204
conichalcite, 237
copper, 188
coral, 165
cordierite, 138
corundum, 134
crocoite, 222
cuprite, 221

D

danburite, 140, 200
datolite, 130, 202
dendritic agate,
  55-56
descloizite, 217
diamond, 133
dioptase, 145, 238
dot and eye agate,
  57-59
dumortierite, 154

E

emerald, 136
enargite, 181
epidote, 241
erythrite, 257

F

fetishes, 147
fire agate, 45
fire opal, 144
flagstone, 160
flame agate, 60
fluorescent
  materials, 148
fluorite, 154, 253
flower agate, 61
fortification agate,
  62-64
fossils,
  animal, 103
  marine, 104-107

  plant, 108
franklinite, 185
fulgurites, 168

G

galena, 180
garnet, 139
geodes, 85-87
glauberite, 205
goethite, 215
gold, 189
granite, 161
green quartz, 37

H

habits, crystal, 174
hematite, 186
hemimorphite, 201
Herkimer
  diamonds, 33
heulandite, 209
hiddenite, 142
howlite, 155

I

idocrase, 143
iolite, 138
iris agate, 82

J

jade, 155
jasp-agate, 96
jasper, 151
jasper
  mottled, 97
  orbicular, 97-98
  picture, 99-101
  spiderweb, 101

K

kammererite, 256
kunzite, 142
kyanite, 252

L

labradorite, 156
lace agate, 65-66
lattice agate, 65-66
lazulite, 249
lepidolite, 255
limestone, 162
limonite, 215
linarite, 247

M

magnetite, 185
malachite, 156, 233
marble, 162
meteorites, 169
microcline, 251
milky quartz, 34
mimetite, 229
mohs scale, 175
moldavite, 130
molybdenite, 180
moss agate, 67-70
mottled jasper, 97
muscovite, 212

N

natrolite, 201
natural display
rocks, 149

O

obsidian, 157
olivine, 142, 239
onyx, calcite, 153
opal, fire, 144
orbicular jasper,
97-98
orpiment, 227
orthoclase, 207

P

pearl, 165
pectolite, 211
peridot, 142
petrified wood,
109-112

picture jasper,
99-101
pink chalcedony, 50
pipestone, 153
plagioclase, 208
platinum, 177
plume agate, 71-73
prehnite, 240
pseudomorphic
agate, 83-84
psilomelane, 213
purple chalcedony,
49
purpurite, 254
pyrolusite, 184
pyromorphite, 234
pyrophyllite, 231

Q

quartz, 140, 157
quartz,
amethyst, 38, 140
aventurine, 37
blue, 38
citrine, 36, 140
green, 37
milky, 34
rose, 39
rutilated, 33
smoky, 35
tiger eye, 36
tourmalinated,
34
quartz with gold, 35

R

realgar, 223
rhodochrosite, 126,
158, 257
rhodonite, 126
rock crystal, 32
romanechite, 213
rosasite, 232
rose quartz, 39
ruby, 134

ruby, star, 127
rutilated quartz, 33

S

sagenite agate,
74-75
sandstone, 160
sapphire, 134
sapphire, star, 127
scheelite, 228
scolecite, 209
seraphinite, 131
serpentine, 158
shell, 166-167
siderite, 227
silver, 177
smithsonite, 243
smoky quartz, 35
snowflake agate, 76
soapstone, 159
sodalite, 127
sphaerocobaltite,
258
sphalerite, 219
sphene, 218
spiderweb jasper,
101
spinel, 137
spodumene, 142,
210
star ruby, 127
star sapphire, 127
staurolite, 218
stibnite, 182
stilbite, 210
sugilite, 128
sulfur, 226
systems, crystal, 175

T

tanzanite, 144
tektites, 170
tetrahedrite, 179
thomsonite, 131,
206

thulite, 131
thundereggs, 88-89
tiger eye quartz, 36
titanite, 218
topaz, 135
torbernite, 235
tourmaline, 141
tourmalinated
quartz, 34
tube agate, 77-80
turquoise, 128

U

ulexite, 205

V

vanadinite, 222
variscite, 129
vesuvianite, 143,
217
vivianite, 250

W

waterline agate, 81
wavelite, 236
wolframite group,
216
wulfenite, 228

Z

zincite, 224
zircon, 138
zoisite, 144

Take Your Collecting Another Direction

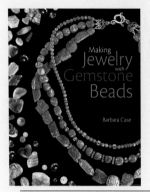

Making Jewelry with Gemstone Beads
By Barbara Case

Another option for some of the many gems and minerals you collect is to transform them into stunning jewelry. This guide offers an impressive collection of 100 projects, of varying skill levels, to help you do just that.

Softcover • **Item #Z1340** • **$19.99**

Big Bead Jewelry
By Deborah Shcneebeli-Morrell

This guide features techniques for creating glamorous jewelry using chunky gemstones in a modern, organic approach.

Softcover • **Item #Z0307** • **$19.99**

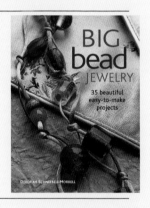

Pebble Pets
By Steve and Megumi Biddle

Create 30 lovable rock creatures with easy techniques including layering rocks with paper, molding details out of modeling clay and creating faux fur. Follow along with the step-by-step instructions to make these cute pets as a family project, or to give as gifts.

Softcover • **Item #Z4292** • **$22.99**